of rail transport and travel

*BBC History Magazine*

700

D0262869

Also by Christian Wolmar

*Engines of War*
*Blood, Iron & Gold*
*Fire & Steam*
*The Subterranean Railway*
*On the Wrong Line*
*Down the Tube*
*Broken Rails*
*Forgotten Children*
*Stagecoach*
*The Great Railway Disaster*
*The Great Railway Revolution*

# TO THE
# EDGE
## OF THE
# WORLD

*To Alan*

## CHRISTIAN
## WOLMAR

Atlantic Books
London

First published in Great Britain in hardback in 2013 by Atlantic Books, an imprint of Atlantic Books Ltd.

This paperback edition published in Great Britain in 2014 by Atlantic Books.

9 8 7 6 5 4 3 2 1

A CIP catalogue record for this book is available from the British Library.

Paperback ISBN: 9780857890382
E-book ISBN: 9781782392040

Text design by carrdesignstudio.com
Maps by Jeff Edwards
Index by David Atkinson

Printed and bound by CPI Group (UK) Ltd, Croydon, CR0 4YY

Atlantic Books
An imprint of Atlantic Books Ltd
Ormond House
26–27 Boswell Street
London WC1N 3JZ

www.atlantic-books.co.uk

# CONTENTS

# LIST OF MAPS AND ILLUSTRATIONS

## MAPS

## ILLUSTRATIONS

13. Japanese troops entering Vladivostok, 1918. akg-images/Interfoto.

14. Farmers and children sell dairy products to passengers. © William Wisner Chapin/National Geographic Society/Corbis.

15. Leon Trotsky, Petrograd station, 1920. © Hulton-Deutsch Collection/CORBIS.

16. Armoured train on the Trans-Siberian Railway. Mary Evans/ Robert Hunt Collection.

17. Pointsman at Novosibirsk, 1929. Mary Evans/Sueddeutsche Zeitung Photo.

18. Children selling flowers to passengers, 1921. © Ella R. Christie/ National Geographic Society/Corbis.

19. Saloon car, 1903. Mary Evans/Sueddeutsche Zeitung Photo.

20. Buryat people at Talbaga station. Mary Evans/Sueddeutsche Zeitung Photo.

21. Third-class in Krasnoyarsk, 1905. Mary Evans/Sueddeutsche Zeitung Photo.

22. Vladivostok station. akg-images/Imagno.

23. Passengers on a platform, 1915. Rex/Roger-Viollet.

24. Yaroslavsky station, 1908. Mary Evans Picture Library.

25. Yaroslavsky station, 1974. akg-images/RIA Nowosti.

26. Railwayman beside snow-covered tracks, 1978. © Hulton-Deutsch Collection/CORBIS.

27. Members of the Young Communist League at Yaroslavsky station. akg-image /RIA Nowosti.

28. Builders of the Baikal Amur Railroad, 01 October 1984. © RIA Novosti /Alamy.

29. Plaque at Vladivostok station. Courtesy of Deborah Maby.

30. Novosibirsk station. Courtesy of Deborah Maby.

31. Circum-Baikal Railway. Francorov/Wiki Commons.

32. *Rossiya* Trans-Siberian train arriving at Ulan-Ude, 2007. Rex.

33. Ulan-Ude station, 2012. Courtesy of Deborah Maby.

34. Christian Wolmar and Deborah Maby. Courtesy of Deborah Maby.

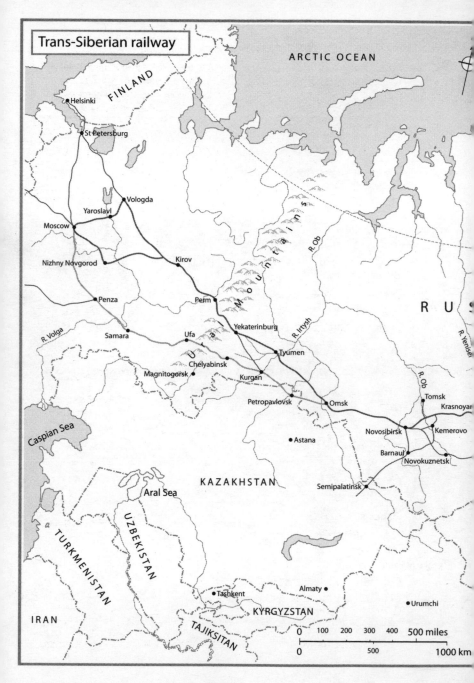

# Trans-Siberian railway

ARCTIC OCEAN

FINLAND

Helsinki

St Petersburg

Vologda

Yaroslavl

Moscow

Nizhny Novgorod

Kirov

Penza

Perm

R. Volga

Samara

Ufa

Yekaterinburg

R. Irtysh

R. Ob

Chelyabinsk

Tyumen

Magnitogorsk

Kurgan

Petropavlovsk

Omsk

R U S

R. Yenisei

Tomsk

Krasnoyar

Caspian Sea

Astana

Novosibirsk

Kemerovo

Barnaul

Novokuznetsk

KAZAKHSTAN

Aral Sea

Semipalatinsk

UZBEKISTAN

TURKMENISTAN

IRAN

Tashkent

Almaty

Urumchi

KYRGYZSTAN

TAJIKSITAN

Mountains

U  r  a  l

R. Ob

0  100  200  300  400  500 miles

0  500  1000 km

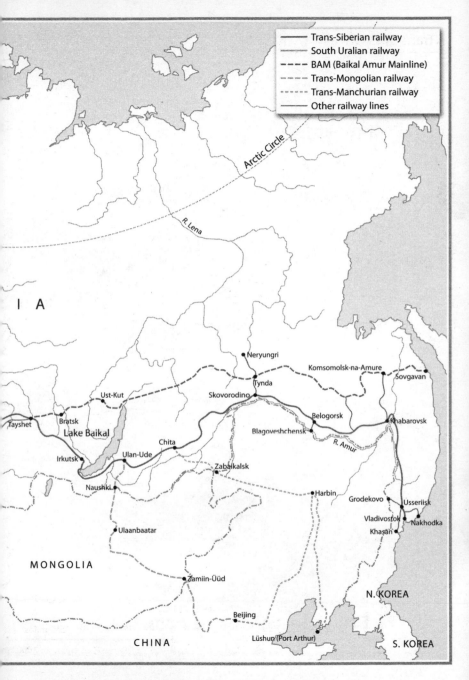

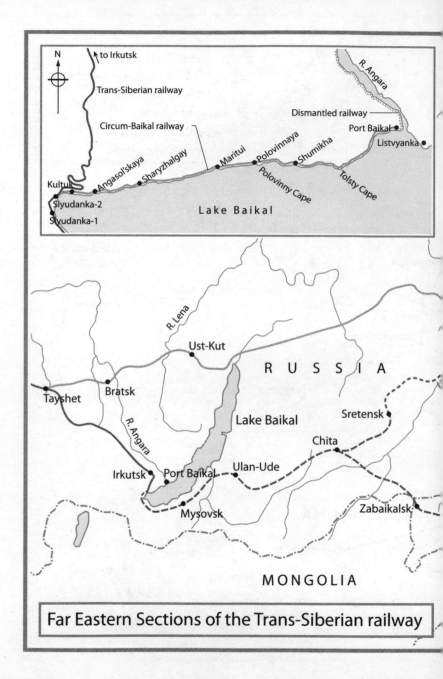

Far Eastern Sections of the Trans-Siberian railway

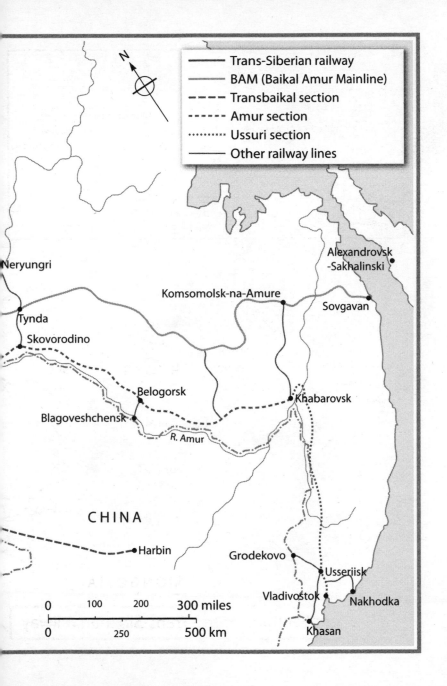

Trans-Siberian railway
BAM (Baikal Amur Mainline)
Transbaikal section
Amur section
Ussuri section
Other railway lines

Neryungri

Tynda

Skovorodino

Belogorsk

Blagoveshchensk

R. Amur

Komsomolsk-na-Amure

Alexandrovsk
-Sakhalinski

Sovgavan

Khabarovsk

CHINA

Harbin

Grodekovo

Usseriisk

Vladivostok

Nakhodka

Khasan

| 0 | 100 | 200 | 300 miles |
| 0 | | 250 | 500 km |

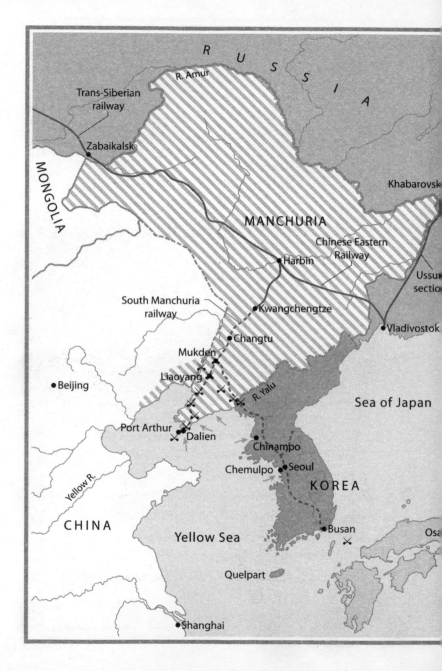

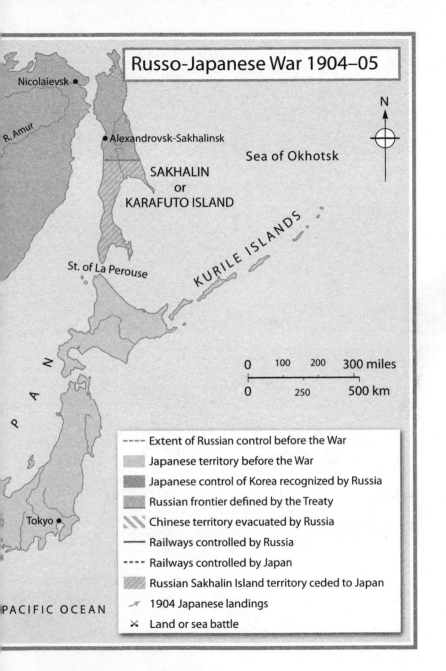

## Russo-Japanese War 1904–05

Nicolaievsk •

R. Amur

• Alexandrovsk-Sakhalinsk

Sea of Okhotsk

SAKHALIN
or
KARAFUTO ISLAND

N

St. of La Perouse

KURILE ISLANDS

| 0 | 100 | 200 | 300 miles |

| 0 | 250 | 500 km |

P A N

P

Tokyo •

- - - - Extent of Russian control before the War

Japanese territory before the War

Japanese control of Korea recognized by Russia

Russian frontier defined by the Treaty

Chinese territory evacuated by Russia

——— Railways controlled by Russia

- - - - Railways controlled by Japan

Russian Sakhalin Island territory ceded to Japan

⤢ 1904 Japanese landings

✕ Land or sea battle

PACIFIC OCEAN

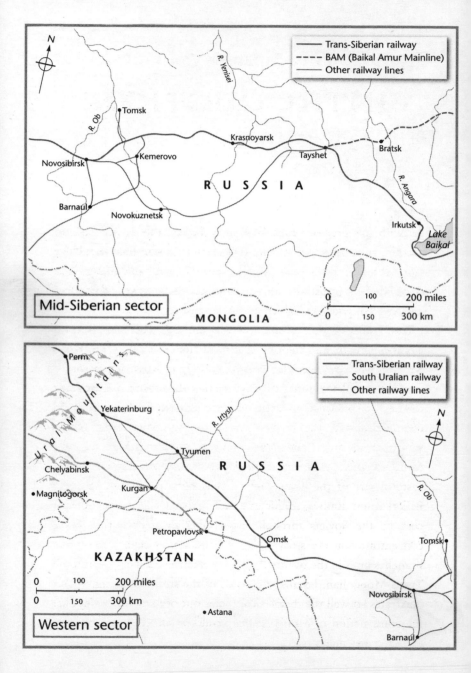

**Mid-Siberian sector**

- Trans-Siberian railway
- BAM (Baikal Amur Mainline)
- Other railway lines

R. Yenisei

R. Ob

Tomsk

Krasnoyarsk

Tayshet

Bratsk

Novosibirsk

Kemerovo

R U S S I A

R. Angara

Barnaul

Novokuznetsk

Irkutsk

Lake Baikal

0   100   200 miles
0   150   300 km

MONGOLIA

**Western sector**

- Trans-Siberian railway
- South Uralian railway
- Other railway lines

Perm

Ural Mountains

Yekaterinburg

R. Irtysh

Tyumen

R U S S I A

Chelyabinsk

Kurgan

R. Ob

Magnitogorsk

Petropavlovsk

Omsk

Tomsk

KAZAKHSTAN

0   100   200 miles
0   150   300 km

Novosibirsk

Astana

Barnaul

# INTRODUCTION

As with my previous railway history books, this is not just an account of a transport system. It is so much more than that. The story of the Trans-Siberian is both a tale of remarkable engineering stimulated by imperial ambition, and also a key part of Russian and, indeed, wider European and Asian history.

The Trans-Siberian is not a single railway. There are several Trans-Siberians, and the one that most fits the name – the route between Moscow and Vladivostok, entirely in Russian territory – was not completed until 1916. Before that the route from Moscow to the Pacific Ocean used the Chinese Eastern Railway, built in conjunction with the Trans-Siberian, through Manchuria, which was part of China (and now known as the Trans-Manchurian). More recently, as described towards the end of this book, the eastern part of the Trans-Siberian has been paralleled with the Baikal Amur Railway, built at great financial and environmental cost by the Soviets through virgin Siberian steppe. This book concentrates on the story of these lines, rather than the various branches built in the twentieth century, such as the Turksib and the Trans-Mongolian, because the focus of the story is Siberia, which illustrates so well the theme that comes out of many of my books: the construction of a railway line results in all kinds of changes, expected and unexpected.

In Siberia's case, the results have inevitably been both positive and negative. In many respects, this is a tragic history. Soon after it was built, the Trans-Siberian was the catalyst for a major war, fought almost on the scale of the First World War, and then became the centre of much of the fighting in the Russian Civil War. Leon Trotsky famously used an armoured train on the line to lead the fight against the Whites, the counter-revolutionary forces in that war, and there was much bloodshed on both sides. In particular, the biggest mistake was to have built the original line through Manchuria, a move that not only resulted almost immediately in the Russo-Japanese War, but was also instrumental in bringing about the Russian Revolution, as it stimulated the failed Russian uprising of 1905.

The Trans-Siberian itself contributed to the epoch-making revolution of 1917. The concentration of resources by an impoverished government on what was perceived as adventurism in the Far East – especially during the building of the Amur railway in the years running up to the First World War – undoubtedly contributed to the political instability in Russia. The Trans-Siberian, therefore, does not merely have a major role in railway history, but its contribution to the wider geopolitics of the twentieth century cannot be overestimated. Without the Trans-Siberian, modern maps of Europe and Asia might have a very different complexion.

The sequence of wars, as well as the mass migration stimulated by the line, were the source of much suffering, and there are numerous tragic stories in this book. But there is also a fantastic, positive tale to be told, one that is too often omitted or simply forgotten in the clichéd view of Russia. The construction and the continued efficient operation of the Trans-Siberian ranks among the greatest achievements of mankind. Indeed, much of this book is about debunking myths. The Trans-Siberian came in for considerable criticism in the West when it was first built. The Russians were portrayed as corrupt incompetents. While undoubtedly mistakes were made and money went missing, this is to deny a magnificent achievement, one of the great engineering wonders of the world.

As I found when I travelled along the line, this is not some little meandering rural railway with the occasional chundering train, but rather, one of the world's great arteries, a piece of infrastructure that transformed not only the region in which it was built, but also the entire nation that built it.

The first chapter sets the scene with an outline of pre-railway Siberia and a short account of the development of Russia's first railways. Indeed, Russia took to the iron road rather late and its backward economic state meant the network grew more slowly than in Europe, despite the vast size of the nation. In the second chapter I explain the reasons why the Trans-Siberian became an important political issue in the latter stages of the nineteenth century, and consider the arguments between the protagonists and the opponents. There were no shortage of schemes put forward, but for a long time Russia's rulers were opposed to the idea. Then, as explained in chapter 3, the mood changed, largely thanks to one man, the great Sergei Witte, the line's successful advocate and a brilliant politician and administrator – a rare combination.

It took about thirty years between the idea for the line first emerging and the decision to go ahead. However, the choice of route through Manchuria was to have devastating effects. Remarkably, as explained in chapter 4, it took barely a decade to build the Trans-Siberian, despite the difficult climate, disease, shortage of materials and labour, and widespread corruption. It was an amazing achievement, although the condition of the completed line did leave a lot to be desired.

The fifth chapter covers the experiences of early travellers, which were undoubtedly mixed and at times perilous. Nevertheless, most came away impressed and there was, right from the beginning, a constant process of improvement. Their accounts are certainly varied and entertaining. Chapter 6 covers the first of several wars fought around the Trans-Siberian: the Russo-Japanese conflict, which was stimulated by the construction of the line and proved disastrous for Russia.

In chapter 7 the impact of the construction of the line is assessed. It transformed Siberia from a place just known for exiles and prisoners into a honey pot for immigrants, who arrived in their millions, encouraged by the state. Industry and agriculture both flourished. Chapter 8 tells the story of the completion of the line using solely Russian territory with the construction of the Amur Railway, the most difficult section, in order to bypass the troubled Manchurian route. The ninth chapter is the account of the civil war on the Trans-Siberian, a bloody and prolonged battle that ultimately decided the fate of the Russian Revolution.

Chapter 10 covers the interwar period, again a time of conflict, and then, worse, the establishment of the Gulags that were to cost the lives of millions of people caught up in Stalin's bloody purges. It also explains the role of the Trans-Siberian in the industrialisation of Siberia, and the subsequent transfer of vast amounts of industry to the east in order to protect it from Hitler's invasion.

The eleventh chapter covers the terrible history of the construction of the *Baikal Amur Magistral* or BAM, the world's biggest railway project, which caused widespread environmental damage and has created a white elephant. Finally, in chapter 12 there is a brief account of the Trans-Siberian in the post-war period and an analysis of its impact on history.

A note on distances. The Trans-Siberian is 5,771 miles (9,288 kilometres) long, according to the famous monument at Vladivostok Station, but over the years the construction of tunnels and the straightening out of curves has reduced its overall distance. It is, therefore, a few miles shorter, but that is hardly significant; although in a sense the Trans-Siberian is a slight misnomer, since it is 9,000 miles from St Petersburg to Kamchatka, the furthermost point of Siberia in the north-east. In other words, the Trans-Siberian does only two thirds of the job. Nevertheless, it is an impressive one. The author of *The Big Red Train Ride*, the late Eric Newby, summed it up best: 'There is no railway journey of comparable length anywhere in the world. The Trans-Siberian is the big train ride. All the rest are peanuts.'

A note on dates. Russia used the Julian calendar until just after the October Revolution (which was actually in November in the Gregorian calendar) and changed to the Gregorian on Wednesday, 31 January 1918, which, consequently, was followed by Thursday, 14 February 1918, thus dropping thirteen days from the calendar. I have, therefore, used dates from the appropriate calendar: the Julian for events in Russia before 1918 and the Gregorian thereafter. Dates in Europe follow the Gregorian throughout.

I make no apology for being inconsistent with translations from Russian spelling. There are variants of almost all names, and I have merely tried to select those best known.

I owe a particular debt to two people. First, to Stephen Marks, not only for his meticulous and fascinating account of the circumstances that led to the construction of the line in his book *Road to Power: The Trans-Siberian Railroad and the Colonization of Asian Russia, 1850–1917*, but also for being kind enough to read the draft and offer numerous corrections and comments. Second, to Bernard Gambrill, who from his Bruges hidey-hole read through the draft meticulously, picking up on errors both stylistic and factual. He also spent a remarkable amount of time digging up hundreds of potential images, and it is thanks to him that the book has such a good selection. My friend Liam Browne researched the section on agitprop trains, which was exceedingly helpful, and several other people have offered advice, including William Aldridge, Jim Ballantyne, John Fowler, Brent Hudson, Andrew Jones, Peter Lewis, Kate Pangbourne, Gordon Pettit, Harvey Smith and John Thorpe, as well as Teresa Glyn, who deserves a mention. There are others whom I am sure I have forgotten, but they will be included in the next edition.

I am also enormously grateful to my wonderful partner Deborah Maby, not only for her support and her practical help in reading the proofs, but, best of all, for accompanying me on the Trans-Siberian in November 2012 for what was quite literally a trip of a lifetime and a fantastic experience. As they say in the guide books: recommended. Thanks are also due to the staff at Real Russia for organising the journey. I am grateful, too, to my agent, Andrew Lownie; Toby Mundy and Louise Cullen at my publishers; and Ian Pindar, the copy editor. I claim, however, all the mistakes.

I dedicate this book to my much-loved and missed rogue of a father Boris Forter (né Kougoulsky, 1896–1976), who would have loved hearing about my trip to his homeland – which, sadly, he was never able to visit after he was forced to leave following the Revolution – and to read my account of this great railway. He was born in Moscow in the year the first major section of the Trans-Siberian was completed, fought against the Austrians in the Carpathian Mountains in the First World War and considered joining the White forces in 1918, a story I relate in the book; but, fortunately (not least for me), he fled to France instead, and later the United States and Britain.

I also dedicate this book to little Alfie, born 114 years later, who already seems to love trains.

# ONE

# A SLOW EMBRACE

There were many reasons for Russia not to have built the Trans-Siberian Railway – and very few to build it. While by 1869 America boasted a transcontinental railway and Canada, more relevantly, followed suit sixteen years later, Russia was different. Unlike most of Europe, which had embraced liberalism to accommodate the needs of industrial growth, Russia remained an absolute monarchy ruled by a conservative tsar through a political system that made no concessions to democracy. Travel was circumscribed by the state to such an extent that rail passengers needed internal passports to travel around the country. Compared with the United States and Canada, Russia was a primitive country, based on inefficient agriculture and boasting little industry. The territory of Siberia – the vast area east of the Urals through which the railway would pass – was sparsely populated and its climate was far harsher than the western regions of Canada and the United States, which had begun to be settled thanks to their transcontinental railways. It seemed to offer little to attract potential immigrants who would be needed to justify the massive cost of constructing the line. Given the likely poor demand for travel the need for the line could, therefore, be questioned.

Then there was the sheer scale of the enterprise. The railway would have to stretch across the whole of Siberia to the port of Vladivostok, a distance of some 5,750[1] miles – 9,255 kilometres

– from Moscow, since it made no sense to stop halfway, given its military rationale was to serve the ports on the Sea of Japan and reinforce the ties between the centre and the most disparate parts of the Russian Empire. As a comparison, the First American Transcontinental, which linked an already well-developed network of lines in the American Midwest with California, required only 1,780 miles of new line when work began in California in 1863. Given Russia's poverty and its feudal, rather than capitalist, economy, neither private firms nor the state seemed in a position to embark on such an ambitious and costly project.

Yet Russia – or rather the tsar – did decide to build the line. The reasons for this momentous decision, as we shall see, were not rooted in any rational assessment of the economic benefits of building the railway, but rather in the tsar's personal motivations and his assessment of its military and political value. The advantage of being an autocratic leader with no need to consider public opinion or pay too much regard to the parlous state of the Treasury, was that he had the power to make such things happen. His word was law and fortunately he had able aides, most notably Sergei Witte, his finance minister, to carry through the work.

This was a familiar pattern. After all, it was a previous tsar, Alexander's grandfather, Nicholas I, who had brought the iron road to Russia in the first place on equally untested reasoning. While the first lines had been laid in both the UK and the US in 1830, Russia was hesitant about joining the railway age. Yet Russia desperately needed railways as the nation was a transport nightmare. The lack of investment and the size of the country resulted in lengthy, heroically difficult journeys, and the severe climate meant that sleighs rather than wheeled vehicles had to be used in winter. There was a scattering of good roads in Russia, notably the St Petersburg–Moscow highway, completed in 1816. One of its early travellers, Princess Maria Volkonsky – the wife of Sergei Volkonsky, one of the instigators of the attempted coup against the tsar of December 1825 – took five days to cover the 450 miles between the two cities when she journeyed east to join her husband in exile. That suggests it was certainly among the better roads of the age in Europe. This was the first of a series of highways that Nicholas had built to link the major towns, but minor routes could be travelled only on dirt roads, which became quagmires when the snow melted in the spring or the rain fell in the autumn.

Despite Russia's primitive economic state, there was a well-organized system of passenger transport on these main roads. The fastest form of transport was that of government diligence, stagecoaches usually drawn by four horses abreast, which carried four passengers inside and three, paying lower fares, outside, together with the conductor and driver. There were, too, slower and cheaper public diligences which carried up to a dozen people, while more affluent families had their own vehicles. The operation of the roads was dependent on the government, which strictly controlled people's movements. Horses had to be changed at government-run post stations located every ten miles or so and supervised by a stationmaster who 'was bound to give preference to travellers on government service. The ordinary traveller might therefore have to wait hours or days for horses to become available, but his trials could be lightened by skilful bribery.'[2]

In Siberia travelling in the sleighs used in winter was infinitely preferable to the summer equivalent. This was normally a *tarantass*, which was rather like a large, shallow basket that rested on flexible wooden poles attached to the axles. The *tarantass*, drawn by two horses, carried up to four people with a seat for the driver but no benches for the passengers, who simply made do with finding space alongside their baggage and loose belongings. The smaller, single-horse-drawn *telegas*, little more than a slightly modified farm cart, was an even more uncomfortable conveyance, used mostly only for baggage, but at times brought into service when *tarantasses* were not available. The one advantage of not travelling in the winter was that large sections of the road could be avoided in the short, ice-free season by using the ferries that plied their trade along Siberia's huge rivers and which, in some parts flowed in an east–west direction. By the mid-nineteenth century large paddle steamboats were also available to passengers, providing reasonable accommodation during voyages that could last 1,000 miles or more.

Indeed, before the arrival of the railways, the rivers had been the backbone of Russia's transport system, even though they were only sufficiently ice-free to be used, at best, for five months of the year. Short river crossings were made on flat-bottomed rafts or barges moored to a chain anchored in mid-stream, but at times large queues developed at key crossing points because there were not enough of them. Nor were these little boats particularly safe or reliable. There were dangers from sizeable ice floes – mini-icebergs, in effect – in the spring, which could send the boat's occupants flying into the water or even sink the craft with invariably fatal results. At times the sheer volume of these floes stopped the service altogether. Indeed, the elements posed an ever-present danger to progress. If the rivers dried up, the large steamboats could become marooned in the shallows for days or even weeks, while after prolonged rain the rivers became too swollen or fast-flowing for safe navigation. Oddly, bridges, too, posed considerable danger. These structures were often crumbling and rotten, and *yamschchiki*, the *tarantass* drivers, excited by what they saw as a challenge, would often accelerate to cross a bridge, judging that they would outpace any collapse – which did not always prove to be the case.

Given the rigours of the journey, optimistic travellers would seek comfort and rest at post houses, which were located about every ten or twenty miles throughout the route, when they could no longer face another night of being thrown around in a *tarantass*.

They were invariably disappointed. These government-run post houses normally consisted of living quarters for the postmaster and his family and a common room for travellers, which was 'about twenty feet by eighteen feet wide, the two sections being heated by a huge brick oven in the dividing wall'.[3] There were a few chairs and tables, but no beds and the 'guests' would sleep where they could on furs and coats, lying on uncarpeted filthy floors inhabited by cockroaches and their predators: large, hungry rats. There were no sanitary facilities, which rarely troubled the local travellers, who did not believe in washing on these voyages, as they thought that 'soap and water sensitized the skin and increased the dangers of frostbite'.[4] A British visitor, Harry de Windt, remarked that while the Russian peasant women would not find it a hardship to remain unwashed for months at a time since that was their custom, the aristocratic ladies who travelled to join their husbands in Irkutsk or Vladivostok found it unbearable: 'The prettiest looked hideous in the early morning hours, with tangled hair, disordered dress and pale, pasty faces, while their diamond rings served to show off the blackness of their hands and nails, which they had probably been unable to wash for days.'[5] With typical Victorian gallantry, he omits to tell us what the less pretty ones looked like.

The first part of the trip from Moscow to Siberia, the route to the Urals – the natural as well as official barrier between Europe and Asia – was relatively easy since the roads were in reasonable condition, but thereafter the going got tougher. Steven Marks, the historian of the genesis of the line, sums it up neatly: 'Siberian transportation west of Lake Baikal was bad, and east of the lake it got worse.'[6] The historic route through Siberia, rather grandly titled the post road – a 'flattering misnomer'[7] according to foreigners who ventured on to it – was known locally as the *trakt* and had been improved in the eighteenth century (using the labour of exiles) to a width of twenty-one feet. For the most part it was merely a line of tall posts or clumps of birch trees to indicate the route through the steppes, just enough for two *tarantasses* to pass safely. There was not only the problem of mud in the wet seasons, but the sheer remoteness of the route meant that any breakdown led to lengthy delays to find replacement equipment. In the winter the sleighs gave a smoother ride, though the danger then was from storms that could trap the unwary between the post houses which would have provided shelter – albeit crude. There was, too, a hidden danger for unwary drivers. Rocks partly covered by snow could shatter sleigh runners, which would be impossible to repair on the spot and leave travellers spending nights by the roadside in freezing conditions with only the furs of the *tarantass* to keep them warm. Traffic, too, could be heavy on parts of the route in winter as the road was 'often blocked by hundreds of one-horse sledges loaded with hide-bound boxes of tea and all roped together to form a single file perhaps a mile long'.[8] It was customary for the drivers in these long chains to fall asleep, given they had nothing to do as they were connected to the next wagon; and therefore the horses, left to their own devices, tended to drift towards the centre of the road – to the annoyance of any traffic coming in the other direction.

*Tarantasses* were limited to a maximum of 8 mph, which was strictly enforced by the government's agents, but this safety measure was not sufficient to prevent accidents, which were more frequent at night. Since passengers in a hurry would be driven at night as well as day in order to cover the huge distances, sleepy or, more often, sozzled drivers would doze off with inevitable consequences. And if the condition of the road and the flimsiness of the carriages were not dangerous enough, travellers lived at constant risk of attack from runaway convicts, who, particularly in the summer, would form into groups, lying in wait near post stations. With little to lose, they were particularly violent and after robbing their victims of money, clothes, weapons and sometimes even the passports that might enable them to return to the west, would often slaughter travellers to prevent them bearing witness.

Given these difficulties it was hardly surprising that it could take a year and sometimes more to reach Vladivostok, the main port on the Pacific that would eventually be the terminus of the Trans-Siberian Railway. In the right conditions, and with money for bribes, the journey could be undertaken much more quickly, but there were never any guarantees about travelling through Siberia. The unexpected mishap was always to be expected.

The term Siberia is, in fact, a rather loose description of the region east of the Urals with a landmass equivalent to the whole of North America, including Canada and Alaska, and Europe put together – some five million square miles, a number that seems almost impossible to grasp – with a population today of forty million. Broadly, it takes in the Asian land mass north of a line drawn between Kazakhstan and Korea, including China and Mongolia. The eastern shores stretch between the Sea of Japan and the Bering Strait, both of which are parts of the Pacific Ocean. Maps barely do justice to the scale of this land mass, because to fit on a page they are generally on a larger scale than representations of other countries, which is justified by the scarcity of towns and villages of any description. It is only by realizing that Siberia encompasses seven time zones,[9] compared with four across the US mainland, that the scale begins to be understood.

The standard Western European assumption of equating Siberia with freezing-cold temperatures is not entirely accurate. The southern parts of Siberia through which the railway runs is broadly on the same latitude as central England and has a humid, continental climate with cold winters – typically averaging −15°C in January – and fairly warm summers. It is, though, the more northern, drier areas where the freezing temperatures that are synonymous with Siberia can be found with, typically, January figures averaging –25°C or worse.

Vladivostok, which is tucked away in the southernmost corner of Siberia near both the Chinese and North Korean borders, is almost ten degrees of latitude south of London. While Vladivostok has a legendary feel to it, like Timbuktu, as if it were some unimaginably distant place, it is, in fact, by no means the furthest point from Moscow. To the north-east there are several thousand miles of land mass, ending in the peninsula of Kamchatka, which scowls across the Bering Strait at Alaska, famously sold to America for barely the price of a tsar's summer residence.

There is an entertaining, if perhaps apocryphal tale that illustrates the scale of the Siberian lands. In the eighteenth century the Empress Elizabeth Petrovna invited half a dozen virgins from Kamchatka to visit her in the capital, St Petersburg. Escorted by an imperial officer, these supposedly chaste maidens were, by the time they reached Irkutsk near Lake Baikal, which was about halfway on their journey, already carrying children fathered by their military chaperon. According to Harmon Tupper, author of a 1960s account of the railway, the Lothario was replaced by a supposedly more reliable fellow, but 'nevertheless, by the time the young mothers reached St Petersburg – nearly 9,000 miles from Kamchatka – their firstborn had half-brothers and -sisters'.[10]

Siberia, of course, remains synonymous with the phenomenon of exile. With justification, since the numbers suffering that fate were remarkably high. Exile to Siberia became a punishment as early as the late sixteenth century, but initially only a few criminals were sent there. At the time, Siberia was the lenient option. The Russians had a penchant for particularly unpleasant and cruel treatment of anyone who transgressed the law or challenged the autocratic rule of the tsars. It seemed a feature of the Russian rulers to devise particularly intricate and painful ways to despatch their victims. Men were impaled on sharp stakes, hanged or beheaded for minor crimes, while flogging and branding were commonplace. Mutilation – such as amputation of limbs or cutting out tongues – was also sanctioned, until, in the mid-eighteenth century the empress Elizabeth Petrovna, the daughter of Peter the Great, decided that the barbarity had to end. She abolished the death penalty and largely replaced it with exile to Siberia. While the death penalty was later partly reinstated, it was used only sparingly and instead most criminals found themselves being sent east. It was not always a blessing for the hapless transgressors of the criminal code. In fact, such were the depredations suffered by many convicts, a swift death in a prison yard might have been preferable.

Broadly, there were two categories of exile: the common criminals and the political activists, who, for the most part, were more affluent and well-educated than the lawbreakers and made up a tiny minority, perhaps one or two per cent. The overall number of people sent to Siberia, though, was quite extraordinary as the system had a dual purpose. While primarily exile was a form of punishment, it also helped to populate the tribal areas of Siberia with Russians in order to solidify the tsarist regime's hold over its eastern lands. That, too, of course, would motivate the construction of the railway. The pace of deportations increased greatly in the early nineteenth century and a reliable estimate is that at its peak in the mid-nineteenth century, up to 12,000 people were sent each year, many bringing their families with them, so that overall, between 1800 and the outbreak of the First World War, around one million people were exiled.

Of course, while being sent to Siberia seems a particularly cruel punishment, the French and British had their own exile systems during the nineteenth century, sending people to far-off colonies rather than internally to a distant part of the same nation. After a hiatus during the First World War and the Russian Revolution, hundreds of thousands were sent during Joseph Stalin's rule, which lasted until the 1950s.

During the early part of this period, exile was, for the most part, a sentence of death. According to Tupper, 'Exiles were herded on foot to Siberia and died by the thousands for lack of food and shelter.'[11] The relatively liberal Tsar Alexander l began to improve conditions for the exiles, establishing stockaded rest houses – *étapes*, as they were known, since French was the language used by the ruling classes – which offered some protection and respite to the travelling deportees. Nevertheless, the conditions remained brutal. Those sentenced to hard labour were sent to the mines beyond Irkutsk, in deepest, north-eastern Siberia (not salt mines, as myth has it, but silver and gold), where some, dreading a lifetime of incarceration and suffering from the brutality of the guards, committed suicide by drinking water in which they had soaked the poisonous heads of matches. Those sentenced to hard labour and a second group, 'penal colonists', were exiled for life, but could become settlers after serving a sentence ranging from four to twenty years.

Despite this, the exile system failed miserably as a way of increasing the population. There is a bit of a mystery here. The numbers being exiled to Siberia suggest that the population should have grown rapidly in the nineteenth century. But census figures suggest it did not. The reason was that most exiles were relatively old – typically thirty to fifty – which meant that by the time they were released to settle they were beyond the age when they could be expected to raise a family. Moreover, there was an inbuilt sexual imbalance resulting from the far greater number of male than female exiles. There was, too, a high death rate, even after various sets of improvements were introduced in the rare brief periods of more liberal rule. While the figures on prisoner numbers suggest that many lived a long time, the jailers who controlled the penal colonies and the mines were effectively a law unto themselves, since they were so far from the capital and therefore routinely failed to report deaths, because they could continue to draw rations and allowances on the part of these deceased prisoners. This was corruption on a grand scale. According to a British Foreign Office report, large numbers of prisoners 'existed only in official lists of the Siberian authorities, who prolonged the lives of thousands of exiles on paper in order to put the money received from the government for their support into their own pockets'.[12] Indeed, that provided almost an incentive to despatch prisoners or encourage them to escape to eke out a miserable existence as a bandit unlikely to survive the winter. The census, however, reveals the real story. The modest increase in the Siberian population during the nineteenth century was, in fact, almost entirely the result of settlement by freed serfs after the abolition of slavery in 1862. There were, too, numerous tribes who had lived there for time immemorial. These were a disparate group, several of whom were nomadic, who had little connection with the Russian state and had their own languages and customs.

The unattractiveness of transport in Siberia to all but a few hardy settlers was, therefore, one of the spurs to the construction of the Trans-Siberian Railway. However, it took a leap of imagination to set out to build a 5,750-mile line, far longer than any other in the world, when Russia's railway system was much less developed than its counterparts in Europe and North America. Russia's first steps to joining the growing number of railway nations were tentative – hardly surprising, given the conservative and authoritarian nature of rule by Tsar Nicholas l. The construction of railways began to be mooted for the first time in Russia in the mid-1820s. As in Britain and continental Europe, man-hauled wagonways had been used for some time in mines and the first horse-drawn railway – a 1.2-mile line carrying silver ore from a mine at the Zmeinogorsk works in the Altai region of south central Russia, near what is now the Kazakhstan border – was built in 1809 by Pyotr Frolov. This line was notable not only as the first to use horses – who could haul three wagons each carrying eight tons of ore, far more efficient than any previous method – but 'for many cuttings and tunnels built to ease gradients, and for the replacement of angle rails, as used elsewhere, by cast-iron convex rails matching corresponding grooves in the wheels of the wagons'.[13] It was, in other words, a very sophisticated railway by the standards of the day, but unfortunately it was in such a remote area of the country that even the tsar was unaware of its existence. It took another twenty-five years before Russia's first steam engine was built, and it was – as in Britain, where the Stephensons, George and Robert, were the main developers – the work of a father-and-son team. The Cherepanovs, Yefim and his son Miron, were mechanics at the iron works of Nizhny Tagil in the Urals, who had previously produced a series of steam engines used to supply power to pumps and over a period of fifteen years had greatly improved their efficiency. In the early 1830s Miron was sent to England, at the time the world's leading trailblazer on steam technology, to learn how to produce an efficient steam locomotive. By 1833 they had produced their first engine, but – just as with similar pioneering efforts in Britain – it was not very successful. Indeed, the boilers of the first two locomotives they produced both exploded, again a common feature of early locomotive development, but the third, completed in 1835, proved relatively efficient, 'able to move faster than a horse, even if it could pull only a smaller load'.[14] It is a measure of the state of Russia in the early nineteenth century that both Cherepanovs were actually serfs, effectively owned by the factory for which they worked. Sadly, their efforts were in vain as the first Russian railways used foreign locomotives.

Hence the elements of building a railway were available in Russia relatively early, just as railway mania was sweeping the European continent and, indeed, the United States. The political will, however, was lacking, despite the entreaties of the small, forward-looking minority of the aristocratic ruling elite, who realized that the railways were the only viable transport option for a vast nation like Russia with the extremes of climate that made roads impassable and rivers unnavigable for large parts of the year. This group of modernists knew that transport costs were an insuperable barrier to the country's economic development. For example, the price of some agricultural produce would be three or four times greater in the major cities than at the farm gate, an increase almost entirely attributable to the high cost of river transport. The development of the nascent iron industry, located near the mines in the Urals where Europe meets Asia more than 1,000 miles from Moscow, was greatly handicapped, as the price of iron products from the region was so high in the major cities that firms found it easier to import goods from Britain or France. The unreliability of the transport system was an added burden. In winter when the rivers were frozen, land transport was possible in theory, but in practice roads were often blocked by heavy snow and ice. The effect of this poor transport network went far beyond simple economics: 'A consequence of this slow rate of movement was that a bad harvest in one province could rarely be compensated by grain shipments from a more fortunate region; hence the frequency in Russia of localized but deadly famines.'[15]

Numerous proposals for horse-drawn railways were put forward in the 1820s, but rejected by the monarch. Support for railways grew following the opening of the world's first modern railway line, the very successful Liverpool & Manchester in 1830, which stimulated the development of rail travel across Europe. While the main long-distance mode of transport in Russia, the waterways, was improving thanks to dredging, the construction of canals and the introduction of steam boats, it was clear to the modernizers that the railways represented the future: 'In the final analysis, Russia's transport needs could be adequately met only by an integrated network of railways.'[16]

It took an outsider, a German, Franz von Gerstner, to convince the tsar to support the building of the country's first railway, the fifteen-mile-long line between what was the then capital, St Petersburg, and Tsarskoe Selo, the tsar's summer residence. Originally, von Gerstner's aim had been much more ambitious. He had put forward a plan for building a network of lines across Russia, and tried to appeal to the tsar by emphasizing that the system would be ever ready to send troops around the country at great speed. There were, too, other influential opponents of the railways in the government. Nicholas had surrounded himself with advisers of a similar conservative bent, such as Count Yegor Kankrin, his long-term minister of finance, who, like many senior officials of the time such as von Gerstner, German. Kankrin, an economist, argued that such a large enterprise would divert capital away from agriculture, where it would do far more to improve people's lives. He also worried about the effect on the traditional carters carrying goods along the highways and on the forests, which would be depleted for locomotive fuel, a rather unconvincing argument given the size and scale of Russian woodland. Nevertheless, his arguments prevailed. Given such powerful opposition, it was no surprise that von Gerstner's proposal was rejected, but the tsar, who had thwarted a coup attempt by the Decembrists in 1825, was ever alert to the military potential of the iron road. He had noticed that there had been a swift transfer of troops by rail from Manchester to Liverpool during one of the perennial Irish emergencies[17] and the parallels between England's tenuous hold over Ireland and Russia's difficult relationship with its Polish province were all too obvious.

As a result of the tsar's interest, von Gerstner was allowed to build the Tsarskoe line to demonstrate the feasibility of running a railway in the harsh Russian climate. Although privately financed, its construction was helped by the granting of various concessions, such as exemption from taxes and the right to collect all the revenues. The six-foot-gauge line (later changed to five foot, the normal Russian gauge) was opened in 1837 with the first train, carrying eight full coaches, taking a mere twenty-eight minutes, an average of almost 30 mph, to reach Tsarskoe Selo. Its extension the following year to Pavlosk, a village sixteen miles further down the line, which, in a rare show of modernity during the dismal period of Nicholas's police state, was a kind of mini-holiday resort with buffets, concerts and a ballroom to entertain the St Petersburg crowds on their day trips. In order to attract people, in a clever marketing ploy, the railway subsidized the public entertainment at Pavlosk, which features strongly in Dostoevsky's *The Idiot*, as 'one of the fashionable summer resorts near St Petersburg'.

Initially the line was operated by a mix of locomotives, imported from Britain and Belgium, and horses, but soon the animals, exhausted by pulling the heavy trains, were put out to grass. The line was an instant success, with people flocking to the railway both out of curiosity and a desire to sample the attractions. In the first year more than 725,000 travelled on the line, an average of 2,000 a day, enabling von Gerstner to pay healthy dividends to his shareholders, since fares were relatively high – though the concerts at Pavlosk were free.

Not surprisingly given the tsar's obsession with retaining power at all costs, the success of the Tsarskoe Selo Railway encouraged him to give permission for a line to be built linking Warsaw, then part of the Russian Empire, with the border of the Austro-Hungarian Empire, which at the time was Russia's staunch ally. The justification for the scheme was largely military, as witnessed by the tsar's insistence on locomotive rather than horse traction, and the line was soon extended by the Austrians to Vienna, the

Hapsburg capital. It was built by private interests, but supported by a guaranteed rate of return from the government of four per cent – a lucrative arrangement for the railway company. And it was soon put to good use by the military when in 1848 Nicholas sent Russian troops along the line from Warsaw to crush a rebellion in Hungary in a particularly bloody and ruthless way.

Despite the clear success of the Tsarskoe Selo line, opposition remained strong within government circles to the creation of a railway network in Russia. The modernists argued that Russia's early steps towards industrialization were being hampered by the lack of an efficient transport system. The most obvious initial route for a railway was to link the two main cities, St Petersburg and Moscow, some 400 miles apart, which had been suggested by von Gerstner, but the opposition voices remained vociferous. Kankrin changed his grounds for opposition somewhat, arguing that long-distance railways were not viable – despite their growth in Europe and America – and that it would be impractical to give the railway companies the right to own serfs – although, again, many American railroads in the South did own slaves.

In a manner familiar to students of British government, a commission was set up to assess the viability of the project and its report, published in 1841, was very favourable to the idea. Nicholas gave the go-ahead for the scheme early the following year, although Kankrin, who represented a strand of conservative, anti-railway opinion that was powerful in both Europe and America, resisted to the last: 'All thinking people abroad consider that it [the Moscow–St Petersburg railway] will realize no profit, will ruin morality and liquidate unproductively capital which could be put to better use.'[18]

In many respects the difficulties and issues facing the construction of what became known as the Nikolayev Railway (later renamed the October Railway following the October 1917 revolution) were to be repeated, on a grander scale, half a century later when the Trans-Siberian was debated. Finding the finance, determining the role of the private sector, seeking engineering solutions and establishing the political ramifications – all these factors would be considered in much the same way for both schemes. Just as with the Trans-Siberian, it was an epic project in terms of railway construction, becoming, on completion, the second-longest in the world under a sole administration, beaten only by the Erie Railroad in New York State. The story of the Nikolayev Railway mirrors, too, the experience of the Trans-Siberian in terms of its purpose, a way of establishing and consolidating state power. And ultimately, in both cases, it was the decision of the all-powerful tsar that would determine the outcome of these discussions.

Although a group of German bankers had been enlisted to finance the construction of the railway, and von Gerstner maintained an interest, the idea of building it with private capital was soon abandoned and the project became a state enterprise with a budget of thirty-four million roubles (around £3.4 million at the time, and broadly 100 times that in today's money). Nicholas was a details man, in the habit of dealing with all kinds of matters that other monarchs would have found far too trivial, and he took an intense, supervisory role in the construction of this key railway, personally chairing the committee that was in charge of its construction, a precursor of the similar one that was established for the Trans-Siberian. The scale of this project was daunting, in a country that was still largely agricultural and barely industrialized. The tsar, of course, had one advantage: serfs who were paid little to work on the line. Such a major enterprise, built mostly by hand, required an army of labour. The best estimates suggest that there were 50,000 serfs employed by the railway at its peak, and perhaps ten per cent of them died, mostly from the periodic epidemics of typhoid and dysentery, which spread through an ill-treated and hungry workforce. In contrast, as we will see, conditions on the Trans-Siberian – built half a century later and after the serfs had been freed – were much better and the death toll much lower.

The serfs were not actually owned by the government, but, instead, contractors working for the project would pay their owners, the large landowners, for their services. The serfs themselves were paid a small sum, but most of it was eaten up by compulsory payments for their food and housing. They worked unbearably long hours: 'The contracts stipulated a working day from sunrise to sunset and the labourers were usually required to work on Sundays and holidays; only heavy rain could be relied on to give them a rest.'[19] As well as being badly fed and poorly housed, the serfs were likely to be flogged if they complained, but the liberal supply of alcohol that was made available to them quelled any potential riots. Those who tried to escape were rounded up by a particularly fearsome gendarmerie, specially established to prevent disturbances.

Nicholas's reputation as an authoritarian figure might be wholly justified, but the oft-told tale about the slightly odd route taken by the railway has largely been debunked. He is said to have ordered the route between the two cities to follow a straight line which he drew using a ruler, and it is indeed straight, apart from three rather incongruous kinks. These are said to have been where his fingers projected over the edge of the ruler, but, in fact, were more likely to have been determined by the difficulties of the terrain through which the line passed. A similar tale arose later over a much longer curve, the Verebinsky bypass, added to the line to avoid a gradient, but since the change was made in 1877 – more than two decades after Nicholas's death – this, too, enters the realm of myth.

The truth or fiction about another feature of the line, its gauge, is more difficult to disentangle. While the Tsarskoe Selo line was six feet, and the Warsaw–Vienna railway used the standard European gauge of four feet eight and a half inches, the Moscow–St

Petersburg line and, subsequently, nearly all Russia's rail network used five feet. The standard explanation is that Nicholas, obsessed with military considerations, ordered the adoption of this wider gauge for defensive purposes, knowing that the requirement to change gauge at the Russian frontier would hamper any potential invader. This explanation has been accepted as conventional wisdom, but the truth is rather more complex. As was common practice in Russia, once the idea of railways took hold, the tsar had sent missions to Europe and the United States to learn more about them. Typically on such trips, the emissaries would return with skilled foreign personnel able to advise them on how to implement new developments. On the American trip, one of these recruits was George Whistler, a former army officer who had worked on several US railroads – and was, incidentally, the father of James Whistler, the illustrious British-based painter. It was reputedly on his advice that the five-foot gauge, common in the early railroads of the United States, was used, since the six feet of the Tsarskoe Selo would have proved too expensive. However, the very fact that Nicholas would have known of the defensive advantages of having a separate gauge suggests that the choice of five feet was made with military considerations at least partly in mind. In the event, the gauge did prove useful for resisting attack, especially during the Second World War, when the German advance was greatly hampered by the requirement to tranship equipment at the gauge break, but it also made life difficult for the Russians themselves when they were the aggressors in the war against Turkey in 1878.[20]

There were numerous obstacles for the project to overcome. As well as slave labour, it required skilled engineers who were in short supply, which meant that most had to come from abroad. Whistler was effectively the chief engineer, but the tsar was intent on presenting the project as a Russian achievement and therefore appointed two of his countrymen engineers to be responsible respectively for the north and south sections. There was such a small supply of home-grown engineers in a country with very few universities and technical colleges that 'the entire graduating class of the Imperial School of Engineering was drafted to the railway in 1843'.[21]

The topography was not easy. Much of the terrain was undulating and intersected by rivers and gorges, as well as deep swamps and dense forests. With the route designed largely as a straight line, extensive cuttings and embankments were required. It was, too, a project on an unprecedented scale. Apart from churches and castles, nothing that required such large numbers of workers and sophisticated techniques had been accomplished in Russia previously. Only the construction of St Petersburg in the swampy marshes of the eastern Baltic by Peter the Great in the seventeenth century could compare in scale with the building of the Nikolayev Railway. Even in terms of railways across the world, this was a major project as few early lines extended beyond 100 miles.

The technology, like the skilled engineers, was largely imported. The tsar had wanted the materials to be sourced in Russia as much as possible, but because of the underdeveloped state of the nation's industry, most ultimately came from Britain and the United States. The mills in the Urals, the heart of the Russian iron industry, proved capable of supplying only a small proportion of the rails and their products were far more expensive, not least because it actually cost more to transport on Russia's terrible roads than the British imports brought in by sea. The locomotives, at least, were largely Russian-built. Nicholas had insisted on domestic production and wanted to use the construction of the country's first major railway to stimulate the creation of a domestic locomotive industry based at Aleksandrovsk, near St Petersburg. The expertise and the design of the locomotives – of which 162 were manufactured – came from America and, initially, so did the craftsmen, but they were required to train locals both to produce the locomotives and to drive them. However, it took until the mid-1850s for the Russians to develop the skills required to take over the enterprise.

The government had enormous difficulties in finding the money to build the scheme. Raising taxes on an already overburdened agrarian population was not only difficult but risked fomenting revolts. Nicholas's constant emphasis on military rather than civil spending led to repeated delays during construction as money simply ran out. The speed of construction was not helped, either, by the tsar's insistence on overseeing decisions concerning even the most minor detail as he kept a tight control on the engineers, both senior and junior, responsible for building the line.

As a result, the line took nine years to complete – twice the expected time – and cost double the original budget, but it proved to be a triumph, as it was used heavily by both passengers and, not surprisingly given the state of the roads, goods. Even though the 400-mile rail journey took about twenty hours, the volume of traffic far exceeded expectations. In 1852, the first full year of operation, the railway averaged nearly 2,000 passengers per day and carried large quantities of freight, mostly flour, grain and livestock. Both the amount of freight and the number of passengers grew rapidly during the decade and the line even became profitable. The high patronage was an impressive demonstration of the need for the railway, especially in the light of the bureaucratic procedures imposed by the tsarist police state, which required every passenger to have both an internal passport and specific permission to travel. A small instance of liberalization encapsulates the nature of repressive tsarist rule. In December 1851, a month after the line opened, Count Kleinmichel, who was in charge of the railway, announced that members of the free classes would no longer require prior police permission to depart from their local station, but instead would merely have to present their passport just before getting on the train. So, in a very small respect, the railway was a liberalizing force, as 'at least the upper classes of Russian society no longer needed police permission for every separate single journey outside of their place of residence'.[22]

Yet the vast majority of passengers travelled in third class, suggesting it was the peasant masses who took to the rails, despite the police procedures. With such a massive bureaucracy, an enduring feature of Russian governance even today, it is hardly surprising that there was little state money available for other purposes. These travellers were encouraged by the surprisingly cheap fares. The cost for third-class passengers was just seven roubles (about fourteen shillings (70p) in equivalent British money of the time), which, though beyond the means of the poorest, was certainly less expensive than similar long journeys on other European railways of the time. There was, too, a real bargain as third-class passengers could travel in freight trains, seated in boxcars with benches, for just three roubles for a journey that took up to forty-eight hours, since their maximum speed was 10 mph. There were only three passenger trains per day, and only one, the daily express, carried first-class passengers; but according to a report in *The Times* in 1865, the higher cost of nineteen roubles was well worth it. Indeed, the standards seemed to match those of the best European and American trains of the day: 'Travellers are received in brilliantly lighted saloons . . . luxurious sofas and armchairs invite the weary to repose . . . when the hour of retiring arrives, the *valet de chambre* conducts the gentlemen passengers [while] smart *femmes de chambre* point out to the lady travellers their bedrooms and boudoirs.'[23] So there was none of the mixing of the sexes that shocked British visitors in America at around the same time.[24]

The St Petersburg–Moscow railway was, on its completion, the premier railway of Europe, far better than its contemporaries, precisely because of the interest in the project taken by the tsar: 'It could be built to such high standards because the government of Nicholas 1 had been willing to utilize the financial resources of the state to the fullest extent, having also at its disposal the services of experienced, competent and honest administrators, a considerable number of well-trained, skilled and resourceful engineers, a large pool of labour, both skilled and unskilled, as well as access to the latest foreign technology.'[25] The result was that Russia had one brilliant railway, as demonstrated by the fact that today's alignment is almost the same as the original route; but because of the high cost and the scarcity of state resources, Russia was slow to expand its rail system.

While undoubtedly a success for those who could take advantage of this new form of travel, the impact of the line took time to take effect in terms of the wider economics of the nation. As with railways across the world, the transport of food and raw materials became cheaper and quicker, reducing the cost of transport by as much as ninety per cent, which greatly reduced the cost of food to urban dwellers. The railway afforded new opportunities for peasants who were able to seek work further from their villages, but because there were initially no connecting branches the effect was limited to those living along the line. There had been numerous suggestions for such branches to connect the railway with neighbouring towns from various local notables, but the government rejected all these plans – another illustration of its hesitant attitude towards modernizing the Russian Empire. Most crucially, the industrial area in the Urals was still not connected with the nation's two main cities, which greatly hampered its economic development.

In the four decades between the completion of the Nikolayev Railway and work starting on the Trans-Siberian, Russia did embrace the idea of a national rail network, but generally with little sense of urgency and at a far gentler pace than its European counterparts. There was no early period of railway mania as occurred in so many other countries which plunged into the railway age with such enthusiasm. Given the limited resources, it was felt that the country could afford to build only one major railway at a time, especially as the lines were being funded from the state coffers. The completion of the Nikolayev Railway encouraged the tsar to order the construction of the St Petersburg–Warsaw Railway, also as a state enterprise. This time there was no doubting its main purpose – retaining control over its troublesome Polish province and supporting the resistance to any attack from the West: 'Unlike the St Petersburg–Moscow Railway, this line was to be built primarily for military and administrative purposes.'[26] A railway to Odessa on the Black Sea from Moscow through Ukraine, the bread basket of the nation with its fertile soil, would have had a much greater economic impact, but Nicholas's priorities were all too clear. And, as Richard Haywood points out in his book on early Russian railways, Nicholas even got his military priorities wrong, because a line to Odessa 'would also have had crucial military value, for the attack by the Western Powers came, not through the Kingdom of Poland, as the tsar had feared, but through Crimea'.[27]

The Crimean War proved a spur for an extension of the railway system. At its outset, in 1853, Russia could still only boast a network of 650 miles, far less than its European rivals, such as Britain, which had almost ten times that number, and this proved a great handicap to the war effort. Crimea, bordering the Black Sea, could be reached only by the traditional water routes, and subsequent recriminations over the defeat focussed on the inadequacy of the transport system. The Russians, too, were aware that the British, in contrast, had built the first ever military railway to help break down the long siege of Sevastopol.[28] Nicholas, a broken man following the early defeats of his beloved army, died during the war and was replaced by his son, the far more liberal-minded Alexander II, who embarked on a major railway building programme.

Alexander, who became tsar in 1855, was able to make use of the terrible debacle of the Crimean War to encourage a period of rapid railway expansion. Unlike his father, he was not hostile to private interests and was far readier to embrace foreign technology. He authorized the creation of the Main Company of Russian Railways, financed by a consortium of mainly French and English investors, but, crucially, with the Russian government retaining the financial risk by guaranteeing a yearly return of five per cent to the shareholders – a kind of state-backed capitalism. This arrangement stimulated a mini-boom in railway construction with several lines being built between the Baltic and the Black Sea, principally for carrying grain and other agricultural produce, including a line linking Kiev with Odessa, and in 1862 the completion of the St Petersburg–Warsaw Railway with a branch to the Prussian border. Helsinki, then part of Russia, and St Petersburg, too, were linked by a railway line. However, the Main Company proved unable to fulfil all its obligations and the relationship between the government and the company was fraught, not least because it was run by a group of French directors based in Paris with a penchant for a luxury lifestyle that did not endear them to their Russian counterparts, who were effectively civil servants. Indeed, 'the formation of the Main Company proved to be very damaging to the future not only of the Russian railways, but of the Government itself'.[29] As was often the way with early railway projects, the Company had underestimated the cost of building lines, partly because of its own incompetence as well as widespread corruption, and repeatedly asked the government for extra loans to complete its various projects. This caused embarrassment to the aristocracy as several ministers and even members of the tsar's family had substantial shareholdings in the Main Company. Following some renegotiations, most of these lines were completed in the 1860s and Russia was beginning to acquire the beginnings of the type of rail network that was already commonplace in Europe.

Although Alexander had a greater belief in free enterprise than his father it still proved impossible to persuade private entrepreneurs to build schemes entirely at their own risk. There were doubts that the Russian economy, still largely based on agriculture and mining, could sustain profitable railways. Despite this, the government had understood the importance of creating a rail network and in 1866 drew up a plan for the expansion of the system. This stimulated the greatest-ever phase of expansion in the Russian railway network, with the mileage of 3,000 miles trebling in the decade to 1877 and doubling again to 1897, a period that included completion of part of the Trans-Siberian. While this boom did throw up a few entrepreneurs – 'railway barons', as they became known – the impetus still came from government; and these railway magnates were more often interested in making their fortunes at the expense of lucrative contracts from the government, rather than through the construction of profitable lines. Indeed, most of the risk of building and operating these railways was taken by the government, as promoters continued to be guaranteed a set rate of return on their investment. As confidence grew in the Russian economy, several private railway companies did emerge, but by and large the government remained involved in most of the network, since no line could be built without its permission and most needed some kind of financial support. The complex system of private and public ownership was rationalized in the late 1880s by the finance minister, Nikolai Bunge, who effectively forced through the creation of a genuine railway network for the first time. Privately and publicly owned railways were forced to co-operate by, for example, using each other's rolling stock where that was convenient and the creation of a unified railway tariff. That set the tone for the construction of the Trans-Siberian, which was to be, unequivocally, a government project.

Unlike the Moscow–St Petersburg Railway, most of the later lines were constructed on the cheap, with sharper curves, insufficient ballast and steep gradients. Bridges were built with inferior material and occasionally collapsed, and rails frequently broke. It was only the fact that the maximum speed was usually 25 mph that prevented a spate of very serious accidents. Stations were often located far from the towns they served, because it was cheaper to route the railways through the valleys rather than the hills on which many settlements had been constructed as a protection against invaders. Many of these same features would be found on the Trans-Siberian.

Despite this, just as had happened a generation before in Europe, the advent of the railway transformed the way of life of local people and was usually welcomed by them. A few curmudgeonly landowners would complain that the noise would disturb their sleep or the smoke would make their animals ill, but for the most part the arrival of the railway was celebrated and peasants from far afield would come to greet the first train. The economics of the area would change as the labourers building the line would need to be fed and grain prices would rise 'sometimes by as much as ten times'.[30] Then, after the line's completion, land prices would rise as it became easier to take produce to market.

The amount of freight carried doubled between 1865 and 1880, then doubled again in the following decade. Much of that was grain, which became an important component of Russia's export trade; and coal, from the Donets Basin, straddling Russia and Ukraine, became increasingly important. Passenger journeys grew, too, but they were highly seasonal, dominated initially by farm labourers and later, as the more affluent classes took to the railways, by what was called 'dacha traffic', the annual trip to the country cottage that nearly every family of means possessed. Russia was still an underdeveloped and backward country, but its railway system was the one aspect of its economy that was, in any way, modern. The system was nothing like as intensive as those in most of Europe or the United States, but nevertheless it was a relatively efficient and effective network that was recognized as being vital to the nation's economy.

Neither grain nor passengers, however, were the real motivation behind the government's interest in growing the rail network – that remained military. The Warsaw line, for example, had been used soon after its opening to put down one of the perennial Polish rebellions. Therefore, despite the government's constant penury due to wars, a desire to have a strong rouble and the slowness of industrial development, railways were seen as a key priority. As Alexander III's war minister later put it, 'railways are now the strongest and most decisive element of war. Therefore, regardless of financial difficulties, it is exceeding desirable to make our railway network equal that of our enemies.'[31] Nothing else can really explain the interest in the Trans-Siberian, which, as the next chapter will show, developed soon after the mid-century.

# TWO

# HOLDING ON TO SIBERIA

As the network of lines was spreading around European Russia, the idea of building a railway stretching deep into Russia's Far East had begun to take hold. But slowly. There were various promoters, idealists and fantasists with a claim to being the first to have set out the concept, and because several of these were foreign, non-Russian writers tend to give undue credence to such claims.

One particularly ill-informed story which has been given widespread prominence is that the first budding Trans-Siberian developer was a British gentleman named Mr Dull, a tale that was simply too amusing for many writers not to repeat. It is, unfortunately, a myth. The fellow in question was actually a Thomas Duff, whose initials had been lost in the retelling of the story but whose descendants have now corrected the misreported account. Certainly, his plan was not dull. Duff was an adventurer who went to China and returned via St Petersburg, where in 1857 he met the transport minister (officially known as the Minister of Ways and Communications), Constantine V. Chevkin, and suggested the building of a tramway from Nizhny Novgorod, 265 miles east of Moscow, east via Kazan and Perm to the Urals, which would have been the start of the Trans-Siberian. Duff had worked out some detail suggesting it would cost $20 million, but would earn a healthy rate of return of fourteen per cent. In return, he wanted a guarantee of four per cent interest from the government. Duff also reportedly said that the tramway could be horse-drawn, using some of the four million horses that supposedly roamed around western Siberia. Despite the fact that even the ever-inventive Victorians would have spotted the impractical nature of the idea, numerous historians have intimated that this was a serious suggestion. Sadly it was probably just a joke born of a casual remark.

In any case, Chevkin, portrayed aptly by Eric Newby as 'a man noted for his irascibility and a masterly obstructionist to boot'[1] – a description that could be ascribed to many of his successors in government who thwarted attempts to modernize Russia – was unimpressed with the idea and showed Duff the door, saying that the scheme 'did not seem realizable because of the climatic conditions'.[2] Duff tried again three years later to no avail.

To overcome the problem of snowdrifts alluded to by Chevkin, a former governor of Tomsk named Suprenenko made a suggestion that was even more outlandish than Duff's wild horses joke – except he was serious. He put forward the idea of a horse-drawn railway enclosed by a wooden gallery all the way to Tyumen, 1,100 miles east of Moscow, and Irkutsk, near Lake Baikal. Not surprisingly, Chevkin showed him the door, too.

At the same time, however, there were serious ideas emerging for railways within Siberia. The first proposal came from a Russian, Nicholas Murayev, the far-sighted and relatively liberal governor general of eastern Siberia. Appointed in 1847, his mission was naked imperialism, to protect and extend Russian interests in the Far East. He expanded Russian control over territory disputed with China in violation of a treaty, increasing the Empire's territory by some 400,000 square miles, almost twice the size of France, including the crucial Amur river route that opened the way to the Pacific. He built countless fortresses to protect these gains and tried to make Siberia's economy more viable by exploiting resources such as coal. Transport – and railways in particular – he realized would be key to maintaining control over the expanded territory and he carved out a forty-mile route from opposite Aleksandrovsk, a newly established Russian post on Sakhalin Island in the sea of Japan, to Sofiysk on the lower reaches of the Amur river, which for much of its length forms the border between Russia and Manchuria. His idea was that this would become a railway, creating a transport route that avoided the mouth of the Amur, which is dangerous to shipping because of the shifting sands. While Murayev, the imperialist, might have been unconcerned that this went through Chinese territory, Chevkin was not – so this plan, too, went into the waste-paper basket.

Then along came a group of three Englishmen whose surnames – Sleigh, Horn and Morison – sound like a dodgy firm of high-street solicitors but whose first names have been lost in the mists of time. They sought to build a line from Nizhny Novgorod right across Siberia to Aleksandrovsk in order to 'facilitate relations between Europe, China, India and America',[3] a laudable aim at a time of international tension in the aftermath of the Crimean War. Like Duff, they too had a financial plan, offering to organize a loan of $25 million in exchange for being given the land and a 90-year concession, but the idea seems to have elicited little interest from the government.

Finally, a New Yorker with a passionate interest in Siberia tried his luck with a more thoroughly developed scheme. This was Perry McDonough Collins, another adventurer and reportedly the first American to cross the entire breadth of Siberia, which he accomplished partly by river. Given the rather odd title of Commercial Agent of the United States at the Amoor [Amur] river by the US government, he was a rather more serious candidate than his predecessors for promoting such a grand scheme, and was, according to various figures like Murayev and the tsar's second son, the Grand Duke Constantine, who offered him support, 'an honest, persuasive and immensely likable self-made man'[4] with a gift for oratory. Collins – bored of his job as a banker and gold-dust broker in San Francisco dealing with the 49ers, the original gold-diggers – had developed an obsession with Siberia, seeing it as a possible El Dorado for American traders. He hastened to St Petersburg, where he met Murayev and various other officials and embarked on his journey through Siberia.

His journey, accompanied by a mysterious 'Mr Peyton', provides an insight into travel on the post road in the mid-nineteenth century and demonstrates how fast it was possible to travel through Siberia, provided the traveller had official support – since he was the lucky recipient of a personal letter from Murayev, which definitely speeded things up for him, and was prepared to endure the hardship of almost perpetual motion. Collins, who had been advised by Murayev to travel in winter when progress was faster, averaged 100 miles per day to reach Irkutsk, a distance of 3,545 miles, in just thirty-five days, travelling on all but seven of them, and in his characteristically meticulous way he reported: 'we changed horses 210 times on the journey, with some 200 drivers and 25 postilions.'[5] There were inevitable mishaps, most seriously when at one point the sleigh plunged into a ditch and the driver was thrown off while the horses bolted. Collins tried to reach the reins, but was unable to do so and the sleigh came to a halt only when the horses smashed into a *tarantass* coming the other way, resulting in the death of one and the total wreck of both vehicles. The horse, notes Collins coolly, was turned into steaks and soup at the next post house and its skin exchanged for a couple of bottles of vodka.

As possibly only the second American[6] to venture there, he was given a hero's welcome in Irkutsk and then proceeded further east, where he sailed down the Amur. During the journey he started putting forward his proposals for a Siberian railway to the Russian authorities. He sent the local governor a letter suggesting a line from Chita, 250 miles east of Lake Baikal, to the Amur river, which would have created a through transportation route to the Pacific and, of course, the United States. He saw the Amur as a way of opening up Siberia to the outside world, from the east. He, too, reckoned it would need $20 million – a figure that, oddly, keeps popping up in these schemes – and 20,000 men to build it. He wanted the government to provide the land and materials in exchange for stock, and it would be offered the right to purchase the line at any stage. The proposal was passed on to St Petersburg, where, inevitably, it ended up on Chevkin's desk. By then a Siberian Committee had been created on which Chevkin sat and he spoke strongly against the idea – who would feed all the workers? he mused – and despite Muravyev's support, the idea was killed off.

Collins fared better with his other proposal: a plan to cross Asia – and, indeed, the world – with a telegraph wire to connect the Russian Empire with both the United States and Europe via an underwater cable in the Bering Strait that separates Russia from the American continent, Alaska and British Columbia.

Elsewhere, telegraphs were springing up next to railway lines, which provided an obvious route for them, but here the idea was for a simple set of wires to run across Siberia. Backed by Samuel Morse, the inventor of telegraphy, Collins obtained a concession from the Russian government to erect the line and also gained permission from the Canadian and US governments. Then, cleverly, he sold his franchises to the Western Union. This was fortunate, because an Atlantic cable linking America with Europe and, eventually, Russia was laid by a rival company without the need to cross the Siberian steppes, so the $3 million that had been spent on erecting wires in Siberia was wasted.

There were also plans from within Siberia for railways that crossed at least a major part of the region. It was not only the obduracy and lack of interest of politicians like Chevkin that ensured the failure of all these ideas, or even the technical difficulties, but more fundamental political considerations. The very fact that a railway could be built changed the relationship between Russia and its wild east. The issue of laying tracks to the Pacific brought up wider questions of the nature of the Empire and the role of Siberia within it, which would be the subject of much debate and controversy over the next three decades. Indeed, the question of the railway became subsumed in wider issues about what to do about Siberia as part of the Russian Empire, an issue that exercised several government committees and commissions and which was given urgency by the humiliation of the defeat in the Crimean War.

While many of the early suggestions for a Siberian railway may have been rather fanciful, the next quarter of a century was dominated by hand-wringing debates about Siberia that took the matter very seriously indeed. At root was the attitude towards this distant province. It did not go unnoticed in Russia that the United States was beginning to establish itself across its vast – but not as vast – continent. It would be wrong to suggest that the question of the Trans-Siberian was entirely dictated by military considerations. As Steven Marks puts it, 'many writers have portrayed the Siberian Railroad as serving exclusively the defence of Russia's Pacific shore and Far Eastern border; but they have overlooked the domestic concerns that affected the security of the Empire and were ultimately as important as the menace of foreign powers'.[7]

In the 1850s the government had established a Siberian Committee, which broadly took the view that the future of the region lay in the gradual establishment of large estates owned by the aristocracy, using the toil of their serfs (who were not emancipated until 1861). It was, in fact, precisely the same kind of bucolic vision that the Southerners tried to defend in the American Civil War – and, indeed, had sought to create in the American West – with ranches and their black slaves. The key concern was that Siberia might declare its independence, secede in the same way as the Southern US states, but with the key difference that it would probably have been impossible for the Russian government to impose its will and reunite the Empire. Stimulated by various political exiles who had, as it were, gone native, such as many of the Decembrists sent there after their attempted coup in 1825, a Siberian regionalist movement had developed. It was not particularly focussed or coherent, but was rather 'a heterogeneous, amorphous movement of Siberian intellectuals who stood in the broadest sense for the interests of their region'.[8] The regionalists saw Siberia as a land separate from Russia, with its tradition of tribalism and different geographic characteristics, populated by people with greater independence and spirit than their western counterparts.

The movement's most charismatic advocate was Nikolai Ladrintsev, who argued that Siberia should have the same kind of future as America and Australia, with a combination of settlers and the indigenous population creating prosperity. Instead, Siberia had 'been left in the tundra, the miserable result of arbitrary administration, dependence on the metropolis, and the central government's exploitive self-interest in Siberia as a penal colony and source of furs and minerals'.[9] This movement was taken seriously in St Petersburg, where it was feared it would lead to the creation of an independent Siberian state, even though that was not necessarily the position of the regionalists. The official response was typically heavy-handed and was aimed at eradicating the very notion of Siberia. Tsar Alexander III (who had assumed the throne when his father, Alexander II, was assassinated in 1881) issued a series of decrees that aimed to accelerate 'the gradual abolition of any sign of the administrative separateness of Siberia and the destruction of its internal administrative unity'.[10] The region was broken up into various administrative entities, which meant that by 1887 the very name Siberia was no longer used for any part of the Empire. The flip side of this was that the tsar supported the construction of a railway to stimulate the economic development of the region.

Inevitably, though, the military aspects of the pros and cons of building a railway featured prominently in the discussions. While the Western section of the Siberian railway could be justified in terms of helping emigration from the overpopulated parts of European Russia, and by the exploitation of mineral wealth, building a line through the sparsely populated territory beyond Lake Baikal could be justified only on the basis of strategic considerations. Nothing raises the temperature of the political debate more than supposed threats from other nations. And, in fairness, with Britain at the height of its gunboat-diplomacy pomp, and the major powers in land-grabbing mood across Asia and Africa, there was no shortage of genuine threats. Russia had extended its empire in the east through Muravyev's efforts and subsequent treaties with China and Japan, imposed largely at the end of the barrel of a gun. But technological developments were also a threat, since improved shipping made it easier for Japan, America and, in particular, Britain – the pre-eminent world power of the time – to see parts of Siberia as potentially ripe for exploitation, especially in the event of a war, given Russia's weak hold over its distant territory. These nations, too, were all keen to establish control over China, which was weak and largely defenceless, and its fate was clearly bound up with that of Russia's Far East.

During the second half of the nineteenth century Russia and Britain were in constant competition for territory in Central Asia and the Far East. Throughout the period between the Russo-Turkish war of 1877–8 and the start of construction of the Trans-Siberian, there was tension between Britain and Russia over the status of Primorye, the region which includes Vladivostok. Indeed, during the conflict Russia had even feared a British attack on its Pacific coast; and in the 1880s the two countries nearly came to war several times over British occupation of Afghanistan, which was intended to create a buffer between its Indian colony and Russia, whose territorial ambitions were creeping southwards. According to Marks, 'the situation was aggravated by the imminent completion of the Canadian Pacific railroad, which would cut the journey between England and Japan from the 52 days it took through the Suez canal to 37 days'.[11] There were even incorrect allegations that the British had built and financed the Canadian Pacific, which was eventually completed in 1885, and these arguments were used to strengthen the case for building the Siberian railway. China, too, came heavily into the equation. Manchuria, formerly an empty buffer zone between the two great Asian empires, was being populated and there was talk of various railways across its territory. In the fluctuating alliances among the major European powers of the era, Britain played complex diplomatic games with China as a pawn that greatly worried Russian military strategists.

The war with Turkey had strained the government's finances but highlighted the value of efficient rail transport to supply an army during a conflict. The railways had proved their worth, too, in battle against Afghan troops in Central Asia. The humiliation of the Crimean War, where the defence of Sevastopol was made much harder by the lack of a railway, was, too, an important consideration. Therefore, by the mid-1880s, many military strategists were pressing for the construction of the Siberian railway as vital to the nation's strategic interests. It was seen as a way of maintaining Russian control in the same way that Britain had established control over India through the construction of a railway network in the aftermath of the Indian Mutiny (1857–8). It was the military potential of railways that attracted the attention of

Tsar Alexander I, as it was becoming clear that the iron road was an essential part of the armoury of both occupation and warfare.[12]

Indeed, the military motive for building the line was both defensive and offensive: 'As military strategists throughout the 1880s discussed construction of a railroad across Siberia, or at the very least from Vladivostok to the Amur river, their ostensible intent was to enhance the defence of Russian territory, but official perceptions of the railroad presupposed that it would also be the means to an offensive, "forward" policy in China.'[13] That reasoning actually engendered some opposition from supporters of the alternative strategy of strengthening the navy patrolling the Pacific coast, obviating the need for a land connection. Nevertheless, the idea of a land connection had far more resonance in government circles, but the high cost was always used by opponents of the scheme, especially finance ministers.

The military imperative was also given a boost by the completion of the Canadian transcontinental in 1885, given the shorter journey time between England and Japan, which was seen as a potential military advantage. Psychologically, for the Russians, the construction of the Canadian transcontinental proved more important than its American predecessor completed sixteen years previously. Canada was a similarly vast, rather underpopulated country and its furthermost province, British Columbia, could well have seceded had it not been for the construction of the line across the new nation. The Russian Far East, like the Canadian West, was remote and semi-detached. If the Canadians could use a railway line to bind their country together, so could the Russians.

Proposals for a Siberian railway were dreamt up by all kinds of characters ranging from the crazy to the pragmatic during the 1870s and 1880s. There was a fellow called Hartmann with an idea for a line from Tomsk, about 1,800 miles from Moscow, to Irkutsk, and then from the other side of the lake to Sretensk, in the Amur basin. He wanted an annual subsidy of $2 million and an eighty-one-year concession. Then there was General Mikhail Annenkov, who had built the Trans-Caspian Railway from the sea to Samarkand, claiming that he could build the line in just six years at the ridiculously low price of $30,200 per mile. Both of these got nowhere, as did even the best schemes of this period.

There were potentially several alternative routes, too. There were proposals for a northern one from Perm to Tyumen on the Tura river; another further south linking Nizhny-Novgorod to Kazan and Yekaterinburg, also ending in Tyumen; and a third from Perm to Yekaterinburg and then to what is now Belozerskoe. The concept moved an important step forward in 1875, when Konstantin Posyet, the transport minister, posited the idea of a railway to exploit the wealth of Siberia. It was the first official document to advocate a line stretching into the depths of Siberia. He argued that Siberia was no longer 'a desolate and terrible country inhabited by convicts',[14] but rather a rich source of resources which could be exploited with a railway connection. He wanted it to run from Moscow right through to the Amur river, but if that were impossible, at least as far as Irkutsk. He wanted it to use the northern route through Perm, rather than existing trade routes through the south in order to spur the development of these areas, which were home to tribes and untouched by civilization. His plan, though, attracted scant support from the committee of ministers, the contemporary equivalent of the Cabinet. Although, Posyet's proposal did not gain the support of the committee, it did decide to go ahead with the construction of a railway from Nizhny-Novgorod along the right bank of the Volga to Kazan and Yekaterinburg, a proposal endorsed by the tsar in December 1875.

This did not mean, however, a Trans-Siberian Railway, but rather a line that stretched just the other side of the Urals. The next decade and a half was a period of fierce controversy and debate over whether the Trans-Siberian should be built and, indeed, why. The discussion over the possible construction of the line was characterized by 'ideological, personal and ministerial divisions, as well as financial exigencies, would keep the issue from being resolved one way or another'.[15] Supporters of the scheme faced an uphill task in winning over the politicians, even though the tsar himself was clearly supportive and the creation of a committee was seen as a way of breaking the deadlock. The Russian system of governance was fraught by divisions between government departments, whose ministers saw themselves as ruling over their particular fiefdom with little reference to their fellow politicians. Difficult matters, like the issue of the Trans-Siberian Railway, were passed on to committees and commissions, whose members always seemed more expert at procrastination than decision-making. As an example, the Baranov Commission, created to look at the inadequacies of the railway system during the Russo-Turkish war, sat for six years after the conflict had ended. Moreover, as with almost every government in the world, ministerial paralysis was made worse by the finance ministry's hostility to any type of spending whatsoever. Posyet's continued support for the Trans-Siberian came up against the conservativeness of the minister of finance, Ivan Alekseevich Vyshenegradsky, who was adamantly opposed to the idea of the railway. Of course, sitting on top of all this chaotic structure, the tsar was an absolute monarch who could simply make decisions on his own. So it was with the Trans-Siberian.

In 1886 the tsar received complaints from the governor generals of both Irkutsk and Primorye, expressing concern that their territory was vulnerable to land-grabbing by the Chinese. Specifically, Count Alexei Ignatiev, the governor general of Irkutsk, warned that large numbers of Chinese were infiltrating Transbaikalia, the region around Lake Baikal, and consequently that a railway was essential to bring soldiers quickly to the area. He proposed a line between

Irkutsk and Tomsk, from where there was river communication with Tyumen, now connected by rail to Yekaterinburg and Perm. In what was clearly an organized piece of political pleading, the governor general of Primorye, Baron Andrei Korff, suggested a 660-mile-long line from the eastern shore of Lake Baikal to Sretensk, on the Amur, from where steamers could reach the Pacific. The two railways would, in effect, have created a Trans-Siberian route.

Somehow, after years of procrastination and debate, this seems to have been the key round of lobbying that led to the decision to build the Trans-Siberian. Alexander III wrote a rather curious note at the bottom of Ignatiev's report, which suggested that he did not realize the extent of his own power: 'I have already read so many reports of the governors general of Siberia and it must be confessed with sadness and shame that up to now the government has done almost nothing to satisfy the needs of this rich but neglected region.'[16] He wanted to see prosperity and peace for Siberia, which he stressed was 'an indivisible part of Russia', and the line would bring 'glory to our Fatherland'. Through the railway, the vast region would be 'Russified' and industrialized. This was, in effect, a decision to build the line, but it would take another five years before the final go-ahead.

While the wider debates over Siberia were taking place, the railway was creeping towards it as Russia was enjoying something of a belated railway boom. By the time that the Trans-Siberian was being seriously considered in the early 1880s, Russia had a network of 14,500 miles – extremely modest given the size of the country. By contrast, at that time the United States, with its smaller land mass, had more than ten times that number, while the tiny Great Britain had about the same amount.

Nevertheless, this represented considerable progress, given that at the onset of the Crimean War in 1853 there had been just 620 miles. By 1866 there were 3,000 miles, and then by 1877 the mileage trebled, and doubled again by the end of the century. The massive expansion of the railway network was, however, largely at the expense of taxpayers and was a terrible drain on the government's coffers. This was because earlier attempts to persuade private companies to build lines entirely at their own risk had failed. While technically all the railway companies in this period were in private hands, in order to encourage companies to build these new lines – which were much needed but inherently uneconomic, since they mostly passed through thinly populated territory – the government underwrote their debts. The situation was exacerbated because several lines fell into the hands of unscrupulous railway barons, whose only interest – in parallel with their counterparts in the United States and many parts of Europe – was to make money: 'No matter how uneconomically or irrationally the railway companies operated, the government was obliged to make up their deficits out of its own treasury.'[17] Worse, much of that money had to be borrowed from abroad, which weakened further the rouble, making imports – which were required to stimulate industrialization – more expensive.

In 1877 the rail network reached Orenburg, near what is now the border with Kazakhstan, and traditionally a staging post for people travelling over the Urals into Asia. More importantly, the Ural Mining Railway opened the following year, serving the industrial region; and in 1880 the bridge over the Volga near Syzran, with the grand name of Imperator Alexander II, opened, bringing central Russia closer to the Siberian steppes.

For the time being, however, the Urals remained uncrossed. There was, nevertheless, a section of railway separate from the rest of the network, east of the Urals. This line, the first in Siberia, was started in 1883 and ran from Yekaterinburg to Tyumen, and by connecting with the tracks to Perm, which had been completed in 1878, provided a link between the Kama and Ob rivers. It opened in 1885, but remained cut off from the rest of the rail network for a decade until the Yekaterinburg–Chelyabinsk line, built as part of the overall Trans-Siberian project, was completed in 1896.

Despite the obvious benefits of this boom in railway construction, which continued to be Russia's main catalyst for industrialization, and despite the tsar's support, the Trans-Siberian project remained stalled. This was down to the vagaries of the tsarist government's administration and, in particular, the ministry of finance's tight control over the purse strings. An absolute monarchy creates an atmosphere in which ministers are constantly manoeuvring to win favour from the ruler. Therefore, control of the construction of the Trans-Siberian – by far the most prestigious government project – became the subject of endless bickering between departments, which meant that it took several more years before the foundation stone could be laid. The war, transport and finance ministries were in a permanent state of struggle, battling it out like a scene from *Yes Minister*. Most ministers were more interested in pushing forward the interests of their own department than those of wider society or even, ironically, of the tsar.

Of course, all the discussions were overshadowed by the question of finance. The minister of finance, Vyshenegradsky, was a fiscal conservative who had made his reputation by reducing costs as a director of two railway companies, and he fought a long and hard rearguard action against the Trans-Siberian project. As Theodore Von Laue, an economic historian, puts it, 'The Imperial will could not prevail over the parsimony of his Minister of Finance.'[18] Following the intervention of the Siberian governor generals, in order to make rapid progress, the tsar called four special conferences in the winter of 1886–7 to consider the many practical, technical and financial aspects of building the line. Then a co-ordinating committee was appointed, only to be scrapped because it proved ineffective, and replaced by a second committee. Vyshenegradsky, whose opposition to the line was based on both fiscal and intellectual grounds – arguing it would bankrupt the nation and was an unnecessary extravagance – not only withheld any significant funding, but manoeuvred to weaken the transport ministry by trying to wrest control of the project for the ministry of finance. He created a department of railway affairs within his ministry in order to sort out the overspending on the railways in government control. By allocating virtually no money for new lines, which he thought ought to be built by the private sector, he even managed, for a while, to stop any surveys on the route being carried out. Vyshenegradsky also enjoyed a piece of good fortune when Posyet, the minister of transport, who had continued to battle away for money to support preliminary work, was forced to resign in 1888 following a rail accident involving the tsar's train, which could have resulted in the deaths of several members of the royal family.

Posyet's departure further delayed progress as the new Transport Minister, General German Egorovich Pauker, was a weak-willed fellow who did not push sufficiently for funds to begin the preliminary work on the project. Pauker died after less than a year in office, and his successor, Adolf von Hubbenet, found it equally difficult to persuade Vyshenegradsky as the rivalry between the finance and transport ministries threatened to derail the project, despite the tsar's support. At root, there was an ideological difference. The ministry of finance was obsessed by keeping a tight rein on the state budget, while the transport ministry had a strategic grand vision that saw the railways as being at the heart of Russia's industrialization. Indeed, this type of row has been repeated countless times around the world over the past century whenever big projects are put forward, and is even echoed in contemporary Britain today with, for example, Crossrail in London, which was on the drawing board for more than half a century before work finally began in 2009.

Vyshenegradsky kept up his rearguard action by suggesting a plan that would involve constructing only those sections of line where no traditionally navigable river was available. This would have reduced the required construction of railway from more than 4,600 miles[19] to just 2,000. It was a bad, old-fashioned scheme, opposed by business interests and engineers, who argued that the need for eight transfers from rail to water would be expensive and slow down the journey. Indeed, it was not unlike the Main Line, a similar early mixed waterway and rail route completed in Pennsylvania more than half a century previously in 1834, which proved to be unsuccessful precisely because it was far less convenient than the railways. Consequently, the idea was given short shrift, but even then Vyshenegradsky had not finished. If the line had to be built, then, he suggested, why should it not be funded by private interests?

Vyshenegradsky had been plotting with General Mikhail Annenkov to obtain funds from French banking interests to build the line. Annenkov, who had fought in several campaigns in Central Asia, was a pioneer in the use of railways in wartime. In the 1880s, while fighting to establish Russian control in what is now Turkmenistan, he quickly built a 1,000-mile section of the Trans-Caspian Railway along the Afghan border in order to speed up the arrival at the front of troops and matériel. It was, indeed, an example of the important role that railways played in the waging of war, and had helped obtain military support for the notion of the Trans-Siberian. The Trans-Caspian showed, too, that railways were not just useful in defending territory, but could also help offensive action. Annenkov realized that the line made sense militarily in keeping the Chinese threat at bay, but he also had potential contacts to fund the line, because his daughter was married to a high-ranking French official. His war efforts, particularly his use of the railway, had earned international recognition, and after making contact with the Rothschilds, the renowned banking family, he put forward the idea of obtaining French money to fund the construction of the line. The Rothschilds, who already had extensive railway interests in France and Italy, offered 300 million roubles, which Annenkov, who wanted to be in charge of the project, felt was sufficient, but his efforts proved to be of no avail. Vyshenegradsky's initial enthusiasm paled and then the committee of ministers came out against the proposal to fund the scheme with foreign money, presumably because of its military importance.

In truth, using the private sector to fund the Trans-Siberian was always unrealistic. The line was to be built in territory that could hardly be more unpromising for railway economics. It was very long and went through underpopulated lands with little likely passenger traffic. While it would transport some minerals and agricultural produce, it was never going to make the kind of decent return on capital which investors, particularly big bankers like the Rothschilds, would expect.

The project, therefore, was to be planned and funded by government. Not everyone believed it was possible, however. The British establishment was particularly disparaging. They laughed at the ability of the Russians to carry out such a mammoth enterprise and, indeed, such was the contempt in Whitehall that a furious British military attaché in St Petersburg rebuked his own government for searching 'for a thousand details to discredit the enterprise in the eyes of Europe'. Instead, he suggested, 'British energy should be directed to obtaining orders for the iron rails, rather than cavilling and carping at a railway extension.'[20]

However, while British contempt for Russian enterprise might have been born of a combination of xenophobia and hubris, a dose of scepticism was probably the right response. The decades of squabbling and controversies that had delayed the decision to go ahead showed that Russia's administrative processes had more in common with the feudalism of the eighteenth century than the modernism of the approaching twentieth. It was, in reality, only the dedication and force of will of a particularly skilled and, indeed, ruthless, politician, Sergei Witte, that saw the project through to completion. All such projects need champions and nowhere was that more true than in a Russia still ruled by the primitive system of absolute monarchy. And Witte proved to be just the right man for the task. A long-time railway manager and briefly transport minister, Witte had been Vyshenegradsky's protégé and was appointed as his replacement as finance minister in August 1892. That appointment meant the right man was in the right place at the right time – one of those fortuitous accidents of history. Otherwise, the Trans-Siberian might have stayed on the drawing board.

# THREE

# WITTE'S BREAKTHROUGH

When Sergei Witte became minister of finance, work on the Trans-Siberian had barely started and there was still a lack of momentum within government circles behind the project. Indeed, Witte found a situation where neither money nor resources had been allocated to the scheme, and there was no clear mechanism to see the project through. He would quickly change all that.

There are not many finance ministers who, like Witte, can claim to have built one of the wonders of the world. There is no doubting that it is Witte who most deserves the accolade of father of the Trans-Siberian Railway. Even though he was no spendthrift, he recognized the importance of the line in several respects. Like many great men, Witte needed a considerable amount of luck to complete the project. He needed, too, the right *Zeitgeist* to push forward a project that had been mooted for so long and yet seen so little progress. Witte was that relatively rare beast in tsarist Russia: a man whose ability rather than his birthright had propelled him to the top of government. Born in the Georgian capital, Tblisi,[1] in 1849, Witte's background was modest; although there was aristocratic blood in his lineage – the odd princess and count – his father, Julius, was merely an official in the local governor general's office. Witte studied mathematics at Odessa University, where his well-received dissertation was on infinitesimal numbers, a choice replete with irony for someone who would later spend billions of roubles on building a railway.

Both his father and grandfather died during his time at university, leaving his family on hard times. Consequently, he had to find a stable job very quickly, which, inevitably, pushed him into the civil service. He joined at the lowly ninth rank (*chin*) in the deeply hierarchical structure, but was always destined for higher things, because of what he called his 'noble' blood – which was somewhat diluted – and because of his undoubted abilities, which quickly attracted the attention of his superiors. His mentor was Count Vladimir Bobrinski, Russia's minister of transport, who counselled Witte against becoming an engineer, arguing with great foresight that the railway needed men with a good liberal education, rather than narrow specialists. So Witte went to work for the Odessa state railway, which at the time was owned by the government. Witte was initially a ticket clerk, but also, according to his memoirs, 'studied freight traffic, worked as assistant stationmaster and full-fledged stationmaster, and acted as train inspector'.[2] It was, indeed, precisely the sort of on-the-job training which was given to bright new recruits by British Rail, except that after just six months he was appointed director of the traffic office, the key role in ensuring the smooth running of a railway.

During the Russo-Turkish War of 1877–8 he claimed in his memoirs to be practically the sole manager of the Odessa Railway, responsible for delivering all the traffic to the front and his efforts came to the notice of the tsar. It was at this time that Witte suffered the worst mishap of his career, when a train carrying recruits crashed down a ravine and burnt out, killing more than 100 men. The disaster was caused by a maintenance crew, who had removed a rail but failed to replace it or, indeed, to put up warning flags during a blizzard. Along with the director of the railway, Witte was held responsible, even though he had no direct involvement in the maintenance of the railway: 'public opinion in those days was envenomed by that spirit of liberalism which is essentially hatred against those who stand out either because of position or wealth, the spirit which animates the revolutionary mob',[3] was Witte's rather revealing explanation. The pair were sentenced to four months' imprisonment, but in the event Witte served only two weeks, thanks to the support of the tsar, who had been impressed by his commendable war efforts, and even then Witte was allowed out of jail during the day to continue going to work.

The Odessa Railway was privatized during the war and therefore Witte found himself working for Jan Bloch, one of the big 'railway barons' of the period, who had made fortunes out of the expansion and operation of what was Russia's biggest industry. By 1886 Witte was running what had become the Southwestern Railway, and his organizational skills were proving to be second to none. He managed to turn the fortunes of the loss-making railway around through his understanding of management and economics. The main obstacle, in his view, was that the railway was run by engineers and they had no business sense, always seeking to spend money on the track and infrastructure rather than realizing the importance of ensuring lines were profitable and, indeed, functioning. This, in fact, is an age-old conflict in railway management, and Witte was adamant about asserting his authority over the engineers, even though he was not one himself.

Witte's progress to the highest echelons of Russian society was not all smooth. Shortly after his arrival to work for the government in St Petersburg in 1889 he found himself a widower when his wife died suddenly, but he soon fell in love with Matilda Ivanovna Lissanevich, the wife of a physician and the daughter of a Lithuanian postmaster. More worryingly, he met her in a *salon* where her reputation was anything but impeccable, with rumours of torrid affairs with numerous noblemen. And, worst of all in the highly anti-Semitic Russia of the time, she was a Jew. Witte ignored the gossip and any religious objections, paid 30,000 roubles for her divorce and married her, despite the fact that such a divorcee with a dubious past could never be admitted at the Court, which Witte now frequented as part of his new post.

During this time Witte also had a brief brush with extremist politics that could have ended his career. After the assassination of Alexander II by left-wing revolutionaries in 1881, Witte was involved in a tale of spying and assassination that would not have disgraced a John le Carré thriller. Witte was moved by what he felt was this terrible tragedy of regicide to help create the Holy Druzhina (Holy Brotherhood), a secret society of counter-revolutionaries. The movement attracted widespread support among the elite, and in a convoluted episode Witte was sent to Paris to spy on an agent, Polyanski, who had been ordered to kill a man called Hartman, one of the plotters involved in a previous attempt on the tsar's life. Witte was supposed to kill Polyanski if he failed, in turn, to kill the plotter. However, Polyanski got wind of the plan and confronted Witte, and eventually after moments of farce involving the two 'apaches' (gunmen) who were supposed to carry out the bloody deed, the crazy plan was called off and Witte returned to Russia, leaving the movement in disgust at such far-fetched activity. He was, in fact, despite his adherence to the absolute monarchy, no right-wing fanatic and, in particular, was outraged that after the assassination there was a purge of Jews from the railway, a policy he called 'senseless nationalism' that destroyed the careers of countless 'highly competent men'.

In fact, Witte very much believed in promoting people on merit and was a pioneer of modern business practice. He was at the same time both a modernist and a traditionalist, a man who wanted to see Russia develop and yet held firm to the concept of absolute monarchy. He realized the key to a railway's profitability was the correct setting of freight tariffs – cheap enough to attract business, but sufficient to ensure profitability. As a result of combining his mathematical knowledge with economic theory, he designed an effective nationally-applied freight tariff. This enabled him to lower freight rates on the line, while increasing revenue, nearly doubling the value of the assets. He wrote a treatise whose title, *Principles of Railway Freight Tariffs*, suggests it did not attract a wide audience, but which was widely acclaimed among railway managers as the seminal work on the subject. Witte saw the potential to tailor railway tariffs to wider political objectives. Previously, the rates had largely been set at a standard rate per verst (a Russian unit of measure slightly longer than 1,000 yards), but to encourage the development of remote areas, Witte argued that the rate per verst should decline for long-distance carriage. This greatly helped the ironmasters in the Urals to make their products more competitive when they had to be shipped all the way to St Petersburg. In such a vast country a more intelligent approach to the pricing of freight was essential. It was, in effect, a way of bringing together the disparate parts of the Empire and would prove to be crucial to ensuring the development of Siberia once the Trans-Siberian was completed.

Witte was not without a sense of humour. In his memoirs he recalls his various predecessors and writes of Posyet: 'He was very honest, but remarkably unintelligent. His ignorance of railroad matters was prodigious. He had a peculiar weakness. His inspection of [rail]roads was confined to an examination of the toilet rooms. If he found them insanitary, he was furious, but if they were clean he felt satisfied and looked at nothing else.'[4]

Witte's ruthlessness was legendary and he was ever ready to put one over on his rivals. He had a network of informants throughout the rail industry, which meant that he seemed to know more about rival railways than did their own managers – a demonstration of the single-mindedness that would be needed to see through the project. Indeed, he was not averse to turning against former allies in order to achieve his aims.

Witte's skills at running railway companies did not go unnoticed in government circles and, in particular, by Vyshenegradsky. In 1889 Witte was given the post of director of railway affairs in the finance ministry, a position deliberately created by Vyshenegradsky to try to impose financial discipline on the perennially overspending railways. The appointment represented a remarkable promotion for the former ticket clerk, who had jumped seven *chin* from his first role in Odessa to a position that conferred hereditary nobility on its post-holders.[5] It was a power move by one government department against another that was typical of Russian administration of the time. Witte managed to wrest most of the responsibility of the railways from the transport ministry, much to the consternation of Hubbenet, the ineffectual minister, who became so angered by Witte's encroachment into his territory that it almost resulted in a duel.

Witte was a conspicuous success. By then the crazy situation of the private railways milking the government had been ended. Instead, the government had begun to construct railways at its own expense, in the way that it would build the Trans-Siberian. It had also nationalized some of the private railways and strengthened its legal powers over the others in order to prevent the leeching of state funds. Despite the mixed pattern of ownership, the railway had, for the first time, become a unified network. Nevertheless, although the finances had improved thanks to these reforms, the system still lost money and Witte set about changing that. In fact, he managed, very quickly, to balance the books, ensuring the railway deficits which had long been a burden on state finances disappeared. He brought together most of the railway functions of government under his control, making the industry far more efficient. The railway deficits that had burdened the state budget soon disappeared, much to Vyshenegradsky's pleasure. It became clear that when Hubbenet was forced to resign from his post because of the failure of the railways to deliver food quickly to the Volga area during the famine of 1891–2, Witte was the obvious replacement and took up the post in February 1892. He quickly began sorting out the mess on the railways left by his predecessor, and in the summer of 1892 he was despatched by the tsar as a troubleshooter to the Volga region, where cholera had taken hold among a population weakened by hunger. He organized the health services, calling on medical students to help, and mobilized the Jewish grain-dealers for the provisioning of the stricken areas. There was no doubting his diligence and courage. According to his own memoirs, he 'travelled from town to town, from hamlet to hamlet, inspecting hospitals and dispensaries, coming in close contact with the patients'.[6]

When Witte was appointed as transport minister, Vyshenegradsky assumed he had now got his own man in the transport ministry, thereby further extending his control over it. He could not have been more wrong. Witte had his own agenda. During his tenure in the finance ministry, Witte had, indeed, robustly cut back spending at Vyshenegradsky's behest, but now he was in a position to push forward the Trans-Siberian project that Vyshenegradsky had so long opposed. Vyshenegradsky's days were, in any case, numbered. His dogmatic policy of maintaining the level of grain exports at the height of the famine in order to obtain hard currency attracted widespread criticism, as it had greatly exacerbated the effects of the famine. Suffering, too, from the after-effects of a stroke, he was forced out of office. In August 1892 Witte, recently returned from the Volga region, was appointed to replace him as minister of finance, a post he would hold for eleven years.

Vyshenegradsky had, ironically, paved the way for the construction of the Trans-Siberian. Thanks to his transfer of powers over railway building from the transport ministry to the finance ministry, Witte was now in control of the process. He had no illusions about the calibre of many of the aristocrats who sought to obtain concessions to build railways or who held government positions thanks to their noble blood. He described them as being made of 'inferior stuff', whose chief characteristic was 'unlimited greed': 'For many years some of these scoundrels and hypocrites have been holding the highest Court positions and, at least outwardly, they have been intimate with the Imperial family.'[7] Consequently, he realized he had to create his own structure to bring about the construction of the line. Work had started the previous year, but it had stopped once the scale of the Volga famine became clear. There was, in any case, no money, thanks to Vyshenegradsky.

For Witte, the construction of the railway was far more than a transport project. He recognized that it would not be a profitable enterprise, at least for many years. No matter. It was an undertaking of overriding national importance that offered huge financial benefits in the long run, both for Siberia and for Russia as a whole, because the line's superior speed would allow the railway to take much of the east–west seaborne freight traffic. The Trans-Siberian was bound up with the wider project of Russia's industrialization. The advantage of improved transport would bring about economic prosperity across a wide range of industries. Russian textiles would be sold far more easily to China, given the proximity of the rails, and Chinese products would cost less in Russia because of the reduced cost of freight carriage. The Trans-Siberian, he pointed out, would also transport Siberian grain, timber, hides, butter and minerals, stimulating Russia's overall economy. They were all the same free-trade arguments that are used today to justify globalization. Witte did not emphasize the military usefulness of the line, which, as we have seen, was a key driving force behind the project, but did say that it would help service Russia's Pacific Fleet and assure amicable relations between Russia and both the Orient and the United States.

The Trans-Siberian was not just about Siberia. Railways were perceived by Witte as the engine for growth of the whole wider economy, and therefore the Trans-Siberian, as the biggest project by far, was its most important driver. The logic of what was effectively a model of state capitalism went something like this: railway construction would stimulate the growth of the heavy metallurgical industry, providing rails and other equipment, protected by tariffs on imports. This, in turn, would stimulate the growth of smaller and lighter industry. This would revitalize the whole economy, especially in urban areas, which, in turn, would raise rural production and prosperity as well, because the wages of industrial workers would be sent back to their families living in the countryside: 'Railroad construction thus served as the flywheel for the entire economy.'[8] Certainly, the railways were by far the country's biggest industry, employing 400,000 people by the turn of the century. Witte waxed lyrical about the effect of the iron road, seeing it as not just an economic force but a cultural one: 'The railway is like a leaven, which creates a cultural fermentation among the population. Even if it passed through an absolutely wild people along its way, it would raise them in a short time to the level prerequisite for its operation.'[9] Witte saw economic success as vital for the stability and long-term future of Russia, and he saw the railways as the essential catalyst for the growth of the economy. The monarchy, which he greatly supported but realized was threatened by revolutionary forces, would be saved if Russia prospered. Whereas in Europe the factories had sprung up first and the infrastructure in the form of railways had followed, in Russia it was the other way around. Railways were laid down to stimulate the development of heavy industry, a perfectly acceptable economic model.

Put simply, therefore, Witte saw the railways as the key to economic success, and the Siberian railway, by far the longest and biggest project, was an essential part of the network's development. To Witte the Trans-Siberian 'not only served the obvious political needs of the state, but also provided a foundation on which to build devotion and respect at home and abroad'.[10] Above all, Witte was desperate to demonstrate that Russia was the equal of the great powers of Europe, able at last to compete with them. It was, in short, 'a quest to satisfy the amour propre of his nation'.[11] Witte promoted the railway to foreign leaders, both to demonstrate its commercial potential once completed, but also simply because it showed that Russia was the equal of – or even better than – its European counterparts.

It was not just Witte's direct influence on the railway which allowed its construction. As Finance Minister he brought stability and growth to the Russian economy, and in many ways was responsible for kick-starting its development as a major economy. He restored confidence in the rouble by linking it to gold, allowing Russia to make large foreign loans to stimulate growth. He promoted the long-delayed industrialization of the country by encouraging manufacturing through reduced tariffs on imported machine tools, while raising tariff barriers on domestic goods in order to protect the nation's fledgling manufacturers. He also, interestingly, created a state liquor monopoly with the ostensible purpose of reducing drunkenness; but, as it turned out, this resulted in a huge rise in tax income for the government, which helped balance the books. The success of his economic policies was such that in the 1890s Russia averaged an 8 per cent growth – albeit from a low base – which was far higher than other European nations at the time. Without that growth, the Trans-Siberian would have remained a pipe dream.

Witte was really not exaggerating when he summed it up as a project 'to occupy one of the first places in the ranks of the most important undertakings of the nineteenth century, not only in our Motherland, but also in the whole world'.[12] That was not much of an overstatement. Nor was his rather immodest suggestion in his memoirs that 'It will not be an exaggeration to say that the vast enterprise of constructing the great Siberian Railway was carried out owing to my efforts, supported, of course, first by Emperor Alexander III and then by Emperor Nicholas II.'[13] There was, in truth, probably no one in Russia at the time better equipped to oversee the project than Witte with his experience of both railway matters and government.

Vyshenegradsky's parsimony and opposition to construction meant that Witte needed every means at his disposal to overcome the enormous obstacles to financing and then building the line. Given the situation Witte found when taking over at the ministry of finance, it seemed highly likely that the project would remain stalled for years, even though work had started briefly and then stopped in 1891. Money, of course, was the top priority. In fact, to this day there remains some mystery about precisely how the line was paid for, because the government economy was operated on the basis of what is called a 'single till' system – in other words, all revenues, including loans, were pooled together, and therefore it is difficult to ascertain which funds went towards paying for the railway. By stabilizing the economy, Witte did manage to obtain foreign loans, especially from France, and there seems to have been a considerable sleight of hand – familiar to the modern reader – about his claims that the government's books were in the black, when, in fact, the opposite was the case. The railway was 'financed out of the surpluses of the ordinary budget, which supposedly had accumulated thanks to its "favourable implementation" in 1894 and yearly thereafter',[14] according to

Steven Marks, but as he implies there was an aspect of smoke and mirrors, which we will never be able properly to fathom.

Finding the money was not, however, the only problem or even possibly the main one. As we have seen, the administrative systems of the Russian government were rooted in eighteenth-century practices, rather than those of an industrialized economy. Almost as soon as Witte took over the finance ministry he set about creating a structure that would enable him to drive through a project on the scale of the Trans-Siberian and related schemes. Witte wrote a paper setting out how the project should be taken forward through the creation of a powerful committee that would run and oversee its construction; and, indeed, would have a wider remit that encompassed not just the railway itself, but other matters in Siberia, such as immigration and town planning, which were inevitably influenced by the advent of the line.

Witte's predecessor, Hubennet, had already mooted the idea of creating a 'special central managerial body' for the development of the project, but it was Witte who ensured that it became a powerful organization able to override, day to day, any doubts raised by opponents. In a masterstroke, Witte suggested the chairman of the committee should be the heir to the throne, the tsarevich Grand Duke Nicholas, who had already played a role in the development of the scheme and would become Russia's last tsar. When Tsar Alexander first gave the go-ahead for the line's construction, the tsarevich was on a grand tour that encompassed Greece, Egypt, India and Japan. The tsar had the clever idea of getting his son to inaugurate the scheme at its eastern terminus, Vladivostok, as a brilliant PR exercise. Consequently, in March 1891 he wrote to his son, in the pompous manner that royals communicate with each other, complete with inappropriate capital letters and long sentences:

Your Imperial Highness, having given the order to begin the construction of a continuous railway line across the whole of Siberia, destined to unite the Siberian lands, so rich in natural endowments, with the railway network of the interior, I entrust You to proclaim My will on this matter upon Your return to the Russian land after Your inspection of the East. At the same time, I desire You to lay the first stone at Vladivostok for the construction of the Ussuri line, forming a part of the Siberian railway, which is to be carried out at the cost of the State and under direction of the Government.[15]

Tsarevich Nicholas, a man of just twenty-three – whose nerves had recently been shaken by an assassination attempt in Japan, when a crazy police agent attacked him with a sabre – was therefore given the task of inaugurating work at the eastern end of the line. In a brief ceremony on 31 May 1891 he wielded a shovel to fill a wheelbarrow with clay soil, emptied it on to an embankment of what would become the Ussuri line and later laid a stone on the site of the station. Vladivostok at the time was not a prepossessing place and was, as Harmon Tupper describes it, 'a slatternly town of muddy, unpaved streets, open sewers, grim military barracks and warehouses, unpainted wooden houses and hundreds of mud-plastered straw huts of the Chinese and Korean settlers, who comprised about a third of the port's 14,000 inhabitants'.[16] Today the station at Vladivostok still recalls this momentous event with images of Nicholas 'the miracle worker' in the waiting room. Once the railway had been given the tsarist imprimatur in such a powerful way, there was no stopping it. The idea, which had been so long the source of debate and controversy in government circles, now attracted popular appeal.

However, as we have seen, the famine and lack of money meant little work was carried out and construction had come to a halt by the time Witte took over at the finance ministry in August 1892. Witte's proposal for a committee of the Siberian Railway with a membership of key officials from across various government departments was accepted by the tsar and effectively had carte blanche to access sufficient funds to see through the project. Witte argued strongly that the Trans-Siberian should be co-ordinated with other projects, such as the building of the Yekaterinburg–Chelyabinsk line, so that metal products from the Urals could be easily brought to the construction sites. He also ensured that the waterways intersecting the Trans-Siberian route were improved to facilitate the supply of building materials during its construction. Since attracting settlers was a key part of the purpose of the line, Witte proposed that this migration should be planned with the establishment of medical – both human and animal – services, churches and other facilities for the incomers. Crucially, too, a land-distribution scheme had to be created to attract them.

All of these matters came within the purview of the Committee. Witte, in effect, by controlling the Committee, thanks to his clever scheming to ensure the right people were appointed to it, effectively ruled Siberia and influenced wider Russian foreign policy: 'The scope of the Committee of the Siberian Railway was far greater than that of its ancestor [a previous similar railway committee], for it was not limited to railroad construction. Its purview and ambitions continued to expand with Witte at the helm; through it he gained control of the Asian policy of the Empire, at least for a time.'[17] Indeed, its specific remit included 'the arrangements for the general economic welfare of Siberia and for the revival of its commercial intercourse with the Asiatic Continent'.[18]

The choice of Nicholas as chairman of the Committee ensured that the line would be built. Witte spent considerable time persuading the tsar that giving such a crucial job to the young man was a good idea. The tsar was dubious, arguing that the tsarevich was still a boy who was not experienced enough to chair such an important committee. Witte, ever the canny operator, suggested that Nicholas's old tutor, Nikolay Bunge, be made vice-chairman of the committee to advise the young man throughout the difficult process of seeing the project through. The tsar was eventually convinced and agreed to the appointment.

Nicholas himself was keen. Unlike any of his immediate predecessors, he had visited the Far-Eastern corner of his homeland and was supportive of the idea that the line would unify the nation. 'Russifying' Siberia was a way of seeing off the 'yellow peril' and the railway would be in the vanguard of that process. As we shall see in chapter 6, these eastern ambitions were to prove extremely dangerous and, thanks to the creation of the Trans-Siberian, bring about a war that almost resulted in the overthrow of the monarchy a dozen years before its eventual downfall. Nicholas, who later as tsar pretty much lost interest in affairs of state and had an almost fatal obsession with detail at the expense of any strategic view, was actually an active and engaged chairman of the committee, and even retained the post when he became tsar on the death of his father two years later. However, he was weak and easily manipulated by Witte, and their good relationship soon soured. Indeed, the future tsar was rather in awe of the genius who was at the heart of everything the Russian government did. Ironically, it was Witte's abilities as a firm and decisive administrator which made him more suited to rule than the rather dull and ponderous future tsar whom he dominated. Nicholas, once be became tsar, was not in a position to sack Witte, knowing that he was essential to the project. However, 'Nicholas felt he was a spectator at Witte's performance, especially in the Far East, where the minister's powerful presence seemed to thwart Nicholas's own ambitions. Witte surpassed everyone and Nicholas grew jealous and resentful.'[19]

Nevertheless, the structure held firm. The Committee of the Siberian Railway was firmly entrenched, having effectively become responsible for ruling Siberia, and even disputes between the tsar and his key minister could not prevent the progress of the project. There was no stopping it. The army of navvies and engineers needed to drive the iron road through the vastness of Siberia and build the world's longest railway could now be mobilized.

# FOUR

# INTO THE STEPPE

The difficulties facing the builders of the Trans-Siberian can hardly be exaggerated. The railway may not have traversed territory that was mountainous like the Alps or the Indian Ghats, nor as barren as the Sudanese desert, through which the British built a railway at almost the same time, but its sheer length and the extreme temperatures endured by the work gangs made its construction an unparalleled feat. To give a measure of the scale, at 5,750 miles it was longer by 2,000 miles than the Canadian transcontinental railway between St John's, Newfoundland, on the Atlantic and Vancouver in British Columbia on the Pacific, and that had been built in stages. The First Transcontinental in the United States, completed in 1869, was much shorter and required a mere 1,750 miles of new railway when work started in 1863, less than a third of the Trans-Siberian's length, because the section in the east had already been built. In contrast, if one discounts the already existing section from Moscow to Chelyabinsk, the Trans-Siberian still required more than 4,500 miles of new railway.

There were more mundane difficulties than the sheer scale of the task. In the steppe neither stone for the ballast nor wood for the sleepers could be procured locally and the rails for the track had to be transported over vast distances from factories in the Urals and European Russia. Massive steel bridges were needed to cross several rivers, and countless smaller ones, mostly made from wood, were needed to ford the vast number of streams and torrents. Much of the land it crossed was swamp, while other parts were permafrost. Worse, the earth was frozen in winter, but quickly became a muddy morass in the spring thaw. While the mountains were not excessively high, several ranges required the construction of long, gently rising curves, since tunnelling, for the most part, was eschewed because of cost constraints. Then, around two-thirds along the route from Moscow, there was the awesome barrier of Lake Baikal, the biggest lake by volume and the deepest in the world, which, stretching nearly 400 miles from north to south and with a mountain range at its southern tip, posed the greatest obstacle for the builders. Labour, too, was a huge issue. Vast swathes of the line went through land that was uninhabited or populated only by nomadic tribes unwilling to engage with the project, so the workers had to be brought in from afar.

There was, in short, nothing easy about the undertaking. In order to rationalize the construction so that the contracts were not unmanageable, the railway was divided into three major sections – the Western, Mid-Siberian and Far Eastern lines. Each of these was further subdivided. The Western and Mid-Siberian were both split into two separate projects in order to speed up construction. The Western comprised Chelyabinsk–Omsk and Omsk to the River Ob, while the Mid-Siberian Railway was divided at the Yenisei river with a section from the Ob and to Krasnoyarsk and then from the other side of the river to Irkutsk. The big bridge crossings over the wide, meandering rivers, such as the Ob and the Yenisei, were left until last, along with the Circum-Baikal, the most difficult part of the route along the mountainous southern shore of Lake Baikal. Consequently it was envisaged that steamers would take the traffic across the lake in summer, while in winter tracks were to be laid across it. The Amur Railway was then to run from the shores of Lake Baikal to the embankment of the Amur river at Khabarovsk; while the easternmost section, the Ussuri Railway, was to go from the other side of the river southwards to Vladivostok. Speed was of the essence and in the east construction on the Ussuri started – or rather restarted – from Vladivostok simultaneously in 1892 with work getting under way on the Western railway. The following year, building the Mid-Siberian began, too, which meant progress was being made across the whole region. In effect, these were all separate but massive railway projects, each of which individually was comparable to the American or Canadian transcontinentals and each posing a different set of difficulties, given the changes in terrain, the varying levels of settlement and the peculiarities of the local climate. Overall, the task was on a far greater scale than any previous or, indeed, subsequent railway project in the world.

All of these projects were overseen by the Committee of the Siberian Railway back in St Petersburg. It would make the key decisions over, for example, the decision of whether a lengthy bridge should be made of steel or wood; finalizing the route, such as the choice of which bank of the Angara river the railway should run along between Irkutsk and Lake Baikal; when work should start on a particular section; and crucially, of course, allocating budgets. However, given the time needed to communicate decisions and the remoteness of the construction sites, it was the chief engineers and their contractors who made all the day-to-day decisions.

The survey work undertaken before construction began had been cursory in the extreme. There was no attempt to select an optimum route, but instead a four-verst belt was haphazardly drawn on the map by the administration in St Petersburg and consequently the surveyors in the field examined only this small swathe, irrespective of whether it appeared suitable. The process was made even more arbitrary by the fact that there were no proper maps of Siberia, which meant the St Petersburg bureaucrats had little information on which to base their route. Given the inadequacies of the cartography covering this vast region, there were many instances where moving the line a few miles in either direction would have provided a far better alignment. According to Steven Marks, 'some members of the Russian Technical Society suspected that even after construction had begun as much as half of the route had not been surveyed in any fashion'.[1] Apparently, on one section of the Ussuri Railway, the survey was carried out by an unqualified local man, accompanied by his two sons and a Mongolian-speaking guide. It was no wonder that this proved to be the most difficult section to build. The Technical Society, one of Russia's leading scientific organizations at the time, pressed for detailed surveys of the whole line to be carried out, backed by scientific evidence. To no avail. The government was in too much of a hurry for such nonsense and, moreover, the 'government engineers denied the incompleteness of their surveys and investigations'.[2] Instead, they pointed out that to build the perfect railway would take a century and they wanted to ensure it was done in a decade. Ultimately this muddling through was probably appropriate for the resources available to the government and proved sensible, even if, undoubtedly, much money was wasted by lack of proper preparation.

The same military and political imperatives which dictated the speed of progress also helped determine the route. The railway was all about getting to the Pacific as quickly and easily as possible, and therefore little attention was paid either to technical factors or to local interests. In fact, this philosophy of getting the job done as quickly as possible had dictated the way the First American Transcontinental railway had been built in the 1860s, except that there it was money and greed which determined the need for speedy construction, since the line was built by private interests supported by huge government grants.[3]

The most bizarre decision concerning the route was that it bypassed Tomsk, the biggest city in central Siberia. The oft-repeated legend is that the surveyors asked unsuccessfully for a bribe from the local authorities to bring the line nearer the city. In fact, the more likely explanation is that they made the decision on geological grounds, because Tomsk is situated in the taiga (virgin forest), surrounded by swamplands created by the flood plain of the huge River Ob, and it would have required a long and expensive construction project to reach the city. A branch line was later built connecting the city with the main line and Tomsk was given the consolation prize of being the administrative headquarters for the Siberian Railway. Several other Siberian towns were bypassed in this way by lesser distances, as the surveyors and the builders chose the path of least resistance. The traditional siting of towns on hilltops or on river bends made it difficult for the railway to gain easy access and in several places there was a river between the station and the town.

The other major decision on the route was to have far greater consequences. Instead of remaining in Russian territory and keeping to the north of the Amur river, it was decided to take a more southerly approach to Vladivostok, through Manchuria, part of China. There were a couple of obvious technical advantages to building what became the Chinese Eastern Railway. It reduced the overall length by 514 versts, more than ten per cent of the entire railway, and, moreover, its supporters argued that the cost per verst would be less, because it traversed easier railway terrain, although as we will see in chapter 6 this did not prove to be the case. However, while technical reasons were put forward to explain the change, the decision was rooted in grubbier political considerations. The notion of building the Trans-Siberian through Chinese territory was, in fact, almost as old as plans for the railway itself. The diehard Russian imperialists had always seen the railway as an opportunity to establish control over the Chinese, confirming Muravyev's land grab mentioned in chapter 2, which they argued would be advantageous from a military point of view either to protect against an attack or to launch one.

Despite this, the original route drawn up in 1891 envisaged the Amur Railway running from Lake Baikal through the Shilka and Amur valleys to Khabarovsk, where it would meet the Ussuri line up from Vladivostok. This Transbaikal route, however, would have to traverse unpromising railway territory, as preliminary surveys completed in 1894 revealed that much of the 1,200-mile Amur Railway passed through hills and river valleys that would require expensive high embankments and cuttings. More than 100 bridges would be needed, including a lengthy mile-and-a-half crossing of the Amur at Khabarovsk. Consequently, the line was going to cost about 90,000 roubles per verst, double that of the Western sections. There were other difficulties, too. The road needed to supply the construction was so poor that virtually everything would have to be transported by river; there was an acute shortage of water in winter; and much of the track would have to be laid on permafrost, a technique about which there were still grave doubts. In truth, however, these obstacles added up to a compelling excuse for building the line through Manchuria, rather than conclusively proving that the Amur Railway was not a feasible option, as demonstrated by the fact it was actually built a couple of decades later.

Witte, in his memoirs, rather disingenuously suggests that since construction of the Trans-Siberian was at that time reaching Transbaikalia, there was a discussion about which route it should take heading east and that he 'conceived the idea of building the railway straight across Chinese territory, principally Mongolia and Northern Manchuria, on toward Vladivostok'.[4] The notion that Witte had just suddenly dreamt up the plan of sending the tracks through Manchuria is a classic example of a politician rewriting history. Building a line through another country's territory was rare in the annals of railway history and, clearly, such a major step would not have been mooted, let alone considered seriously, unless a lot of groundwork had been covered in advance. In fact, diplomatic considerations between the three major powers in the region – Japan, China and Russia – were at the heart of the decision. Tension had built up between the weak Chinese Empire and the Japanese for much of the latter part of the nineteenth century, and this had exploded into a brief war in 1894, which was won easily by Japan. As part of the reparations, China had to pay a vast sum, which Witte arranged to be met with a loan from French bankers and which he also pledged Russia would indemnify.

As an expression of gratitude for Russia's benevolence in arranging and guaranteeing this loan for reparations, the Chinese sent Li Hongzhang, a very senior politician who had led the army during the fighting, as its representative to the coronation of Nicholas II. Witte, informed that Li was arriving by way of the Suez Canal, machinated to ensure that he was not met by any European politicians during the trip, so that they could negotiate the terms for the railway through Manchuria on his arrival in St Petersburg. Witte despatched an envoy, Prince Esper Ukhtomsky, to intercept Li at the canal. There was no shortage of princes in tsarist Russia and, in truth, Ukhtomsky was a pretty minor one, but nonetheless his rank made him a suitable greeter for the Chinese aristocrat and he proved successful in steering Li to St Petersburg before any English or German diplomats could seek him out.

Witte describes a hilarious and fruitless initial encounter with the Chinese grandee, where both sit drinking tea and then Li smokes his pipe, lit by a coterie of attendants, and the conversation never gets beyond the level of repeatedly expressing interest in the health of each other's emperor and their families, with 'no attempt to talk business'. At the second and subsequent meetings, however, an arrangement that was hugely advantageous to Russia was negotiated. Witte stressed how in the recent war with Japan, the Russians had sent troops, but due to the lack of a railway line, they reached the front only once the war was over. In the future, a railway through Manchuria would enable Russia to make military interventions far more quickly and help protect Chinese interests. He even went so far as to say that 'Japan was likely to assume a favourable attitude towards the railway, for it would link her with Western Europe, whose civilization she had adopted',[5] a suggestion that would later prove to be completely unfounded. Indeed, since part of the treaty envisaged mutual support in the event of an attack from Japan, that claim had very little credibility even at the time it was made.

Witte was certainly the consummate diplomat and his strategy worked. The Chinese granted the Russians permission to build the tracks in what was pretty much a straight line from Chita, 250 miles east of the lake, to Vladivostok, but Li refused to allow the railway to be built directly by the government. Instead, a scheme was devised whereby the line would be built by a supposedly private company, the Eastern Chinese Railway Corporation, which was, as Witte points out in his memoirs, 'completely in the hands of the government'; and, even better, since it was nominally a private corporation, 'within the jurisdiction of the Ministry of Finance' – in other words, Witte's very own bailiwick. China agreed to cede a strip wide enough for the construction and operation of the railway, as well as land for sidings, depots and stations on which, remarkably, the railway would have its own police force able to exercise 'full and untrammelled authority', even though it was on foreign territory. For their part, the Chinese insisted the Russians were not to go south of the line of the railway, a requirement to which Witte readily agreed, although this pledge was, in fact, broken almost as soon as construction started.

All these negotiations were carried out in secret, much to Witte's satisfaction: 'Not the slightest information penetrated into the press regarding our secret agreement with China.'[6] The secrecy was probably just as important to Li as it was to Witte, since the treaty greatly favoured the Russians which was why construction would be affected by the Boxer Rising (1899–1901). Witte, in fact, admitted as much: 'The terms of the railway concession granted by China were very favourable for Russia.' The Russians were granted a concession of thirty-six years to run the railway, but even after that it would have been very expensive for the Chinese to reclaim it, with Witte himself admitting that in the thirty-seventh year it would have cost the Chinese 700 million roubles [£70 million] to wrest back control. Despite the appearance that this was part of an expansionist programme by the Russian Empire, Witte insisted this was not the case: 'Under no circumstances was the Trans-Siberian to serve as a means for territorial expansion,'[7] he wrote afterwards. However, even if that were true, the perception of the decision to build the Chinese Eastern Railway would undoubtedly lead Japan to the opposite conclusion. In the event, the railway was the source of no little tension between all three nations and would lead to several disputes and even conflicts.

The first part of the Trans-Siberian line to see picks wielded after the false start of 1891 was on the outskirts of Chelyabinsk, the easternmost point of the existing railway, about 120 miles south of Yekaterinburg, but now destined to be the gateway to Siberia. The construction arrangements were run along conventional lines, with an engineer being appointed who would then either organize the work himself or, more commonly, bring in contractors. The majority of these contractors were large concerns employing hundreds or even thousands of men, although there were, too, a few small outfits allocated a particular task. This first section – the Western Siberia sector, stretched from Chelyabinsk to the

Ob river bank, opposite the town of Novonikolayevsk, which was created in 1893 by the arrival of the railway and named in honour of both the tsar and Saint Nicholas, as a way of hedging bets between religion and monarchy, but is now known by the Soviet-imposed name Novosibirsk. To make the task more manageable, this long section was split into two at Omsk, about halfway along. The man appointed to build the West Siberian Railway was Konstantin Yakovlevich Mikhailovsky, a veteran of the Crimean War and a noble of Ukrainian extraction. He was an accomplished and experienced civil engineer who had built the well-regarded Alexander Bridge over the Volga, which opened in 1880. Mikhailovsky was provided with little more than a map with a thin straight line stretching across the plains for about 900 miles, as Harmon Tupper describes: 'He was prepared for heavy frost that limited the all-out working season to only four months, but he had not anticipated such a crippling shortage of wagons, carts, horses, barges and steamers.'[8] On this Western section, where the land had largely been deforested centuries ago, it was the shortage of wood that created the greatest difficulties, since there was only one usable forest and that was 200 miles east of Chelyabinsk. Consequently, much of the wood had to be imported from distant parts of European Russia, as were the rails and other manufactured parts.

The other materials were available locally, though often at a high price, but it was the lack of workers, particularly those with skills, that was the greatest source of difficulty for the contractors. Inevitably, the labour demands of the whole enterprise were always going to outstrip the capacity of any local supply. There was little mechanization, which, in truth, had only recently become a regular feature of contemporary European and American railway construction, and consequently, the Committee of the Siberian Railway had estimated that this first stage of construction, involving the Western and Mid-Siberian lines, would require 30,000 navvies for earthworks and a further 50,000 skilled and unskilled labourers for all the other types of work. While on this first section unskilled labour was more readily available than further east, with about eighty per cent being recruited locally, skills were in short supply, as Tupper describes: 'Even in the relatively well-populated agricultural districts between Chelyabinsk and Omsk, artisans were hard to come by, for the peasant settlers lacked technical skills. In grazing country, nomadic herdsmen refused to leave their cattle, which they prized so highly that it was their custom to inquire politely after the health of one's beasts rather than that of one's family.'[9] Using local workers had the added disadvantage that they were wont to return home at harvest time, whatever the needs of the railway, creating shortages at just the period when conditions for railway construction were optimal. As a result, Mikhailovsky's contractors were obliged to seek workers not only from European Russia, but Turkey, Persia and Italy as well.

The work was onerous, but conditions were far better than for the poor serfs who had built the Nikolayev Railway between St Petersburg and Moscow half a century before. In the summer most of the labourers simply camped out in tents, but in winter, when there were far fewer labourers in the gangs, since work was confined to bridge and station construction and other secondary tasks, they were housed in portable log cabins or covered railway wagons. Hours were long during the brief summer. From May to August the men were expected to work from 5 a.m. to 7.30 p.m., an exhausting fourteen and a half-hour day, broken only by an unusually generous lunch break of an hour and a half. In the winter the working hours were confined to daylight, but since the line is surprisingly far south – virtually all of the line is within five degrees of the latitude of London and much of it is actually south of that – it meant seven or eight hours were the minimum even in deepest winter, although the cold and the snow were limiting factors to laying track. The schedule was six days a week, and while holidays were respected, when they fell on a weekday, time had to be made up the following Sunday, effectively obviating any advantage. Food was basic, usually a meat or fish stew at lunchtime, served from a huge iron kettle, often with a vegetable side dish, and doled out with the help of wooden spoons, which each worker kept in his boots. Dinner was thin gruel and bread with a small amount of butter or lard, and a little wine was given out on holidays. The standard obviously varied from contractor to contractor, with some (particularly on the Ussuri line) serving inedible food that led to complaints and even revolts, but broadly the fare seems to have been fairly good. It was not, however, free. The cost was deducted from the wages, but even then the men were left with reasonable amounts, since good pay was essential to attract sufficient numbers of workers. According to a contemporary source, 'unskilled workers in western Siberia, for instance, earned up to eight times more on the Trans-Siberian than they normally had earned as farm hands in the employ of old settlers'.[10] Skilled workers fared even better. Masons, most of whom were Italian, could earn up to 100 roubles (around £10) per month by working hard, an excellent wage at the time.

It was, inevitably, dangerous work. The death rate, for which the best estimate is two per cent, may be shocking in today's terms, but compared favourably with other contemporary massive projects, such as construction of the (never completed) Cape to Cairo railway or the digging of the Panama Canal, when at times it reached thirty per cent. The estimate, however, could be either an underestimate or, equally, an overestimate, as it was subject to inaccuracy in either direction. On the one hand, the Soviet historians who documented the story of the construction of the line after the Revolution tended to exaggerate the harshness of the conditions for their own political ends, seeking to portray the evil regime of the tsar as negatively as possible. Then again, unscrupulous paymasters were tempted not to report the death or disappearance of a worker so they could pocket the wages; and, moreover, contractors did not necessarily report all accidents, since it made them look bad.

The conditions at times were almost unimaginably tough. Working on the swampy sections, often knee- or even waist-deep in mud, was not only onerous but risky. Mosquitoes were a constant menace and source of disease during the hot months, although the line was too far north for malaria. Apart from the occasional outbreak of cholera – and, later, on the Chinese section, plague – there were none of the terrible epidemics characteristic of similar projects undertaken in the tropics.

The most perilous task was building the bridges, especially in winter, as the men had to perch high above the river or the surrounding embankment, with no safety equipment and open to the elements. A contemporary observer, L. Lodian, found that there was a curious way of estimating likely casualties: for every million roubles spent, the contractors reckoned on one death. Consequently, as typically a large bridge would cost four million roubles, there would be an expected four fatalities. Lodian remarked that in private conversations the death toll on the bridges seemed to be greater, more like three or four deaths per million roubles spent, but that was too embarrassing for the authorities to acknowledge. He suggested the cause of the high toll was that the steeplejacks on the bridges 'would allow their body temperature to run down more than they were aware, with the result that some of them would make a slip or find they could not get their numbed fingers to grasp a support in time, and down they would go'.[11] The ever-phlegmatic Russian peasants would see such accidents as a matter of course.

Alexander III (1845–1894), the tsar of Russia from 1881 who initiated the Trans-Siberian project.

Sergei Witte, the father of the Trans-Siberian.

Before the completion of the line around Lake Baikal, passengers and freight had to transfer to ferries such as the SS *Baikal*, which was built by the Newcastle firm of Sir William Armstrong, Whitworth & Co., one of the few British contributions to the project. She was able to carry a whole passenger train and two goods trains across the frozen lake at thirteen knots, through ice up to three feet thick.

Due to the shortage of labour, convicts and exiles were used on several parts of the line and earned remission from their sentences in return for their work. Here they are seen working on a bridge over the river Khor in 1900.

Великій Сибирскій путь.—Grand Chemin de la Sibérie. № 3.
Мостъ черезъ р. Ушайку.

The building of the Trans-Siberian required the constrution of hundreds of bridges using a variety of unusual techniques, such as this steel structure built in a design known as 'fish-bellied truss'.

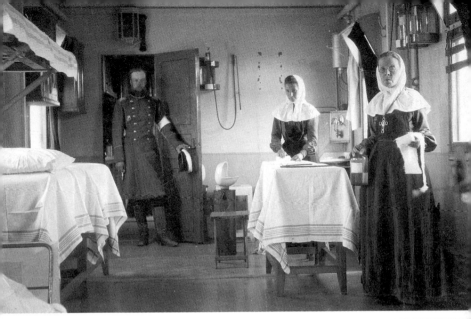

*Above*: The construction of the Trans-Siberian was the trigger for the Russo-Japanese War of 1904–05, which ended in an overwhelming Japanese victory. This hospital train of the Russian Red Cross helped evacuate wounded soldiers along the Trans-Siberian.

*Right*: The line was used, too, for the transfer of Japanese prisoners in the Russo-Japanese War.

*Below*: A rare moment of light relief during the Russo-Japanese war as local people in Manchuria entertain Russian soldiers.

The major bridges, such as this one over the Ob river near Novonikolayevsk (now Novosibirsk) being inspected by engineers, were the last part of the line to be completed.

Although the Trans-Siberian was built much later than most of the world's railways, little mechanisation was used, as shown by this picture of men preparing and laying sleepers.

As soon as sections of line were completed, they became part of a bustling railway that was heavily used right from the start.

The arrival of the first train at Irkutsk Station, 1898, which was actually located across the wide Angara river from the town as building a line over it was reckoned to be too expensive.

The Trans-Siberian was the focus of much fighting in the Russian Civil War and troops of several nationalities, such as the Japanese seen here entering Vladivostok in 1918, became involved, though essentially as non-combatants.

Farmers and children sell dairy products to passengers on the Trans-Siberian, a photograph taken from a collection by William Wisner Chapin for a series in the National Geographic called 'Glimpses of the Russian Empire' in 1910.

Leon Trotsky, on the left, at Petrograd Railway Station, March 1920. He played a major role in ensuring victory for the Communists in the Civil War, using an armoured train as his base.

Armoured trains like this one were used extensively by both sides in the Russian Civil War. This one was originally Russian but was captured by the Czechoslovak Legion in its successful campaign to gain control of the Trans-Siberian.

A pointsman at Novosibirsk, 1929.

Children sell flowers to passengers on the line in May 1921 soon after it reopened following the Civil War.

The steel bridges over the larger rivers were based on designs which Russian engineers had copied on journeys to the United States, where many had travelled to learn bridge-engineering skills; and the results, functional rather than elegant, bore faithful resemblance to their American counterparts, not least because some were supplied in kit form by the United States. The bridge piers had to be particularly strong to withstand the pressure from the rivers in the spring when the smallest meandering stream mutates into a fierce torrent, bearing huge ice floes that would demolish any lesser structures. Many were fitted with special guards to divert the ice away from the support. Siberia's major rivers are immense, wide and fast-flowing, and consequently the bridges spanning them were the last part of the railway to be completed. While the rest of the railway was designed to minimal standards with little attention being paid to the long-term effects of skimping on materials, the bridges were made of far sterner stuff and no risks were taken with them. On completion of the longer ones, four locomotives together with a heavily laden wagon each were sent halfway across the span and stationed there for two hours to assess the stresses and bends.

God, too, was called upon. Before opening to regular traffic, the major bridges were always blessed in a grand ceremony overseen by the local priests. The entrance of the bridge was adorned with a little shrine celebrating a popular saint at which trains slowed down to give passengers the opportunity to throw a few small coins in the bowl provided for the purpose in order to guarantee safe passage. Consequently, thanks to the skill of the engineers – and possibly divine intervention – the bridges have held firm during the whole history of the line, while, ironically, the priests would have done better blessing other sections of the railway, which were subject to frequent fatal accidents in the first few years of operation, as we shall see in the next chapter.

Bridges could not be avoided, but tunnels were. There are still, today, very few on the line, although some have been created to reduce the mileage. Lodian travelled 2,000 miles eastwards along the line before encountering one. Indeed, initially there were no tunnels on the whole line west of Lake Baikal: 'The Russian railway engineer will sooner blow up a small mountain than make a tunnel, leaving a yawning chasm between the rocks; for tunnels, like houses, always have something the matter with them.'[12] Tunnels were expensive and difficult to build, and it is only on the Circum-Baikal line, built a few years later than the main sections of the railway, where there is a concentration of them.

Further east, the make-up of the workforce was very different. Nicholas Mezheninov, who was the engineer in charge of the second main section, the Mid-Siberian Railway, where work started in 1893, faced even greater difficulties recruiting sufficient labour than his counterpart Mikhailovsky. Consequently, in the absence of any local contractors, Mezheninov organized most of the labour directly. Here the line traversed principally primeval forest, the endless taiga, with very little human habitation, fewer than one person per square mile, and previously accessible only by river, as the route did not follow the old post road. Most of the workers were brought in from European Russia, but Mezheninov realized that there still would not be enough and decided to take the risk of recruiting from the only major source of labour available: the convicts and exiles who had been sent to Siberia. It proved an excellent decision. From a prison in Irkutsk, the terminus of the Mid-Siberian section, a group of 1,500 prisoners were requisitioned to fell trees and build earthworks and the wooden bridges used to ford small streams. For the prisoners there was a great incentive in addition to the meagre pay of twenty-five kopeks per day (one quarter of a rouble, which did, at least, cover the luxuries they craved, such as tobacco and sugar, and the illegal vodka sold by the guards): for every eight months a prisoner worked on the line, his sentence was reduced by a year. Even better, for the political prisoners, who were always treated in a different way, two years were knocked off for every one they worked on the line. Later, too, the prisoners' wages, which were only around a third of the level paid to free labourers, were increased to the same rate, an incentive that greatly improved their productivity. Escape into the taiga offered only the prospect of an early death and consequently there were few runaways and most of the prisoners proved to be exemplary workers. There was, too, a clever punishment regime to deter offenders. Prisoners were divided into an *artel*, groups organized tightly for self-protection and, indeed, self-policing. It was a point of honour that a member should not escape and if they did all the prisoners belonging to that *artel* were punished. The convicts were understandably more frightened by their colleagues than by the guards.

Further east, on the Transbaikal, which ran from Lake Baikal to Chita, and the Ussuri between Vladivostok and Khabarovsk, the use of convicts was even more widespread and necessary. The native people, who formed the majority of the local population and were mostly nomadic hunters, were not interested in working on the railway and all other attempts to find workers foundered. Chinese contractors agreed to provide 15,000 labourers from China, shipping them in when the water of the Golden Horn – the part of the Pacific near Vladivostok – melted in the spring, and taking them back to their homeland in December, just before it froze over again. It seemed a perfect arrangement, since work on the line had to stop in the midst of winter when the earth became frozen; but, oddly, unlike on the first American Transcontinental, where the Central Pacific was virtually saved by hiring a large number of Chinese labourers who proved to be remarkably effective workers despite initial doubts about their size and strength, on the

Ussuri they proved to be unsuitable for railway construction. They were unreliable, refusing to work in the rain because they suffered in the damp climate, and their terror of the local tigers, while understandable, caused disruption. According to Harmon Tupper, this fear meant that as soon as there was 'the slightest hint of a tiger in the vicinity, they stampeded in squealing hysteria and huddled in camp until driven out by the labour contractors' musclemen'.[13] While that description may have an element of racial stereotyping, the poor progress on the line compared with the other sections is testimony to the inadequacy of the local labour force.

Troops, too, proved to be unwilling railway construction workers. Orest Vyazemsky, who had the contract to carry out the construction of the line, commandeered several thousand soldiers to work alongside the prisoners, but they considered it menial labour beneath their dignity and conducted what in the days of strong unions and weak managements would have been called a 'work to rule', backed by their officers, who condoned their inactivity.

Consequently, the prisoners provided the core of the workforce on the Ussuri section. There had been some hesitation about using convict labour on the Ussuri because of a bad experience in 1891, during the brief period when construction had started, following the tsarevich's initial ceremonial stone-laying. The government had sent from Odessa to Vladivostok a shipload of 600 convicts sentenced to hard labour to build the Ussuri Railway, rather than serve their sentence on the prison island of Sakhalin; but while their performance had been satisfactory, they were not properly guarded and many escaped into Vladivostok and neighbouring towns, where they were held responsible for an increase in robberies and murders. When work restarted in 1892 under Vyazemsky, the Committee of the Siberian Railway was more careful, requiring the local regional governors who were responsible for the prisoners to weed out those who were known recidivists or had committed severe crimes. Overall, at the peak, about 13,500 prisoners and exiles were employed on the railway, perhaps twenty per cent of the total workforce, and, because they had no alternative, they were a stable core, unlike many of the free hired labourers who would disappear at harvest time or when they simply baulked at the conditions. Research carried out after the completion of the line showed that just over a quarter of the workforce were foreign, mostly Chinese, and just over a third came from European Russia, which, given the use of prisoners, meant that less than twenty per cent of the labour was provided locally by free workers.

Given the difficulties, the pace of progress was really remarkable. On the Western Siberia sector, Mikhailovsky shrugged off all the supply and labour shortages and managed to reach the west bank of the Irtysh river, opposite Omsk, 500 miles from his starting point, within two years. Mikhailovsky was very much a hands-on manager, travelling up and down stretches that were already built in a converted first-class carriage in which he lived. He was often accompanied by his eighteen-year-old daughter Eugenia and her friend Vera Pokrovskaya, who actually lived long enough to tell Tupper personally that Mikhailovsky was 'a steady worker and a strict disciplinarian',[14] necessary requirements for all the head engineers. Tupper's description of the work was therefore first-hand: 'In the field, logs for ties [sleepers] were tediously hand-sawn by two-man teams, which worked a saw back and forth through a horizontally propped-up tree trunk. A few horse-drawn excavating machines had been imported from the United States, but for the most part soil for earthworks was extracted with picks and shovels, then carried in barrows, often wheelless, along a plank.'[15] As for the shovels, 'some were entirely of wood and lacked even a strip of tin on the digging edge', while a thick piece of wood with a stick driven into it served as a sledgehammer to break up the soil that was mostly still frozen. The supports for the countless small wooden bridges, which were made of wood, were pounded into the ground by a big boulder hauled by a pulley held by a tripod of trees tied together, like the tepees of Native Americans. These bridges were built quickly and barely held up progress, but where longer spans were necessary a team of workers would proceed by boat and continue clearing the path ahead, while another group stayed behind to build the crossing.

Mikhailovsky's achievement was all the more impressive because simultaneously he was driving the other section of the railway, the 385 miles from Omsk towards the Ob. Here the problems were different, because the railway was driven through the inhospitable Barabinskaya steppe, described by Tupper as 'a vast expanse of greenish plains dotted with shallow lakes and ponds, where coarse reeds and sedge grass concealed swamps, peat bogs and, here and there, patches of firm ground'.[16]

It was much rougher work than on the plains between Chelyabinsk and Omsk: 'The men hacked through jungles of nettles eight feet tall; chopped down groves of birch, willow and aspen; dug canals to drain marshes and divert underground springs; built dikes and sank trestle pilings into beds of slime; and brought from the rear untold tons of fill for a solid track foundation.'[17] On the last day of August 1895, just three years and three months after the start of work, the line to the Ob was completed. That left only the half-mile-long bridge over the Irtysh, which was completed in March 1896, effectively extending Russia's rail system deep into Siberia for the first time.

Mikhailovsky had built almost 900 miles of railway through terrain for which the term 'inhospitable' could have been coined, using primitive methods and suffering acute labour shortages. Moreover, he managed the task below budget, an achievement for which he was thanked by the Committee for the Siberian Railway. Not surprisingly, Tupper found that Soviet railway experts he met in Leningrad 'declared without a moment's hesitation that the greatest civil engineer in tsarist Russia was Constantine Yakovlevich Mikhailovsky'.[18]

This might be slightly unfair to the engineers in charge of other sectors of the Trans-Siberian, whose task was made more difficult because of the longer distance supplies needed to be transported. Progress was also being made on the Mid-Siberian section, though the harsher conditions meant it was slower. The difficulties posed by the taiga through which this 1,130-mile section passed were different. It was hillier territory, heavily forested, and what an early Swedish explorer described as 'dark and impenetrable'. The shade from the trees meant that the thaw which started in late May in western Siberia was later, with the surface remaining hard until mid-July, giving precious little time for carrying out the groundwork necessary to lay the base for the tracks. Even then, in the brief summer interlude, conditions were not easy since even a little rain turned the whole forest into a muddy swamp.

Mezheninov, the chief engineer, undoubtedly faced even greater difficulties than his counterpart further west in all aspects of railway construction. Not only was the terrain harder, but supplying this middle section posed greater problems than for any other part of the line. Until the completion of the West Siberian, all supplies had to be shipped from European Russia through the Urals and then by a circuitous river route to the construction sites. As Witte had envisaged, the Trans-Siberian project was not just a matter of building a railway, but encompassed a host of other improvement schemes for Siberia, from clearing rivers and draining land to creating new towns and erecting schools and churches. Initially, therefore, millions of roubles were spent on improving the waterways along which the materials for the line were transported, as rivers were widened, dredged and cleared of obstructions to allow the barges to pass through unimpeded. On the route of the railway, however, the vast number of streams and rivulets created further difficulties as every one had to be forded. One particular part of the steppe prone to flooding required the construction of eighty-two bridges in just forty-four miles. In total, from Chelyabinsk to Irkutsk, 635 single-span and twenty-three multi-span bridges were built. The overall length of the metal bridges was more than six miles, and while the single-span bridges were originally in wood, they were later replaced by metal ones in a clever technique devised by an engineer, Nikolai Belebubsky, to avoid having to close the railway. The longest bridge, over the Yenisei river at Krasnoyarsk, was 850 metres (2,790 feet) and won a gold medal at the Paris Exposition Universelle in 1900, while the Ob bridge at Novonikolayevsk was 640 metres (2,100 feet).

To compound the difficulties faced by the construction gangs, everything from horses and carts to ballast and the right kind of wood was in short supply. The sad irony was that the timber that was available in such abundance from the endless taiga was largely useless as it was not strong or durable enough. Sleepers laid with local unseasoned wood lasted barely a year or two, and consequently suitable timber had to be brought in from forests as much as 300 miles away.

Mezheninov was under added pressure, too. Witte and his committee were so impressed by Mikhailovsky's progress that they decided to bring forward the date at which they wanted the whole line completed to 1899, albeit still with the need for water transport connections over the major rivers and Lake Baikal. Mezheninov had originally hoped to work eastwards, finishing the first section from the Ob to Krasnoyarsk on the Yenisei and then to start work on the rest of the route through to Irkutsk (or, as usual, on the other side of the major river, the Angara). However, Witte's insistence on speed meant that the Mid-Siberian needed to be completed within five years rather than seven and this forced

Mezheninov to begin construction of this second section earlier than planned. Worse, he had hoped to work from both ends at the same time, but a belated inspection of the Angara, the river that flows out of Lake Baikal near Irkutsk on which he had depended for transport, ascertained that it was unnavigable, because of shallows and rapids for the barges that would be needed to carry rails and other material. His difficulties were compounded by the bankruptcy of a foundry in Irkutsk, which he had hoped would supply rails, and consequently he decided to have only one crew working eastwards from Krasnoyarsk.

Not surprisingly, as a result of these combined difficulties, this was the section of line on the whole Trans-Siberian project on which most corners were cut. The twin pressures of lack of supply and the imperative for speed meant that everything was skimped. Mezheninov deliberately designed the railway to save money, increasing the tightness of the curves and the steepness of the gradients. Embankments were not built as wide as specified, nor as high above the ground as necessary; ballast was used far too sparingly and the weight of rails, at just under fifty lb per yard, was roughly a third less than the standard used on railways in Europe and America. All this stored up trouble for later and the early years of the Trans-Siberian were characterized by an almost constant need for repairs and a continuous programme of investment to make good the inadequacies of the initial line.

Nevertheless, Mezheninov achieved what many disparaging railway engineers in the West would have thought impossible. He completed the Mid-Siberian Railway – from the shores of the Ob, where the town of Novonikolayevsk was beginning its rapid growth, to the Angara embankment facing Irkutsk – in just five years, amounting to more than 200 miles per year, which was particularly impressive given that the extreme conditions left so little time for track-laying. Mezheninov also, incidentally, built the branch line into Tomsk, despite the difficulties of the terrain, which resulted in the fifty-four-mile-long route taking eighteen months to complete. The cost was more than covered, to the satisfaction of the Committee for the Siberian Railway, by the savings that Mikhailovsky had made on the West Siberian.

This first section of the Mid-Siberian – from Novonikolayevsk to Krasnoyarsk – opened in January 1898 and a year later regular services ran all the way through to Irkutsk, well ahead of the original schedule of mid-1900. Unlike Mikhailovsky who had managed to complete his section under budget, the Mid-Siberian cost far more than expected, despite all the skimping – but that was hardly surprising. Even food for the workers and forage for the horses had tripled or more in price during construction, as a result not just of increased demand but an acute local crop failure, while all other supplies were expensive due to shortages and the distance they needed to be transported. The very presence of so many labourers would inevitably push up food prices, as local suppliers cashed in. Consequently, wages had to be increased to allow the men to have enough to feed themselves and, in reality, it was miraculous that the project was not even more over budget given all these difficulties.

In the east, work on the Ussuri section, barely 500 miles long and running through territory that was flat and seemed to be relatively easy, progressed the slowest. It was not only the usual difficulties in finding the right type of labour, but materials too were hard to obtain given the remoteness of the region. Everything had to be shipped from Odessa on the Black Sea, a journey through the Suez Canal that took at best forty days, and often more. Moreover, Vyazemsky's men were hampered by the variable climate. While it was to be expected that work would grind to a halt in the sub-zero temperatures of midwinter – although this area's proximity to the sea means it is far warmer in winter than in deepest Siberia – it was the summer rains that caused the unexpected delays. The terrain may have been flat, but it was awfully wet. Constant deluges turned the worksites into huge mudfields, and pictures reveal a scene not unlike a First World War battlefield, with men and beasts covered in black muck. The Ussuri river, along which the railway ran for long periods, rose thirty-two feet at the height of the thaw, submerging and at times washing away track that had been laid, and another river, the Iman, also broke its banks with all too frequent regularity. Just to make life even more difficult, the damp conditions fostered a Siberian strain of anthrax that spread rapidly among the horses and then in an equally deadly way to the men in contact with them, while the mosquitoes which attack humans in this region are legendary for their prevalence. Vyazemsky was also hampered by the failure of many of his labour contractors to do anything other than pocket the money they were given to provide workers for the line. Vladivostok was the equivalent of an American frontier town, full of dodgy entrepreneurs and criminals, and it was difficult at times to tell them apart. In his desperation to sign up sufficient numbers of workers, Vyazemsky agreed contracts with a wide variety of these contractors, who were mostly merchants, and retired officers or civil servants, but many simply never fulfilled their side of the bargain and policing these arrangements was simply beyond the ability of a committee a continent away in St Petersburg. So in the face of these problems Vyazemsky can be forgiven to some extent for his tardiness.

Most of this section was built by the team working northwards from Vladivostok, but again a couple of bridges – over the Iman and the Khor – were left until last, while the main construction gang progressed towards Khabarovsk. A second camp was eventually established, and its crew built the first forty miles heading south from Khabarovsk. It was not until November 1897, when the bridges were finally completed, that the line could open to regular traffic. The difficulties encountered in construction were reflected in the cost of the Ussuri, which, at 85,000 roubles per mile (£8,500) was about a quarter more than the average combined for the Western and Mid-Siberian sections. This was still very cheap. As a point of reference, early railways built in Britain cost around £30,000 per mile and in the United States on average around £15,000 (though with considerable variation).[19]

The Transbaikal was the last major section of the Trans-Siberian to be started. It was envisaged that the line would run 700 miles from the eastern side of Lake Baikal at Mysovsk to Sretensk on the Shika river, via Verkhneudinsk (now called Ulan-Ude) and Chita, the capital of the Transbaikal territory. Work on the Transbaikal started in 1895 under the direction of Alexander Pushechnikov, the chief engineer, using materials delivered from the east, via rail and river from Vladivostok to Sretensk.

This was more mountainous and rocky territory than encountered further west, and consequently the line had to follow the meandering and steep-banked Ingoda and Shika rivers. At times the cliffs hewn out over eons by the river had to be blasted with explosives, a perilous but effective process. Despite the freezing temperatures in winter, where around Chita, for example, the average daily high for the three coldest months is about -15°C, work continued throughout the winter thanks to the dry and mostly clear days. The cold meant that work was hampered by the lack of water and labourers had to melt vast quantities of ice for their own use and to keep the horses – and indeed the locomotive boilers – watered.

Ironically, though, it was excess of water which delayed the whole project and caused untold damage. In July 1897 a series of huge downpours overstretched the whole river system and caused widespread flooding. The damage to the railway was extensive. More than 230 miles of newly laid track were affected, and in the worst incident, near Sretensk, a huge landslide swept away more than a dozen bridges and several miles of track. Again, the lack of a proper survey contributed to the extent of the damage as it would have provided an assessment of the likelihood of flooding on particular sections.

Other mishaps included an extreme drought in the summer after the flood and an outbreak of Siberian anthrax, which killed many horses and a few men, but, worse, led many workers to flee the work camps. Two of the main contractors pulled out, claiming to have incurred huge losses. Nevertheless, Pushechnikov reached Sretensk and opened the line provisionally in January 1900 and to regular traffic that summer.

Pushechnikov was also in charge of building the short section of line from Irkutsk down to Lake Baikal, a distance of about forty miles. Here plans were changed at a late stage. Originally, the idea had been to build a pontoon bridge across the wide Angara river, enabling trains to reach the town proper, and then run alongside the river down to Listvyanka on its western shore. However, the Angara, which is the only river that flows out of the huge lake and is half a mile wide at its source, proved fiercer and more unmanageable than expected. A pontoon bridge seemed a perilous option and therefore alternative ideas were considered. Prince Mikhail Khilkov – the minister of transport who took an active role in overseeing the project, though he mostly followed Witte's bidding – decided that the southern bank was easier and shorter, and consequently the railway never reached the Irkutsk side of the river, a situation that pertains to this day.[20] Easier it may have been, but easy it was not, as a comprehensive survey would have revealed. This short stretch of line down to Port Baikal on the lake did not in fact open for regular traffic until the summer of 1900 because of the difficulties of construction. As Tupper describes it, 'where they had expected to build on easy slopes, they were forced to blast out precipitous rock to create a shelf for the roadbed [trackbed], and where there was earth instead of rock, retaining walls had to be piled up against the seven-feet-a-second sweep of the Angara along its banks'.[21]

While originally the idea had been to build a Circum-Baikal Railway along the southern shore, this had long been rejected by the Committee. Instead, for once responding to a relatively detailed survey, the engineers realized it would be very hard to build a line in this mountainous coast and decided on a steamer service across the lake, which would be a much cheaper option. However, the lake may be the deepest in the world, but it nevertheless freezes over; consequently, in winter they envisaged laying temporary tracks on the ice for the trains, as was done to link Kronstadt, on the island of Kotlin in the Baltic, with St Petersburg twenty miles away. Khilkov managed to persuade his colleagues on the committee that a vessel with a steel hull was necessary, rather than the cheaper wooden boat they initially suggested, as it would act as an icebreaker to keep the shipping lane open as long as possible.

Enter, therefore, the main British contribution to the construction of the Trans-Siberian, albeit still a minor one. Of the dozen shipbuilders who submitted bids, W. G. Armstrong, Mitchell & Company of Newcastle[22] were successful and quickly sent over an icebreaker in kit form in no fewer than 7,000 carefully marked packages, which arrived in Listvyanka, a small resort town on the lake, in late 1896. However, due to difficulties finding sufficient local skilled labour and the discovery of numerous missing parts, it took more than three years for the team – led by a marine engineer and four foremen from the Tyne – to assemble the 4,200-ton *Baikal*, which began operating across the lake in the spring of 1900. Although an ungainly ship, described by Tupper as a 'slab-sided hybrid that combined the physical features of a tubby polar icebreaker and a top-heavy excursion boat',[23] it was nevertheless an impressive sight, the biggest train ferry in the world outside the United States, and delighted locals were eager to take their marriage vows in its chapel. The *Baikal* could carry 800 people – separated into three classes – and she could accommodate the coaches of a whole passenger train and up to twenty-eight fully loaded freight cars.

At Khilkov's request, a second smaller ship, the *Angara*, was commissioned to operate in tandem across the lake with the *Baikal*, with accommodation for a mere 150 passengers and no space for rail coaches in her bowels. The ships each operated two round trips a day in fair weather, but, despite their relative comfort, crossing Lake Baikal was an unwanted delay for most passengers. The ships struggled in the storms that whip up quickly on the lake and the *Angara* proved to be too light to break up the ice as effectively as its sister ship. It could only proceed if the *Baikal*, only half-loaded and with no carriages in its hold, broke up the ice in front to create a path.

Even in the summer, passengers could be held up for days at the ports, waiting for a crossing as the ships were marooned by bad weather, and in the winter on many occasions passengers had to make the thirty-mile crossing in a sledge; a perilous journey on ice that occasionally would suddenly break up, creating gaps that would prove fatal for anyone falling into them. On other occasions, journeys were curtailed, the passengers having to disembark and continue by *tarantass* across the ice because the *Baikal* could not force a way through. The other option, of driving trains across temporary tracks on the ice, proved fanciful and was not even attempted until the Russo-Japanese War (see chapter 6), with fateful results.

Of course, building the railway was more than just laying tracks across the Siberian steppe and involved setting up a ferry service. Railways need stations, sidings, signalling systems, depots, locomotives, rolling stock and much more. The advantage of this massive project being initiated and developed by government was that these facilities could be standardized and built to set specifications. Stations had to be at most fifty versts (thirty-three miles) apart – which actually was double the distance allowed on the rest of the railway network – to ensure that facilities were available for passengers in the event of breakdowns and for maintenance of the track, and there had to be a small repair depot every 100 miles – essential given the unreliability of the locomotives.

The stations and other buildings had to comply with the railway's own architectural style, created by a special design-drawing workshop that had been part of the ministry of transport since 1842. It created a typology for the industrial, passenger and office buildings that were part of the railway. That did not mean the buildings were identical, but rather that they had the same design features. It was, in modern-day parlance, a brand, rather like that created for the London Underground a few years later. Passengers waiting for trains will have been grateful that double glazing and strong insulation were, right from the start, provided as standard.

There were no fewer than five categories of stations. Initially there were no first-class stations, as even established towns like Omsk, Krasnoyarsk, Irkutsk and Chita were categorized as second class, but at least they were provided with stations that were built in brick with eclectic combinations of Russian and Western motifs. Apart from a few third-class stations, all the rest were built in wood. They did not lack charm and individuality: 'The architecture was spared from presenting an overall impression of boring predictability. This meant there was a great variety of modified versions to be seen. These wooden buildings were the closest to the traditional native architecture and were constructed in the same manner as the houses in villages and towns.'[24]

The design team did not always get it right. Many country stations lacked covered space to store grain awaiting shipment, which meant it spoiled when there was heavy rain, and was easily stolen. Nor did the two lowest categories of station have any waiting rooms. Passengers were allowed to wait in an employee's house, which was precisely a mere 592 square feet, but that was probably sufficient since there were rarely hordes waiting for trains in these remote places.

Railway colonies quickly developed around the stations to house employees. The railway was effectively creating new communities with a distinctive style: 'The whole of the complexes, buildings and structures of the Trans-Siberian formed a huge architectural entity, a sort of ensemble. The use of the same design, materials, details and decoration along the entire track created an architectural unity and integrity, which was further strengthened by the application of identical colours. Wooden buildings were painted in green and light brown, while others were in red and white, using brick and plaster for decorative details.'[25]

Although there was corruption, incompetence and shoddy workmanship, the railway was completed remarkably quickly. Yet there was a tendency among Western writers, from whom much of our information about the line's construction emanates, to decry the Russian efforts, a contempt that long predated the building of the Trans-Siberian. Martin Page, writing in the 1970s, encapsulates that well: 'Holy Russia, belonging neither to the industrialized West nor to the exotic East, and understanding neither, seemed to imagine that the building of the railway would somehow miraculously make it a major power in both. As it was primarily an exercise in chauvinism, foreign experts were rigorously excluded from even the smallest participation in the project from the outset through to its completion. The Russians lacked the human resources to carry it through competently by themselves, and the results of their attempting to do so were deplorable (and faithfully recorded in the railway journals of the West, whose editors appear to have viewed the prospect of the project's failure with relish).'[26]

There were many other similar comments, both contemporary and more recent, born of ignorance and prejudice. This attitude, particularly prevalent at the time of the building of the Trans-Siberian, has survived, despite the fact that its completion in less than a decade was an achievement on a par with any of the other great engineering projects of the nineteenth century which do not attract the same churlish criticism. A more accurate view was expressed by the authors of a book on the role of the railway in the Russo-Japanese War: 'In many respects, the railway-building involved with both the Trans-Siberian and the Chinese Eastern Railway was the acme of planning, execution and technology. The construction of the railways was carried out economically, with noteworthy achievements in planning and engineering.'[27] As proof of this, the Trans-Siberian was built around fifty per cent more quickly than the Canadian transcontinental which had inspired it. Indeed, *The Engineer* magazine in Britain praised the Russian bridge-building skills in an article in 1897, observing that 'the Russian engineer is rapidly rising to a place amongst the better engineers of Europe'.[28]

Moreover, as we have seen and contrary to what Page says, there was much foreign expertise called upon to help design many features of the railway, such as bridges and other structures, stations and depots. The building of the Trans-Siberian, as befitted a project of this size, was, in fact, a truly global enterprise involving European and, in particular, American suppliers, and it had a lasting impact. Much of the steel for the line was actually manufactured in the United States and many Americans made their fortune producing rails, locomotives and bridge components for the railway. Braking systems, for example, came from Westinghouse and the New York Air Brake company: 'American steel-rolling mills, machine-shops and forges for the manufacture of rails, locomotives and bridge components expanded and grew rich on the contracts that were negotiated with the Russian government for this mammoth enterprise.'[29] The Russian industrialization stimulated by construction of the railways, particularly the Trans-Siberian, was based on American expertise: 'The Trans-Siberian Railway, it was calculated, was supporting no fewer than 128,000 American family members.'[30] The impetus given by the construction of the Trans-Siberian to the American metallurgical industry had, indeed, a long-lasting effect, helping the Americans to overtake the British in many parts of the world as the main suppliers of materials for railway construction. British engineering input, on the other hand, was largely confined to the building of the *Baikal*, though Royal Engineers did supervise some of the more complex building tasks; also, like the French, the British supplied considerable capital to the Russian government, some of which undoubtedly helped to fund the Trans-Siberian.

In other words, the Trans-Siberian was a great stimulus to the global capitalism that was still establishing itself as the dominant economic ethos at the end of the nineteenth century. There is no little irony in that since in many respects the construction of the line was more Soviet than anything the communist dictators would later achieve. It was a monument to state planning and state funding of major projects. Witte may have strengthened capitalism and private industry in Russia through his adept handling of the economy as finance minister, but that was in the name of furthering the interests of his Motherland, not to boost the profits of private enterprise. He understood that a measure of capitalist enterprise was needed, but that ultimately it had to be subservient to the needs of government, and the Trans-Siberian is a testament to that philosophy.

The cost of the railway was undoubtedly increased by corruption – that deep-seated ill of tsarist (and, indeed, modern) Russia. With the committee overseeing the project thousands of miles away in St Petersburg, tight financial control was an impossibility. Nevertheless, the routine nature of the corruption and waste was still remarkable. The extensive use of contractors was at the root of much of it. A few large contractors monopolized the work and were often responsible for a wide variety of tasks which were specified vaguely, allowing for a lot of leeway. Supposedly, any contract worth more than 5,000 roubles (£500) was supposed to be authorized by the Committee, but in practice this rule was avoided by simply allocating lots of identical contracts, each below the threshold. Marks cites the example of a supplier of wood for the Western Siberia section receiving '36 separate contracts for a total of 180,000 roubles'.[31]

The work of the contractors, who were mostly local peasants with a bit of entrepreneurial nous, was essentially unsupervised. They were simply handed contracts to build a particular stretch of track without any competitive tendering process and even then they often asked for extra payment, once work had begun, as they knew that there was no alternative supplier because the imperative was to get the job done quickly: 'Having set his own high price, the contractor then called for even larger payments, and to keep him on the job, the construction chief often approved the requests without higher authorization.'[32] Advance payments were routinely made and were often, as we have seen on the Ussuri Railway, simply pocketed by the supplier, who did not fulfil his contract. With very little supervision of the work, contractors boosted their profits by skimping on material or building to below the required standard, resulting in embankments that were too narrow, insufficient ballast, inadequate drainage and a host of other failings. Profits of thirty per cent were routine and the cost of supplies was often charged at sixty per cent more than contractors had paid for them. Many contractors prospered as a result, and one who worked for Pushechnikov was honest enough to tell him:

'By recommending me for contract work on the Circum-Baikal line, you have made me rich.'[33]

Using a small number of big contractors may have been expensive, but it seemed to suit everyone, even if it meant increased costs. The accountants charged with overseeing the contracts turned a blind eye to this sort of abuse. It made their job easier because it meant they had to deal with fewer suppliers. Effectively, the corruption was institutionalized: 'It got the job done quickly (regardless of costs) and relieved them [the chief engineers] of additional expenditures of time, direct responsibility for the labour force, and the detailed supervision of works (for which they lacked the requisite knowledge).'[34] Moreover, the central administration back in St Petersburg was happy, because there were fewer disputes between suppliers and the engineers who had the main contract.

There is a paradox here. The story of the struggle over the construction of the railway presented in this chapter seems to contradict the incontrovertible fact that the line was actually built, and completed remarkably quickly. But as ever with such stories, it is the hardships and disasters that make the news and are the focus of contemporary accounts, while the steady and uneventful progress of the various sections across the Siberian steppe attracted little attention. The true story, however, is that day after day, week after week, tens of thousands of workers mostly armed with little more than pickaxes and shovels created this monumental railway.

As well as vast numbers of men, the other requirement to maintain progress was, of course, money. And there seems to have been no constraint on the amount available. Witte may have been finance minister, but he was no parsimonious Vyshenegradsky-type figure. He and the tsar realized that the railway would have value only if it were finished. Consequently, once the project was underway, sufficient funds were always made available to ensure its completion. Witte recognized that the construction had been achieved at a heavy price for both the Russian economy and the people, but never wavered from his determination to see the project through. Witte put up taxes that helped pay for the railway and did everything to boost exports, which created shortages at home: 'The Siberian Railroad required huge sacrifices on the part of the Russian population, a sad fact that Witte more than once acknowledged.'[35]

The line, therefore, did not come cheap. Indeed, the ultimate cost was inevitably far greater than the original estimate. The Committee's original budget was around 350 million roubles (£35 million), just under 50,000 roubles per verst, and this had included the Amur Railway, which was not, in fact, completed until 1916. Without taking into account its replacement, the Chinese Eastern Railway – which was very expensive, as we shall see in chapter 5 – the total cost amounted to around 850 million roubles, an overrun of around 150 per cent, and the cost per verst was double the projected average at more than 100,000 roubles. That figure, produced in 1901, however, also includes operating losses for the first three years. Nevertheless, these calculations are probably underestimates, given the opaque nature of the government's finances, and the single-till system of government accounting described earlier, which makes it difficult to identify specific sums of money set aside for the project.

However, in terms of the development of Siberia and the establishment of Russian rule over its huge territory, the exercise was undoubtedly worth it. The railway, as we see in subsequent chapters, continued to grow and be improved, and remains a key part of the region's infrastructure. There was, though, one saving which should be considered in assessing the costs and benefits. The railway obviated the need to build a road connection between Moscow and Vladivostok and indeed it was not until the late twentieth century that there was anything like a reliable route for motor vehicles. The existence of the railway made such an investment unnecessary and that saving needs to be taken into account in any assessment of the cost. Moreover, on the positive side, while the cost may have been higher than expected, so was the usage. Right from the start both local people and long-distance travellers were desperate to use the trains, even though these pioneers journeyed in conditions that were far from ideal.

# FIVE

# TRAVELS AND TRAVAILS

The completed – or rather almost completed – Trans-Siberian which emerged at the turn of the century was not a gleaming new railway exemplifying the cutting-edge technology of the age. It was, rather, a meandering, single-track line with more curves than an average mountain pass and more rickety than a rope bridge. It was slow and unreliable, but it could nevertheless lay claim to being the longest and greatest railway ever built. It was far too glib to conclude, as Tupper did, that the Russians had 'done a first-rate job in building a third-rate railway'.[1]

Tupper's comment is typical of writers in the West who, as mentioned in the last chapter, had a tendency to criticize the new railway out of hand or (far less often) to overpraise it. The most balanced early assessment was given by William Oliver Greener, writing in 1902, whose conclusion was in the curate's egg mould: 'There are poor sections; none is either very good or very bad; some are much better than others.'[2] Greener, almost uniquely among the early critics, recognized the constraints under which the builders had operated, whereby 'everything has been accurately calculated; but everything, too, has been made just as specified in the calculated minimum [in the engineering textbooks], and no margin allowed for possible differences of soil and material'. As a result, there were inevitable instances of subsidence, landslides and spreading of the rails, causing derailments. Greener highlighted the problem of the lightness of the rails, particularly on the eastern sections, which were unsuitable for the heavy locomotives needed to pull the trains, and which slowed down services because running fast places more pressure on the track and consequently leads to breaks. While Greener observed that the line may well have been built more cheaply had foreign contractors been used, he recognized that by keeping it as a Russian enterprise, 'the Russians have gained what they needed badly: practical experience in carrying through engineering work of the first order. In this way, if in no other, the State benefits.' He was sanguine and balanced, too, about the region: 'It was not the Eldorado some picture it, nor is it the desolate waste some consider it . . . [It] is just plain, commonplace country, such as one expects to find in any great British colony.'[3]

With the completion of the Transbaikal and the establishment of the ferry service on Lake Baikal, as well as the erection of the bridges over the major rivers, such as the Ob and the Yenisei, the Trans-Siberian was open for business. From Moscow and Chelyabinsk, passengers heading east in the summer of 1900 could travel by rail all the way to Irkutsk and then down to the lake at Port Baikal, where, after a steamer crossing, they could continue by train again from Mysovsk to Sretensk on the Shilka river; then by riverboats for almost 1,000 miles through to Khabarovsk, where they could take the Ussuri Railway, which ran through to Vladivostok. The journey took a minimum of six weeks, far shorter than the old post road, but nevertheless quite a trek, and there were at times lengthy delays due to breakdowns, accidents and shortage of rolling stock. There could, too, be a long wait for a train as the line's capacity was extremely limited; at first it could accommodate just three trains per day in each direction. Massive backlogs of freight for which there was an immediate demand frequently built up, as passenger trains were given priority. Even the official guide to the line admitted to the early lack of capacity, suggesting in its rather stilted style that: 'The means at its [the West Siberian Railway's] disposal were far from sufficing for the transport and conveyance of the passengers and goods which presented themselves.'[4]

Despite this, there was no shortage of early riders, including numerous foreigners, who provided comprehensive and at times breathless accounts of their experiences. Many local people took to the trains, too, travelling between Siberian destinations, and numbers exceeded expectations. Before the bridges were completed, many sections were opened to provisional traffic, in which passengers travelled in fourth-class carriages attached to work trains and were ferried across rivers. In winter sometimes temporary tracks were laid across smaller rivers and streams, but this was recognized as risky, so passengers disembarked and trudged across the ice. Prince Khilkov was eager to open completed sections of line, despite their poor condition and in August 1898 services started operating between Moscow and Krasnoyarsk, an eight-day journey provided there were no mishaps, from where, after crossing the Yenisei by ferry, passengers could reach Irkutsk (or rather the other side of the Angara from the town) by train.

In 1896, its first full year, the West Siberian Railway carried 329,000 passengers, including 169,000 emigrants. By 1902, when most of the railway was open, a million passengers were carried and the class breakdown shows that this was very much a service used by ordinary local people. Only 8,000 took first class, while 140,000 enjoyed second and the rest were almost equally split between third and fourth.

This was railway travel at its most basic. Arnot Reid, who described his journey from Peking (now known as Beijing) to St Petersburg in a book published in 1899, complained that he had to wait for three hours in a snowstorm before the ferry crossed another bridgeless river, the Oka. He also objected that there were no timetables – a train simply left Irkutsk every other day, and 'when it would arrive at any particular place no one seemed to know'.[5] There was no first class as yet, and Reid did not realize that as there was a shortage of second class, too, there was a first come, first served system to obtain a seat in the compartments. Consequently, he was forced to spend the first twenty-four hours of the journey sitting on his luggage in the corridor. However, in many respects Reid found the journey enjoyable, particularly the opportunities to purchase food at stops: 'At many stations there were outside stalls kept by the country people and there one could get excellent cold roast chickens, partridges, blackcock and other game.'[6] Together with the French brandy and Crimean claret he had brought along, Reid ate well, which was fortunate since he reported that the train took four days to cover the distance between Krasnoyarsk and Irkutsk on the Mid-Siberian, an average of less than 7 mph. At best the speed limit was twenty versts per hour (12 mph) for passenger trains, and just twelve versts per hour (8 mph) for freight, a rate that was well below the norm in European Russia and elsewhere at the time. Indeed, in many places a fit jogger would have outpaced the train, because of the further speed restrictions necessitated by the poor condition of the track.

Reid, at least, survived without mishap. The railway had been so poorly and quickly built that it was a hazard to passengers. Early travellers faced genuine danger. In 1901 some ninety-three people were killed and 500 injured in a total of 524 accidents, though most of these were just simple derailments of freight trains. The catalogue of failings was almost endless. Everything that could go wrong on a railway did – with the exception of major bridge collapses, due (as mentioned before) to the higher standards insisted upon. Smaller wooden bridges would sag under the weight of trains; rails would disappear into the mud as areas expected to be permafrost melted in the summer; the badly ballasted track, with the sleepers on straight sections at times having been laid on the mud with no stone to support them, would break under the strain; the rush to build the line cheaply meant that curves were far sharper than the standard requirement by the government and consequently trains had to reduce speed or risk careering off into the countryside; the steeper than specified gradients meant that trains of only 16 freight wagons were the maximum load for a single locomotive, rather than, as expected, twice that number; and where cuttings had been carved out of hills too parsimoniously, great lumps of earth were wont to fall on the tracks, sometimes blocking the line. In the early days there were large stretches of track with no trees to protect them, and, until the government later planted birches along the line, snow drifts were a persistent hazard in the winter and often required the train crew to dig out the locomotive with their shovels, an operation which could take many hours. There was more, too, more than can be listed, and it was surprising that any trains – let alone the three a day scheduled initially – ever got through. Breakdowns were a daily occurrence and delays of a day or two were routine. Indeed, the railway authorities warned travellers to build in contingency time to their journeys. Photographs of accidents, generally to freight trains, found their way into the European and American press, and were given ironic captions such as 'The usual accident on the Great Siberian Railway', increasing the undeserved contempt with which the Trans-Siberian was viewed in the West. It was not only accidents and breakdowns that caused delays. The railway had necessarily employed large numbers of unskilled men, who paid little regard to the needs of a timetable – when there was one. At every station it seemed that the driver and his mate were greeting long-lost friends and the custom was that they shook hands with all the local staff, lingering over small talk and tea. On saints' days, it was common for the whole crew to desert the train to pray at the chapels provided at every large station.

Some of the incidents were indeed spectacular. According to one early traveller, Richard Jefferson, the very first locomotive to run between Martinsk and Achinsk on the Mid-Siberian fell into a river when the tracks collapsed under it, necessitating months of repair. For Jefferson, who travelled along the line in the winter of 1896/7 when the Western section had just been completed apart from some bridges, the journey was not short of adventure. Jefferson was hoping to make his fortune from the gold mines in central Siberia and travelled the whole length of the completed section. The high point came when he reached the Chulim river, relatively small by Siberian standards, but still wide enough, as he described it, to 'make two of the River Thames at London Bridge'.[7] The bridge to the town of Achinsk was not yet complete, but in the eagerness to open the railway a temporary arrangement had been made: 'A quarter of a mile from the river, the rails diverted from the main road [alignment], and continued down the slope and so on across the ice to the Achinsk side.' Jefferson was rather relieved when the train stopped and 'the conductor came up and requested us to descend and walk to the other side – cheerfully remarking that if the train went through [the ice] only he, his fellow conductors and the engine drivers would be drowned.' Jefferson doubted whether the ice was solid enough to take the weight of the locomotive and the fifteen heavy carriages that made up his train, and trudged happily across 'a cheerless waste of ice' from where, 'over the river, we could see the glint of the sun on the brazen dome of a church in Achinsk, with the twilight gathering in its greyness behind. The half-finished bridge stood out on our right, gaunt and spidery, and nothing around us but the eternal white of the snow.' One can almost feel the cold.

Followed by the crowd of passengers wrapped up in furs that made them look like 'gigantic bales of wool', Jefferson watched the train crossing the ice. The locomotive slowly descended the incline towards the river, whistling and snorting, where, ingenuously, the local trackworkers had secured the sleepers to the ice by freezing them on with water obtained from a hole they had carved into the frozen river. When the first carriage clattered on to the ice, there was another crunch, but the ice held firm, watched with casual nonchalance by the passengers, and within five minutes the train rolled into Achinsk.

At least the river did not amount to an insuperable obstacle for Jefferson and his companions. In the late spring, when enough ice had melted to prevent trains from going over it, the ferry boats could not cross either, because of the danger from huge ice floes, and consequently passengers could be held up for weeks. Similarly, until the ice was strong enough in the late autumn, there was a period when crossing proved impossible, too. Even when they were functioning, the ferries that operated in the summer were a source of great delay, as they had been before the line was built, since all the passengers had to pile on them with their baggage and the little boats invariably had to make several trips across these wide expanses of water.

As a measure of the slowness of travel in the early days the journey of 120 miles between Achinsk and Krasnoyarsk, which was at the time the end of the line, took Jefferson's train all night and part of the morning: 'Through the night we went, toiling over mountain passes, through deep glens or in and out of gigantic forest glades, but with that eternal snow everywhere, with nothing which was inspiring or inspiriting.' The bridge over the Yenisei was not yet completed – it took three years and at its peak 94,000 workers to build – and therefore Jefferson and his companions had to take a sledge into town and continue their way towards

Irkutsk in a *tarantass*. Jefferson also had a brilliant and not entirely unconvincing explanation for why the line was built in such poor condition. He talked to an engineer who had worked on the line, who explained that in effect it was a sophisticated job-creation scheme: 'We are engaged to lay this railway. It is to be finished all the way in about three years' time; after that what are *we* going to do?' As it turns out, Jefferson's interlocutor was spot on. For the first decade or so, the line was in a constant state of repair and improvement, especially after its inadequacies were highlighted by the Russo-Japanese War (outlined in the next chapter).

Earlier in the journey, a couple of days out of Tomsk, Jefferson's train had broken down and he learnt that it would take at least several hours to repair. Instead of waiting, along with a companion, he walked the fifteen versts (ten miles) to the nearest station, and was rewarded by being the first passenger to tuck in to the buffet which the stationmaster had prepared in anticipation of the train's arrival; like an overfed cat, he fell asleep in the waiting room, which proved far more comfortable than the rattling train.

These repasts, copious at times and wholly inadequate at others, were essential given the absence of dining cars in the years before the line was fully open. If there were no local sellers, as could happen in winter, then travellers without provisions would go hungry. On one trip, Annette Meakin, an English gentlewoman (as she termed herself) and her mother, travelling on the Transbaikal section just before it opened fully to the public, was horrified to find only fourth-class accommodation available. To escape the peasants who had crowded into their carriage, they were reallocated by a French-speaking guard to a luggage van with some kindly soldiers, but found only milk, tea and bread to satisfy their hunger during the four-day trip.

At other times the military, notably the top brass, were less helpful to casual travellers. Another early adventurer, William Oliver Greener, travelled in a train on which the army officers bought everything in sight at the stations; on one occasion a greedy general appropriated forty eggs and seven bottles of milk, leaving nothing but salt fish for the mothers on the train with babies to feed.

Jefferson had booked first class, but found that not all the trains provided it, so he spent several nights on the hard boards of third. Many early foreign travellers, like the Meakins, had the same experience and therefore, unusually, they ended up in third or fourth class, which was rarely a happy experience. The Reverend Dr Francis Clark, a New England congregational pastor, travelled from Sretensk eastwards to Lake Baikal at around the same time as Ms Meakin and her mother, in the summer of 1900, when it was still not fully open to regular services. He was lucky, travelling in what was a third-class compartment with hard, unupholstered seats and three tiers of wooden sleeping shelves, only five feet long. In fact, he was fortunate again: on a visit to the Novosibirsk Railway Museum in 2012 I saw gloomy carriages from the 1900s that had three layers of hard metal shelves for sleeping on and cell-like grille doors. Clark found accommodation at the back of the train, which was far worse than the coaches he was travelling in: 'Others, which might be termed fifth class are simply boxcars with no seats, and marked on the outside to carry twelve horses or forty-three men.[8] (Usually, in fact, they said simply forty men.) Clark describes the wide range of different people using these carriages in a manner somewhat bereft of Christian charity: 'If these were fifth-class cars, there were plenty of sixth- and seventh-class people – some in rags, and many in tags, but few in velvet gowns.' He describes them as having 'unmentionable parasites' and that 'odours indescribably offensive made the air thick and almost murky', which grew ever worse as the journey continued.

In 1900, to attract more passengers like Clark, the government launched a de luxe first-class service through to Vladivostok, operated by a combination of private and public enterprise. Prince

Khilkov announced ambitious plans to run these luxury trains between Moscow and both Vladivostok and Port Arthur, the deepwater port on the Liaotung peninsula in Manchuria that had been leased controversially from China, and oddly named after a Royal Navy officer who docked there to repair a frigate and now called Lüshun, for tourists and travellers to the Far East. These were intended to be even better than the similar luxury trains that had become commonplace in Europe over the past couple of decades such as the famous Orient Express. In fact, to create the service Khilkov entered into a partnership with Georges Nagelmackers, the man who had created the Orient Express and other similar services around Europe, and who was charged with providing some of the trains, while others were operated directly by the Russian government. Nagelmackers, a brilliant self-publicist and genuine pioneering railway entrepreneur, used the Paris Exposition Universelle (a world fair held in 1900 to celebrate the achievements of the previous century, notably the construction of the Eiffel Tower) to give visitors a foretaste of a luxury journey along the Trans-Siberian.

Nagelmackers did not just plonk a few carriages into the exhibition area, but rather visitors to the Universelle were treated to a 'railway experience'. They could purchase a meal in the restaurant car for a mere five shillings (25p), but the real treat was the exhibit devised by Pawel Pyasetsky, who was specially commissioned by the railway to demonstrate the 'experience' of travelling on the Trans-Siberian. To give a sense of movement to the 'passengers' tucking in to their three-course meals, the artist devised an elaborate arrangement outside the windows of the dining car to give the feeling of a virtual train ride. A moving panorama was created by means of an elaborate series of belts moving along at varying speeds. The front one travelled rapidly, carrying mundane features such as sand and rocks, while the next, slightly slower, had plants such as shrubs and brush. Behind that, there was a third, again somewhat slower, showing distant scenery while the fourth, which rolled along slowest of all, was Pyasetsky's masterpiece, a set of watercolours on lengthy scrolls, with scenes that he had sketched on trips along sections of the railway that had been completed early.

These watercolours included scenes from the cities of Moscow, Omsk, Irkutsk and Beijing and the idea was to give viewers the impression that they had journeyed along the whole railway. The show actually lasted forty-five minutes and there were nine separate scrolls with a total length of around 900 metres (almost 3,000 feet).[9] The exhibit and the panorama won a gold medal at the Universelle, as did the Eiffel Tower and, rather more prosaically, Campbell's soup.

The de luxe services were not intended to make money for the railway, but were a means of influencing European opinion and to counter the criticism in Western circles that the Trans-Siberian was a white elephant and an inadequate, ramshackle railway. The construction of the Trans-Siberian had always been seen by Witte as a way of putting Russia on a par with its European counterparts, and impressing those rich enough to travel on luxury trains was a key part of that strategy. Yet at first the inadequacies of the railway meant it had quite the opposite effect. Therefore, to induce Europeans to travel its full length – as an alternative, for example, to the sea route to China – the trains were not only to have all the required facilities, but also they were to be relatively inexpensive. The promotional material produced for the Paris Universelle had, in fact, suggested a remarkably cheap price of just £12 for the first-class sleeper express fare between Moscow and Vladivostok.

And what luxury was on offer! Nagelmackers had four carriages specially built for the exhibition, which, he boasted, provided facilities 'equal to the special trains reserved in Western Europe for the sole use of royalty'. It was not an entirely idle boast. The coaches each accommodated just eight people in four two-berth compartments, which all had an en suite bathroom, and decorated in the manner of a private St Petersburg salon. Every carriage had a drawing room and a smoking room, and was fitted out in a different period style: 'one was decorated with white-lacquered limewood, mirrored walls, a ceiling frescoed with figures from Greek mythology and embroidered curtains. Another was in the style of Louis XVI, with bulging furniture of gold-embellished oak; a third was French Empire, and a fourth imperial Chinese.'[10] Every conceivable facility which had ever been put on luxury trains in Europe and America was promised. There was to be a library stocked with books in four languages, a music room with a full-sized grand piano, a hairdressing salon and even an exercise room complete with static bicycle and a rowing machine. For photographers, there was to be a darkroom, though that was probably intended to be as much for the convenience of the censors as the passengers, since tsarist Russia remained very much a police state. And for worshippers, there was the church carriage, an 'ambulatory basilica', complete with icons, curved windows and an ornate altar.

The journey was advertised as enabling passengers to get to Beijing in two weeks, but this was highly optimistic in the early days, given the frequency of breakdowns and overall slowness of the track. A series of early improvements had been made by the time these luxury trains started operating, thanks to an improvement programme promoted by Prince Khilkov, who had realized that the inadequacies of the line were a potential source of international embarrassment. Almost as soon as each section of the line was completed, improvements had to be made to ensure it was functioning properly. This was particularly true of the difficult Transbaikal section, which for much of its route was effectively a mountain railway carved into the sides of valleys on a narrow roadbed. Khilkov had managed to persuade the Committee for the Siberian Railway to invest a further eighty million roubles (£8 million) to make these immediate improvements and these funds enabled the worst of the defects to be remedied. It was not only the condition of the railway that was problematic, but also the lack of capacity caused by insufficient passing loops and sidings. Inevitably, the extra money took time to be sanctioned, but by early 1899 Khilkov had ordered the construction of new marshalling yards and passing loops, as well as an increase in the number of carriages and the improvement of the track so that the maximum speed on better sections was raised to 23 mph, rather than the original 13 mph. As a safety measure, many of the wooden bridges used for fording small rivers and streams, were replaced by far hardier steel structures and the light rails on sections where a break could prove fatal, such as curves, were removed in favour of heavier track, though still lighter than the norm in Europe.

To encourage foreign travellers and to help them while away the interminable hours once on board, the Russian government produced a 500-page *Guide to the Great Siberian Railway*, which was available in French, English and German as well as Russian. Full of photographs and tables, it set out a rosy picture of Russian rural life, describing the various people on the lands crossed by the train in sufficient detail to satisfy the most fastidious anthropology student and all in a slightly stiff, if grammatically precise, translation. There was, too, a surfeit of material on animals both domestic and wild. The Kirgiz horse, for example, 'is endowed with an unpromising exterior, but has inestimable qualities. The thoroughbred possesses the following characteristic marks: a middle height (about 2 arshins); a short back (12 vershoks), a well-proportioned, muscular and expressive head . . . ' and so on.[11] Meanwhile, the Kirgiz people hunted wolves by chasing them down, 'and after a race of 15 versts, the wolf is run down exhausted' and despatched with a stick or whip.

The guide also demonstrated that the Russian obsession with detailed figures for grain harvests and factory production predated the Soviet era. There were endless tables providing a host of statistics, such as the weight of goods (in puds, the Russian measure which is around 36 lb) imported into Vladivostok and Nikolaevsk, the number of horses, cattle, sheep and other farm animals in the various districts around Chita, and the acreage sown in each of the districts around Tyumen, precisely the kind of thing Eric Newby in his book *The Big Red Train Ride* describes having to bear on his numerous tours of Soviet collective farms. It was born precisely of the same desperate drive rooted in the Russian soul to demonstrate that whatever the Europeans could do, they could do just as well or even better. Given the length and occasional tedium of the journey, presumably the guide must have been a useful soporific when passengers retired for the night and found sleep troublesome as they were rocked by the bumpy track.

The best train was reserved for the tsar. According to a contemporary account, it 'surpasses in magnificence the *train de luxe* lately built for the German Emperor. It is a palace on wheels.'[12] There was at the time a kind of silent competition between Europe's royal families over which would have the most luxuriously appointed train. It seems the tsar won with what was, in effect, a luxury hotel on wheels: 'The walls of the drawing room are covered with pale rose silk, while the royal bedchamber is hung with light-blue satin, the furniture being covered with cretonne of the same colour. Each of the sleeping salons has a bedchamber attached, as well as a dining room upholstered with chamois leather.' There was a nursery, complete with a playroom for the children with 'fair-like, swinging cots'. Best of all, the train had its own 'palatial' cattle carriage. Apparently, the tsar's medical advisers recommended that milk from the same cow was better for his daughters, so along for the ride were two Holstein cows.[13]

In fact, the other de luxe travellers fared much less well than the tsar and even rather below the expectations raised by the Paris Universelle exhibition. There was only one de luxe train a week, leaving Moscow for Irkutsk on Saturday evening, while routine services departed daily at 3 p.m. Because the de luxe did not stop at so many stations, it took only nine days, two faster than the daily trains, but Nagelmackers had rather pulled the wool over the eyes of his Russian partners by using standard coaching stock for the Trans-Siberian – adapted for Russia's wider gauge, of course – rather than the elegant stock that had been on show in Paris. Oliver Ready, an Englishman who travelled on the line in 1902, paid £34 10s (£34.50 or around £3,600 at 2013 prices) for the whole journey from Moscow through to Port Arthur and then a boat to Shanghai, but that suggests the promotional rates promulgated in Paris had crept upwards. Nor did the facilities on the train live up to the hype, but were akin to other first-class accommodation in Europe, rather than the 'fit for royals' standard that had been promised. However, Ready, in an account published soon after his trip, had few complaints, although he found the dining car 'far too small' and was annoyed that he had 'to wait far too long for meals'.[14] Nevertheless, he found that on the whole journey, 'the food on the train was good' and it was supplemented, at times, by 'the most delicious milk and cream I have ever tasted [which] were brought in bottles by women and girls for sale to passengers at very cheap rates'.[15]

Another early passenger, Harry de Windt, travelling in 1901 was even more positive: 'This train was truly an ambulant palace of luxury. An excellent restaurant, a library, pianos, baths, and last, but not least, a spacious and well-furnished compartment with every comfort, electric and otherwise (and without fellow travellers), rendered this first étape of our great land journey one to recall in after days with a longing regret.'[16] For de Windt – who noted that the military element on the train were busy cheating a hapless Jewish fellow out of his money at whist – it was one long party. No one, he said, knew what time of day it was, because they all kept to St Petersburg time, but nor did anyone care: 'Our piano is a godsend and most Russian women are born musicians. So after *déjeuner* we join the fair sex, who beguile the hours with Glinka and Tchaikovsky until they can play and sing no more.'[17] Yet, in contrast, another early traveller, Michael Myers Shoemaker, complained that the piano was only used as repository for dirty dishes and that the library confined itself to Russian novels and a few dog-eared French and German books. These days, the on-board service of meals is at appropriate local times, but the timetable is expressed in Moscow time and consequently all station clocks show the time in the capital, which has been known to catch out the unwary traveller.

Some of the other early passengers had rather more profound complaints. The pastor Francis Clark, who had travelled in what he felt was cattle class earlier in his trip, continued westwards in June 1900 on one of the first trains de luxe to depart from Irkutsk and was haughtily dismissive of Russian efforts to operate luxury train services: 'It was luxurious, indeed, compared with the fourth-class emigrant train on which we had just been journeying, but it is still many degrees behind the best American trains.'[18] The train consisted of the Russian wood-burning locomotive, a baggage carriage in which there was, oddly, a bath tub, and then a dining carriage divided into two sections – one with small tables for two or four people, and the other with observation windows and easy chairs for the smokers. There were two set meals a day, a two-course lunch at 1 p.m. at one rouble and a dinner at 6 p.m. for a rouble and a quarter, while à la carte food was available all day from a rather limited menu. The rest of the train was made up of two second-class sleeper cars and one first-class sleeper, although Clark could discern no difference between them. In fact, Clark was pleased with his compartment.

Each one, he noted, accommodated either two or four people, 'with a window, a table, and a wide and very comfortable berth for each person'. The cars were 'handsomely carpeted and upholstered in blue plush, covered, for the sake of protection, with red striped denim', and, with plenty of space for baggage and many convenient hooks for clothes, 'one could make himself as comfortable and have almost as much room as in an ocean steamer's cabin'. Indeed, rather contradicting himself, he wrote that 'this arrangement is far superior to America's more promiscuous and public Pullman sleeping car', which at the time were open plan, as demonstrated in the famous Marilyn Monroe film *Some Like It Hot*.

Annette Meakin, too, compared it favourably with her experience of the Canadian Pacific, as, feeling ill, she 'retired to my bed for three days' and was left in peace. In contrast, she said, 'had I taken ill on the highly praised Canadian Pacific, I might never have lived to tell the tale. Every morning I should have been forced to rise at an early hour and sit upright for the rest of the weary day on the seat into which my bed had been transformed.'[19] She likened the Russian trip to a kind of '"Liberty Hall" where you can shut your door and sleep all day if you prefer it, or eat and drink, and smoke and play cards if you like that better'.[20] She was particularly impressed with the little electric reading light, and the bells which on one side summoned the servant to clean the room and on the other a waiter to provide food. There was, she noted, none of the hurry and rush that characterized rail travel in Europe and North America.

Clark also reckoned the cost was around a quarter of what he would have paid for a trip across America, a shorter distance, in a Pullman. It was, though, far slower, 14 mph on average including stops and at one point, for a couple of miles, a Siberian 'cowboy' raced alongside Clark's train, easily keeping pace until 'he pulled up with a careless wave of his hat, as though he did not consider it worth while to race any longer with so slow a rival'.

Clark was offered a bath in the baggage car, but baulked at the cost of a rouble and a half. He also complained at the absence of English books in the library, apart from 'two or three fifth-rate novels in paper covers, evidently contributed by previous travellers'. Although de Windt, travelling in January, liked Siberia and its whiteness, which he found 'a smiling land of promise and plenty, even under its limitless mantle of snow', the landscape was just too 'dreary' and monotonous to recommend to tourists. Nevertheless, they came in substantial numbers and mostly reported back favourably on their experience.

These conflicting reports by early travellers suggest that there was much variation between trains on the Trans-Siberian. Some of these passengers were fortunate to enjoy their journeys on services that were well-managed and kept clean, while on others clearly the staff could not be bothered to carry out their duties properly. One suspects that the seventy-five cents charged for Pastor Clark's bath was a neat little scam on behalf of the crew, as no one else mentions having to pay. Moreover, as explained above, while some of the trains were provided by Nagelmackers, others were operated by the Russian state railway, which varied in standard. In fact, it was ever thus. When I travelled on the line in 2012 the experience was similar, very much dependent on the particular staff on duty and the 'culture' created by the train manager. Moreover, I discovered that the trains which operated the *Rossya* service, which, westwards, was denoted Train No. 1 (and eastwards No. 2) and ran the whole route from Vladivostok to Moscow, were fitted out to a much higher standard, with TVs in every compartment and softer upholstery for the bunks, than the 'local' trains which covered only part of the line.

Finding the right type of worker in these early days was not easy. Siberia had little industry and consequently few people – apart from the government officials largely recruited from European

Russia – had any experience of working for a wage, let alone in a huge organization like the Russian state railway. The Trans-Siberian needed huge numbers of people. In 1902 the railway had 14,700 employees and, incidentally, 750 locomotives and 550 passenger carriages, much of it second-hand stock commandeered from existing lines in western Russia.

Indeed, it was harder to find suitable staff to operate the railway than it had been to build it. Most of the recruits were of poor quality. The prospect of living in remote Siberia was not an enticing one for railway employees in western Russia. It was not only the remoteness and harsh climate of Siberia; the scarcity of consumer goods, the high cost of living and, in the early stages, the lack of schools were added deterrents. As a result only the least well-qualified railway workers or those with poor employment records moved eastwards. Even the higher wages that were on offer could not attract sufficient competent employees.

The native peoples, many of whom led nomadic lives, were not interested in paid employment and consequently there was only a small pool of potential local labour: 'From its own small population, Siberia offered a contingent of illiterate or half-educated exiles and former convicts.'[21] So desperate were the railways that many of the watchmen hired to guard property at night had been sent to Siberia in the first place for robbery. Others who were given jobs that required them to deal with passengers had committed violent crimes, while murderers and rapists were employed on track maintenance work.

The railways did not help the situation by making life difficult for those they did manage to recruit. There was no mechanical signalling system in the early days and consequently each section of track was guarded from small log cabins up to a couple of miles apart. The signaller would come out at the approach of a train and, standing to attention because every train represented the supreme authority of the tsar, unfurl a green flag – or hold up a lantern at night – to show that the section was clear. One can only imagine what life was like for the signallers in these remote parts of the railway, who would have to trudge miles along the track to take up their posts or return home.

As for brakemen on the freight trains, the railway did not provide brake vans to accommodate them. According to L. Lodian, the railway journalist, the men had to hold on to whatever was available: 'The poor train-hands huddle up in their sheepskins, settle down on their perches and try to get the best shelter they can from the icy blasts of 20 to 40 degrees below zero. They can't even get a nap – so cold is it. So they can only yearn for the next station, when they can get a chance of rushing in for a warming and some hot tea.'[22] Their salary, according to Lodian, was just twenty-eight roubles per month (£2.80), which, he reckoned, was barely enough to live on.

It was not surprising, therefore, that many of the new recruits, faced with the extremes of the climate and the prevalence of disease, did not stay long in the job, with the result that there was a constant shortage of labour. On some parts of the railway there was an eighty-seven per cent annual turnover, representing an almost total change of staff every year.

Nor was it surprising that corruption thrived in these conditions. It was, in any case, endemic in Russia and all kinds of scams quickly developed on the Trans-Siberian. The need to bribe officials to carry out their jobs was universal and indeed institutionalized: 'Bribes were demanded and given openly, usually with receipts indicating they had been paid. They were mandatory for hiring, for transfers, for raises, to prevent imposition of penalties and for hauling freight.'[23] And then there was theft. All stores were prone to go missing, but coal was particularly vulnerable. One estimate suggests that only twenty per cent of the coal stored at Omsk was actually consumed by locomotives, with the rest sold by railway workers to boost their wages. Thanks to black market sales, local institutions such as schools and even the city's government buildings were heated with the railway's coal.

The ineffectiveness of the management contributed greatly to this situation. According to Steven Marks, 'the railroad's management was centralized to an absurd degree.'[24] The Western part of the railway up to Irkutsk was administered from Tomsk and the eastern part from Khabarovsk, but the local officials were granted precious little authority. The legendary bureaucracy – another endemic Russian trait, like corruption – was made worse by the strict oversight of every decision, even small requests for extra money, by the Committee of the Siberian Railroad sitting at the other end of this vast nation in St Petersburg. For example, every grant made to employees hurt in an accident or the families of those killed was considered by the Committee, even though the payments amounted at most to a few hundred roubles.

Despite the dubious origins of many of the railway workers, travelling through Siberia on the newly built railway was not actually hazardous, since even the train crashes mostly involved freight trains and those killed were invariably railway workers. The very name Siberia elicited unwarranted fears and guides like Baedeker's recommended travelling with a revolver, but this was unnecessary and, indeed, could be a source of danger. Baedeker, in fact, seemed to do everything possible to put people off travelling on the line. The guide suggested bringing all kinds of equipment which was, in fact, available on the trains, such as towels, soap and even 'a portable India-rubber bathtub'. To avoid suspicion from the police, only novels should be taken and any political books avoided. Hotels were said to be prohibitively expensive and thieves lurked around every corner. In fact, while care clearly had to be taken, these early travellers reported mostly extreme kindness from their fellow passengers and rarely spoke of any fears of attacks.

Moreover, travel along the Trans-Siberian was soon going to get easier. All the early travellers aiming to reach Vladivostok had to take two boat journeys, one across Lake Baikal, the other on the rivers from Sretensk to Khabarovsk. The two remaining links that would provide a through railway via Manchuria – the Chinese Eastern Railway and the Circum-Baikal round the southern side of the lake – were envisaged to be built within a few years, but both proved troublesome. Indeed, the Chinese Eastern Railway was, according to one analyst, 'primarily the cause of the Russo-Japanese War and was instrumental in bringing about the Russian Revolution'.[25] Quite a claim for a modest single-track railway just over a thousand miles long.

# SIX

# CASUS BELLI

The choice of the Manchurian route might have seemed clever from both a practical and a strategic point of view, but that decision was bound to cause problems, and so it proved. The two sections in Russia connecting the railway with Manchuria proved relatively simple to build. In the summer of 1897 work started on a seventy-mile line, stretching eastwards from the Ussuri Railway near a town now called Ussurisk, north of Vladivostok, towards the Manchurian border at Pogranichny, and was completed two years later. From the west, Pushechnikov, who was still involved in completing the Transbaikal, began work around the same time on the longer Western section from a point between Chita and Sretensk towards the border. Under pressure from the Russian government to speed up the job because of its desire to have a continuous railway line all the way through to the Pacific, he completed the 215 mile line to the frontier town of Manchouli by 1901, a year earlier than planned. Both these relatively easy sections opened quickly to traffic, even though initially they were effectively branch lines that did not serve anywhere significant.

The main section through Manchuria involved a delicate diplomatic situation which was fluid and potentially dangerous. In 1898 the hitherto covert imperial ambitions of the Russian government afforded by the railway came to the fore when it concluded an agreement to obtain the whole of the Liaodong peninsula in southern Manchuria from China on a 25-year lease. This arrangement belied Witte's previous statements about the Chinese Eastern Railway not being part of an agenda to colonize Manchuria. The Russians had designs on Port Arthur and neighbouring Dalny (now Dalian) at the tip of the Liaodong peninsula, which are, unlike Vladivostok, warm-water ports open all the year round. Ever since the agreement to build the Chinese Eastern Railway had been signed with Li, Russia had begun establishing itself in Manchuria as the dominant power. Harbin, the key town and headquarters of the railway, quickly assumed the identity of a Russian provincial capital and a flood of Russian incomers arrived to set up the administration of the railway.

Russia's invasion by stealth of Manchuria was part of the machinations by all the great powers at the time – notably Germany, France, the United Kingdom and the United States – to establish trading centres and colonies in the Far East. Ports were the key to such expansion, as they afforded both a toehold and access to the hinterland. Russia appeared cleverly to have got in there first, but its every move was being watched carefully by its rivals, who were waiting for their opportunity to pounce. The pretext for Russian involvement had come in November 1897 when Germany grabbed Tsingtao, a port on the East China Sea, under the guise of defending its missionaries after two had been killed by local people resisting attempts to spread Christianity. Russia's response was brazen. In March 1898 the Russians strong-armed the Chinese into the leasing agreement for the peninsula and the foreign minister, Count Mikhail Muravev, immediately organized the takeover of Port Arthur. As part of the arrangement, the Russians promised to build a railway to connect the port with the Chinese Eastern Railway at Harbin, effectively creating a through-railway route all the way from Moscow to eastern China. The Russians claimed their takeover of the Liaodong peninsula would protect Chinese interests against the Germans and other European powers, but this was a paper-thin excuse that did not fool anyone. The takeover was clearly part of a wider imperialist strategy that was in clear violation of the treaty negotiated with Li. Witte had been expressing his honest view when, during the negotiations to build the Chinese Eastern Railway, he had told the Chinese that Russia harboured no such intentions, and therefore was genuinely horrified by the military action. He wrote afterwards in his memoirs: 'The Chinese Eastern Railway was designed exclusively for cultural and peaceful purposes, but jingoist adventurers turned it into a means of political aggression involving the violation of treaties, the breaking of freely given promises and the disregard of the elementary interests of other nationalities.'[1] Witte was so angered that he offered his resignation to the tsar, but this was turned down. He was far too useful to lose, although eventually his career would founder on the issue of Russia's Far East policy.

This complex political situation provided the backdrop to the construction of the line, and did not make the task of the builders easier, since there was considerable hostility towards the Russians from local people. Construction of the Manchurian section of the Chinese Eastern Railway began in 1897 under the responsibility of a very experienced Russian engineer, Alexander Yugovich. If the various sections of the Trans-Siberian presented daunting prospects to the builders in the initial surveys, the near 1,000-mile-long Chinese Eastern Railway through Manchuria undoubtedly surpassed them. The railway was to run through mountainous, inaccessible country and there were no maps available to plot the route in advance. The few roads were in poor condition and turned into impassable quagmires in the rainy season. The rivers were unbridged and carts could only cross them at fords or on pairs of small boats lashed together. There was a shortage of timber on most of the route and insufficient stone on the eastern section.

The surveyors reckoned there were no fewer than fourteen major waterways, frozen for four months, that would require bridges. Moreover, whereas the main route of the Trans-Siberian was built with no significant tunnels, eight lengthy ones were required, with the longest, through the Great Khingan Range in the west, envisaged to be two miles long. The hostility of the natural terrain was exacerbated by the hostility of the local people, especially in the hilly areas which were controlled by local warlords.

Not only was there a shortage of materials, but, again, there was no local labour to build the line. Local people did not speak Russian and few interpreters were available to enable them to come to work on the railway. The need to import labour and materials led to an innovative construction plan. Rather than building the line conventionally, Yugovich's Number Two, Stanislav Kerbedz, put forward a novel strategy. Given the lack of access, he decided, with Witte's acquiescence, to lay a crude, rough track through the territory on which a temporary railway could be laid to provide access, so that material, more sophisticated tools and equipment and, indeed, the workers – Russian artisans and thousands of Chinese 'coolies' (hired labourers) – could be brought in to carve out the railway formation and lay the track bed to create the permanent way, with the labour force reaching a maximum of 200,000 at the peak of construction. The first wave of labourers started carving out the track alignment in August 1897, westward from the Ussuri, while others travelled by rail and steamer to reach Harbin, which grew from village status to – by 1903 – a sizeable town with 40,000 inhabitants, half of them Russian.

Given the need for haste, money was always made available by the Committee to ensure rapid progress and that allowed work to be carried out simultaneously at more than twenty sites, each covering a section between fifty and one hundred miles long. As on the Transbaikalia Railway, large stretches of permafrost had to be broken up using explosives or thawed with fires stoked by wood that in many parts had to be brought in from hundreds of miles away. Many of the difficulties encountered on the Trans-Siberian were repeated, such as spring floods washing away sections of newly built line, but nevertheless progress was remarkably rapid thanks to the resources thrown at the project.

However, apart from the elements, there were two further barriers to the construction of the railway: disease and rebellion. In order to consolidate Russia's land grab of the Liaodong peninsula and Port Arthur, work had started in the summer of 1898 on the 550-mile-long South Manchuria Railway, the name given to the line between Harbin and Port Arthur. Russia was already fortifying and developing the port into a naval base and marine coaling station for its Far East Fleet and merchant navy, and needed the railway to supply it. The line traversed the most populated area of Manchuria and soon after the start of construction a particularly virulent epidemic of bubonic plague broke out at Yingkou, about 200 miles north of Port Arthur. Thanks to swift action by the Russian authorities, the outbreak was largely contained, but the epidemic caused panic among the Chinese labourers across the various construction sites and many walked off the job. There was, too, a cholera outbreak in southern Manchuria in 1902, which spread up to Harbin and along the line. This time many Russian workers caught the disease, and again panic set in, resulting in the loss of much of the summer construction period at several sites.

There was a suspicion in Chinese circles that the Russians were making an unnecessary fuss about the difficulties of building the Chinese Eastern Railway and that this was all part of an imperialist plot. A former manager of the line, Chin-Chun Wang, writing in the 1920s, reckoned that most of the railway was relatively easy to build, apart from the long tunnel under the Great Khingan and a bridge at Harbin, and that it was effectively 'gold-plated' in order to attract Russians to come and live in Manchuria: 'There seems to be much evidence to fortify the impression that unnecessary lavishness in the spending of money was generally encouraged. Enormous sums were spent for the erecting of magnificent residences, numerous barracks, palatial club-houses, magnificent churches and schools, etc., all with the idea of inducing Russians to settle along the Chinese Eastern.'[2] It was this, he suggested, rather than the difficulties in construction, that led to the huge cost of the railway, which reached 400 million roubles, about £40,000 per mile, much more than the Trans-Siberian itself, because all these extras were rolled up into the overall cost. That rather makes light of the construction difficulties, since 912 steel bridges, as well as 258 in stone, were required to build the line, but Wang is correct in asserting that the very high cost was due to the fact that the railway was envisaged as more than just a transport system. What is not in dispute is that the Russians used the construction of the line and the need to guard it as a way of driving a Russian wedge into Chinese territory and effectively colonizing Manchuria. The Railway Guard that had been agreed in the negotiations between Witte and Li was more like a small army than a police force, given that it quickly built up to an establishment of 25,000 men.

The very existence of the railway, with its ability to transport people across the continent so quickly, changed the military dynamic of the whole region. Within a few days a bunch of Cossacks, traditionally used to impose Russian power at the local level, could be transported on the railway to wherever there was trouble. In effect, Russia did precisely what Witte had promised it would not, using the railway as the driving force for an occupation. This became apparent with the onset of the Boxer Rising in 1899. Right from the start of construction there had been raids by outlaws – known as *hunghutzes* (literally, 'redbeards') – who attacked local inhabitants and extorted protection money from travellers. Indeed, this was a semi-legitimized system, because merchants intending to travel in the countryside could buy insurance in offices in Manchuria's main cities, and in return they were provided with documentation and little flags to attach to their vehicles which ensured immunity from attack. These raids, however, were insignificant compared with the level of attacks when the Boxer Rising spread northwards with the Chinese Eastern Railway as a key target. The Boxers were a group of conservative nationalists with a mystical bent, since they believed that with enough effort and discipline it was possible to learn to fly. They were, briefly, given encouragement by the Dowager Empress Cixi, who ruled China at the turn of the century, which resulted in an intensification of their assaults on foreign targets. They destroyed much of the South Manchuria Railway around Mukden and Russian workers fled in terror of being massacred. There were attacks, too, on the Chinese Eastern Railway as both lines were seen as an overt expression of the hated foreign invasion.

Overreacting to bandit attacks had already provided the perfect cover for expanding military involvement and the Boxer Rising gave Russia further ammunition to establish control over Manchuria and widen its territorial control. In fact, despite the attacks, according to Witte, the Boxer Rising was never strong in Manchuria and could easily have been seen off by the Railway Guard. Witte saw through the subterfuge: 'Our army behaved in Manchuria as a conquering country, thus preparing the ground for catastrophe. The forces of the Boxers in Manchuria were practically insignificant.'³ Despite the army defeating the Boxers and summarily executing any *hunghutzes* they came across, the War Ministry insisted on a strong presence in the country, exacerbating tensions. The Russians did not help their cause by committing a series of outrages against the local population. Most notoriously in July 1900, at Blagoveshchensk on the Russian side of the Amur river, the army, seeking to enforce the deportation of all the local Chinese, simply drove them, men, women and children, into the river at gunpoint and all but 160 of several thousand[4] were drowned. This was by no means the only recorded instance of war crimes committed by Russian troops and, inevitably, they led to further conflict and violence. Yugovich, the engineer, was unequivocal about Russian intent, later writing: 'It is an open secret that from the very beginning of the campaign it was the desire of the military party not only to punish the Boxers, but also permanently to annex Manchuria.'[5]

Despite the attacks and the damage to the line caused by the Boxers, work proceeded thanks to Yugovich's army of Chinese labourers. By November 1901 it became possible, at last, to go by train from Moscow to Vladivostok, with the exception of the ferry or sled journey over Lake Baikal, and to reach Port Arthur by way of the South Manchuria Railway. The Chinese Eastern Railway was, however, by no means complete. The main tunnel was unfinished, with trains routed on a tortuous line around the summit, and many of the bridges were temporary, rickety affairs. Moreover, it was a slow railway with a limited capacity. The railway, single-track throughout, was planned for an initial capacity of ten trains in each direction daily, but there were insufficient loops where trains could pass to reach that target and the maximum speed was 14 mph, although that fell to 10 mph on hilly sections. Consequently, Yugovich's job was not finished. With extra money granted by the Committee, in the knowledge that a war with Japan was a distinct possibility, a crash programme of improvements was instituted. Almost 150 new sidings – essential both to accommodate waiting trains and to increase the potential to carry freight – were built, but a plan to double-track the line throughout was put on hold, because of the imminence of the war.

The conflict was made inevitable by the increasingly jingoistic posturing of a group of hawkish Russian generals who gained the support of the tsar. They were intent on an expansionist policy that was bound to lead to confrontation, despite Witte's persistent opposition and warnings. Witte had already counselled that once the Boxer Rising was put down in 1901 the Russian troops brought in to support the Railway Guard should return home. The Great Powers were all concerned at Russia's presence, especially given their own ambitions in the Far East, and were clearly not going to allow the Russians to establish hegemony over the whole region. The doves still seemed to hold sway in 1902, when a treaty with China that involved the withdrawal of Russian troops by September 1903 was concluded, and Witte visited Manchuria that summer to assess the situation. After he returned home, however, it became clear that the Russians were not sticking to the agreement and only part of Manchuria was evacuated.

The tsar himself resisted a total withdrawal. Instead, he sent a bellicose new adviser, General Pyotr Bezobrazov, to the Far East (in a luxurious train, Witte noted sourly) and seems to have been taken in by what Witte called 'grandiose fantastic schemes of exploiting our Far Eastern possessions, among which they reckoned Manchuria and northern Korea'.[6] Bezobrazov indeed had designs not just on Manchuria, but also on Korea, the neighbouring peninsula to Liaodong. The Japanese had expansionist designs on both Manchuria and Korea, too, but probably would have settled for the latter, but the tsar favoured Bezobrazov's aggressive intent over Witte's more cautious approach.

The intervention of Bezobrazov ensured that war broke out. He portrayed Witte's desire to pull out the troops as a sign of weakness and the tsar sided with him. Witte resigned from the government, warning of war. Negotiations between Japan and Russia over their respective territorial ambitions in the region inevitably foundered and the tsar failed to understand that Japan was not sabre-rattling. The completion of the Trans-Siberian, and, more precisely, the building of the China Eastern Railway and its southern extension, was (as Witte had warned) a provocative act. Japan was duly provoked.

Like many wars it started almost by mistake, through misunderstanding rather than any desire to fight. The Russians did not believe that Japan seriously intended to attack, while, for their part, the Japanese were convinced Russia would accede to its demands. Tupper sums it up brilliantly: 'In broad terms, the Russo-Japanese War resulted from the competition of two nations for mastery over alien territories to which neither had the slightest shred of legal or moral right.'[7] Both nations' assumptions about each other proved wrong and in February 1904 Japan launched an attack on Port Arthur, and after several attempts to take over the port eventually landed an army on the Liaodong peninsula.

The timing of the Japanese was not accidental, but was prompted by its concerns that the Trans-Siberian and the Chinese Eastern Railway, when completed and improved, would be able to deliver large numbers of troops rapidly to Manchuria. The Japanese wanted to take advantage of the lack of ability of the recently-completed railways to carry the burden of war, and the fact that the Circum-Baikal was not due to be completed until 1906 was crucial in the decision on the timing of the attack. The supply line between Moscow and Manchuria was five or six weeks long, rather than the ten days or so when the lines were functioning efficiently. In a way, Russia was paying the price for not having carried out the Trans-Siberian project much earlier, given that the idea had been more than forty years in gestation. Had the line been completed, say, twenty years earlier, when Japan was only just emerging from its isolation, it would not have been in a position to prevent Russian territorial ambitions. Now, unfortunately for Russia, Japan was a well-organized and growing military power.

By the time the war began, the Chinese Eastern Railway had been improved, but was by no means fully operational; neither the main long tunnel nor many sidings and bridges had been completed and therefore it still had a much reduced capacity. As for the Trans-Siberian, despite a continuous programme of improvements, it was still suffering from the economies that had been made during construction, and remained a slow railway with insufficient capacity. Most crucially, as the Japanese had cannily realized, the fact that there was still no railway route around Lake Baikal created the most serious bottleneck of the whole system, and it was no surprise that chaos ensued on both sides of the lake as soon as war was declared.

Supplies built up at Baikal Station, waiting to cross the lake on which three separate paths had been laid. First, there was a route marked by poles for sledges, which mainly carried officers, given that capacity was limited for the forty-mile crossing. It was not as comfortable as it sounds. Even the officers had occasionally to get out, because the ice on the lake freezes in big slabs, which made it impossible for loaded sledges to cross. Secondly, there was a path for the foot soldiers, who would march across the ice into the blizzards. Their only respite was the rough temporary huts erected every four miles, which dispensed tea and soup, and provided medical treatment for those with frostbite. Then, later, once the ice was deemed solid enough (the lake does not freeze until January) a temporary rail line was laid, a perilous task for its builders as there were crevasses and gaps that could prove fatal for the unwary. Indeed, at first it was thought that locomotives would be able to haul the trains all the way across the frozen lake, but one of the first to attempt to do so plunged through a weakness in the ice caused by a hot spring with the loss of several men and, of course, the engine. Thereafter, locomotives were not risked and, instead, horses and men had to haul the wagons across the white expanse, a task at which even Sisyphus might have baulked.

Consequently, since the capacity of the ice railway was only a fraction of the amount of freight daily arriving at Irkutsk and Port Baikal, they soon filled up with supplies and groups of waiting men. According to a contemporary report the stations were packed with 'mountains of cases, pyramids of bales, containing articles and provisions of which the troops already in Manchuria are in sore need'.[8] Moreover, there were terrible scenes in the other direction as refugees fled the conflict. The correspondent of the *Standard* observed chaotic scenes on the trains heading westwards: '[There were] no lavatories, no food to be got along the line, hardly any water, no milk and 600 children of all ages huddled together for warmth, and crying with misery and hunger. It is one of the most pitiful sights of warfare, and a mere forerunner to the woes behind.'[9] It would not be the last time that great suffering would be seen along the Trans-Siberian, as subsequent events during the Russian Civil War and the Second World War will show.

Even before they reached the bottleneck of Lake Baikal, the troops had endured terrible journeys. Only the officers were provided with sleeping cars and upholstered seats and they even had access to one of the lavishly decorated church cars. In contrast, the other ranks were transported quite literally in cattle class, packed into freight vans lined with felt and some – but by no means all – had been fitted with a stove. There were narrow wooden benches for the troops to sit on, but they had to sleep on the floor. Cossacks, the mounted shock troops of the Russian army known for their hardiness, shared their wagons with their horses, which were stabled at each end of the van, while they sat in the middle. Trains generally carried around 1,100 men, as they consisted of twenty-eight wagons, each with room for forty men or eight horses. Most of the time there was not enough food for the men, because only haphazard arrangements had been made to feed them through mobile canteens. There were widespread complaints, especially as most of the time the ordinary soldiers could not afford to buy food from the sellers who rushed up to their trains at the main stations[10] – one soldier moaned that they had survived on 'little but hard black bread, foul soup and hot tea'[11] for the whole journey. The authorities, recognizing that these conditions would leave the men in no state to fight if they had to endure them continuously for the full two-week journey to Irkutsk (which sometimes was much longer), decreed that for every three days of travel there would be one day's rest. At best, it took troops thirty days to reach the Manchurian front and often as much as fifty, because of delays and breakdowns.

Work was, in fact, well underway on the Circum-Baikal when war was declared, but as it was by far the toughest stretch of the route on which to build a railway – harder even than the Chinese Eastern Railway – it was nowhere near complete by the time the Japanese attacked Port Arthur. One of the members of the Committee for the Siberian Railway was only slightly exaggerating when he expressed the view that the line 'surpassed in difficulty and amount of work all those constructed in the Russian Empire up to the present'.[12] The Committee had sanctioned the building of the Circum-Baikal line in 1898 and the survey work which began the following year confirmed that it would be a daunting task as there were '50-odd miles of precipitous cliffs broken by capes, ravines, bays and narrow shelvings'.[13] Overall, the railway required more than two hundred bridges and thirty-three tunnels to cover its 163-mile length and a measure of the number of curves and switchbacks was that this merely brought the railway a mere forty miles eastwards. Replaced later by a more direct route, the surviving sections are today a major tourist attraction.

Under the direction of Alexander Pertsov, another of the dynamic and intrepid engineers who were responsible for building the Trans-Siberian, a diverse labour force of around 9,000 workers – principally Turkish, Persian and Italian, in addition to the

Russians – was brought together and set about the arduous task of building the line along the shore from Port Baikal to Kultuk on the east side of the lake. The main obstacle was the fact that the cliffs went straight into the lake, with no beach. Consequently, the construction teams needed to build a shelf for the railway, which had to be at least fifteen feet above the lake to avoid the waves washing over the track during the fierce storms that are a regular feature of this massive lake cum inland sea. Dynamite was used extensively to create the roadbed for the railway, but this was inevitably a slow and perilous process. As with the other sections, winter prevented most activities such as track-laying, though tunnelling and bridgework could proceed.

Originally the Circum-Baikal had been scheduled to be completed in 1906, but the imperative of the war meant that Pertsov and his fellow contractors were asked to speed up the work. The workforce was increased by fifty per cent and vast amounts of money were thrown at the project. Remarkably, the first test train managed to run on the line in mid-September, just over six months after the outbreak of the war, but it derailed ten times and, to the embarrassment of the contractors, the chimneys on the carriage ventilators had to be removed because one of the tunnels had not been built to a sufficient height. A few days later, Prince Khilkov on his test train was more fortunate and his progress was delayed by just one derailment, though the train ran at barely 5 mph, because of concern over the state of the tracks. As a result of the need for speed and the difficult terrain, the cost of the completed railway was exorbitant, even higher per mile than for the Chinese Eastern Railway, amounting to seventy million roubles (£7 million), when immediate and necessary improvements are included, which averaged £43,000 per mile.

Given the country was at war and the line covered one of the most remote parts of Siberia, there was little fanfare to greet the achievement of having, at last, completed a railway which connected Moscow with the Pacific Ocean. The date of Khilkov's inspection, 25 September 1904, is rarely quoted in accounts of the line's construction. There was no golden spike, as there had been with every American railway of note, or celebratory fanfare of local townspeople, since there were none. Therefore, there was no one to take stock of this momentous achievement. More than 5,500 miles of railway had been built in just over thirteen years since work had started in May 1891, an annual rate of 414 miles. The Canadian Pacific, which had been Russia's benchmark, was built a bit quicker, at around 466 miles per year, but it was less than half the length and its builders did not face the same difficulties bringing in either labour or materials. Russia could, indeed, take pride in the completion of this momentous engineering feat, even if little attention was paid to it by the outside world, given the remoteness of the line and the outbreak of war.

The opening of the line made a huge difference to Russia's military capability, since the need to transport troops and matériel had led to renewed efforts to improve the ramshackle railway. Money was now found to remedy many of the problems resulting from corners having been cut to ensure the line's rapid construction. A programme of major improvements was initiated, including the widespread replacement of light rails with heavier ones; the construction of more than 200 extra sidings to allow trains to pass each other and to load freight wagons; the introduction of extra rolling stock and locomotives (often seconded from other Russian railways); and the rerouting of parts of the track to avoid the steepest inclines. Together with these developments, the opening of the Circum-Baikal allowed the army to pour men into the theatre of war. From a maximum of three daily trains in each direction, by the end of the war the Trans-Siberian could cater for up to 16 pairs per day. At the outbreak of the war 125,000 Russian troops and border guards were stationed in the Far East, and by the end some 1.3 million had been taken by rail to the region. The Japanese force numbered 300,000 at the start of the war and they were reinforced by twice that number by the end, largely brought in by rail. In effect, the railways, which had been the cause of the war, also became responsible for the vast numbers fighting and consequently dying, because of their ability to deliver men and supplies to the front. Indeed, the very manner in which the war was fought, with massive amounts of troops on both sides facing each other, was a direct result of the railways' ability to deliver constant, steady flows of men to the front line.[14] At times these vast armies even dug trenches, a kind of precursor of the methods that would lead to the lengthy stalemate on the Western Front in the First World War, and consequently the Russo-Japanese War became the subject of intense study and scrutiny by the military preparing to fight that much larger conflict.

Of course it was not only the Russians who made use of the railways. The Japanese not only rapidly built a railway in Korea to help transport troops and supplies to Manchuria, but after overcoming the Russian resistance in Port Arthur they took over the Russian-built South Manchuria Railway. The Russians had, at least, not made the mistake of leaving any locomotives behind, and since Japan operated on a radically different gauge – three feet six inches instead of the Russian five feet – at first they had to use teams of Chinese labourers to haul the trains along the line. Eventually, the gauge was changed and the Japanese made intensive use of the line.

However, the improvements to the Russians' railway supply line came too late. The Japanese might not have expected the Circum-Baikal to be completed so quickly nor for the improvements to the Trans-Siberian to be made so swiftly, but they were ready to pour enough men into battle to ensure victory. Their supply line was far shorter than that of the Russians, who would have been hampered by its length even if the railway had been working perfectly. The Japanese, conscious of the need to finish the war decisively before the Russians could build up too big an army, were able to dictate the timing and location of the war's decisive battle at Mukden in February and March 1905. There were 620,000 troops in the field – 350,000 of whom were Russian – the greatest number up to that point in a single battle in the history of warfare and the Japanese, despite their slightly inferior numbers, were able to triumph.

The construction of the line through Korea and the adoption of the South Manchuria Railway by the Japanese highlighted a tragic irony for the Russians. This not only gave the Japanese easy access to Harbin but, theoretically, there was now a railway line that went into the heart of Russia from a foreign and potentially hostile land. The war taught the Russians a hard lesson: the very railway they had built in order to further their imperial ambitions could be used against them: 'The railway system Russia had constructed provided it with the capacity to threaten Japan, but the capture and control of this system would have provided the latter with the capacity to launch a rapid and potentially unstoppable counter-offensive, with the railway line allowing the transport of supplies and men in the same way that Russia had achieved at the early stages of the war.'[15] In truth, it was not quite as easy as that. Taking over a defeated adversary's lines is difficult, as the Japanese found out when having to change the gauge of the South Manchuria Railway, and the notion that an alien army, even one as adept at using the railways as the Japanese, could harness the Trans-Siberian to ride into Moscow was far-fetched. However, as we see in the section on the Russian Civil War in chapter 8, whoever controlled the railway would control Siberia.

Nevertheless, the added capacity of the line and the threat it posed to future Japanese expansion were undoubtedly helpful to the Russians in the peace negotiations brokered by the Americans at Portsmouth, Maine, in September 1905. Their lead negotiator was the ubiquitous and rehabilitated Sergei Witte, who charmed the American public, which helped his negotiating position. The Japanese, aware that the Trans-Siberian was now a much more effective railway than at the outset of the war, accepted a deal that did not reflect their overwhelming military victory. They did, however, obtain control of the South Manchuria Railway, ensuring that Russia was denied access to Port Arthur, the casus belli. The war also exposed to the Russians the foolhardiness of relying on the Chinese Eastern Railway to reach the Pacific. Attention started to be paid to the building of the alternative Amur Railway, although it would take a decade before it was completed providing at last Russia with a route across the nation entirely on its own territory.

Despite the unexpected and somewhat unmerited concessions gained at Portsmouth, the anger in Russia that had long been brewing over this awful war, which had resulted from naked imperialist ambition, almost caused the collapse of the tsarist regime. There had been growing unrest in Russia for some years, with the tsar refusing to compromise on ceding any of his power. A massacre of peaceful demonstrators in St Petersburg in January 1905 with a death toll of more than a hundred exacerbated the tensions and the defeat at Mukden further intensified the protests. Throughout the year, there was a sharp increase in the level of organization and militancy of strikes and protests, which threatened to bring down the government. Revolution, however, was averted by the October Manifesto, a proposal drawn up by, inevitably, Sergei Witte, to create a *Duma* (parliament), which attracted the support of the less radical protesters and kept the tsar in power for a dozen years, even though he later repudiated the document and ensured the *Duma*, when it was created the following spring, had very limited powers.

The chaos following the end of the war made journeys on the Trans-Siberian even more eventful and haphazard. The English poet and member of the banking family, Maurice Baring, heading west from Irkutsk on the Trans-Siberian Express in October 1905, reported being stuck for four days at Samara on the western side of the Urals during the height of the troubles. At first, it was relatively calm and passengers were given money to buy provisions, but those in third class, who had only been given chits to redeem for food, looted the refreshment rooms and took away all the rations. Eventually, an officer who knew how to operate the telegraph system wired ahead and was granted permission to proceed. According to Baring, 'we found a friend, an amateur engine-driver, and an amateur engine, and we started for Penza.'[16] Inevitably the engine broke down, but another was found and Baring arrived in Moscow fortuitously just as Witte's charter had been issued, which meant that peace for the time being resumed.

In the aftermath of the conflict there was no shortage of generals, notably General Aleksey Kuropatkin, the Minister of War, ready to blame the inadequacies of the railway for the defeat. He argued that had the railway been in a better condition he would have been able to deliver more troops to Manchuria and won the day. This was a very simplistic reading of the situation. Of course, the Trans-Siberian had its inadequacies, but the general's accusation underestimated the fact that waging a war at the end of a 5,000-mile supply line was always going to be difficult, however well the railway functioned. In fact, it was a bit rich for the generals to blame the railway given their own failings. They repeatedly used the wrong tactics, sending thousands of men to their deaths by failing to recognize that weaponry had changed dramatically since Russia's previous major war, the Russo-Turkish conflict of 1877–8. While the Japanese had modernized their command structure and ensured their men fought on full stomachs, the Russians still treated them as serfs with little regard to their needs. Moreover, the Russians' failure to make effective use of modern weaponry, such as machine guns and improved artillery, hampered their ability to counter the Japanese attacks. As the key academic work into the role of the railway during the war suggests, 'while Russia was so ineffective in applying advanced technology in the military sphere, its railway-building was virtually a model of success in this, the most advanced and exacting of technologies'.[17] The Russians' skill at building railways had not yet transferred to other spheres, as Witte had hoped it would.

In fact, the conflict had been misconceived from the start. The existence of the railway proved too much of a temptation for Nicholas, who launched a war that proved disastrous not only to the nation but ultimately to his regime: 'It defied common sense that Russia would embark on a military campaign – a full-scale war, no less – at the most distant end of its territory, with whole sections of the population disaffected and agitating for far-reaching political change.'[18] Witte, in fact, suggested at the time that it had been the hard-line interior minister, Vyacheslav von Plehve, who had advocated the launch of a short sharp war to distract attention from Russia's internal turmoil and rally the population to a patriotic cause. It was an error made repeatedly throughout history by bellicose politicians. Von Plehve paid the ultimate price for his plan and for other mistakes, such as tacitly encouraging attacks on Jews, when he was blown to pieces by a bomb thrown into his carriage in St Petersburg in July 1904.

Blaming the railway was to misunderstand what had happened in the war. As the same academics noted with some irony, 'Russia had been able to transport more than 350,000 troops over thousands of miles and then maintain them in the field over many months, an achievement that would have given satisfaction to an administration with better credentials of efficiency than Russia's.'[19] Leon Trotsky, as we will see in chapter 8, was able to learn from these failings and used the Russian railways, particularly the Trans-Siberian, to great effect. Meanwhile, the Trans-Siberian was returning to normal and benefitting from the improvements its inadequacies highlighted by the war.

# SEVEN

# THE NEW SIBERIA

While the railway may have been conceived by its principal promoters as an imperialist and military enterprise, the impact on Siberia was no less profound. For all its failings and inadequacies, the Trans-Siberian had a transformative effect on the region, beyond even the expectations of its most ardent supporters. The clearest change was the rapid increase in population, thanks to increased migration from European Russia. The Siberian migration was, according to its chronicler Donald Treadgold, the greatest movement of people in history up to that time, other than the arrival in the United States of vast numbers of Europeans during the nineteenth century. While the increase in Siberia's population started before the railway was built, the pace of immigration rose dramatically as a result of its construction, and for a decade or so after the completion of the first section in 1896 there was a virtual stampede to settle in Siberia.

The railway allowed mass travel to Siberia for the first time, opening it up to colonization; it also changed the nature of the region, resulting in the population doubling between 1896 and 1921. As Harmon Tupper concludes, 'The railway ran at a heavy loss to the Treasury; ordinary passenger trains were late, crowded and dirty beyond belief; the bulk of stationmasters, ticket clerks and train crews were given to slipshod ways and excessive drinking; but in enormous counterweight, the Trans-Siberian opened up the country and brought unparalleled benefits to hundreds of thousands.'[1]

Settlement of the region by emigrants from European Russia had always been a key part of the justification for its construction. The fact that the Committee for the Siberian Railway had been given control over the colonization process as part of its remit demonstrated that it was integral to the purpose of building the railway. Apart from construction of the railway itself, colonization occupied most of the Committee's attention and, indeed, took up most of the rest of its expenditure. The Committee's resettlement programme was based on a study of how Bismarck had attempted to 'Germanize' Prussia's conquered Polish provinces through colonization. Other experiences of mass colonization in United States and Canada were also scrutinized for the lessons that could be gleaned. It was, in short, 'demographic engineering on a mass scale'[2] and it was devised by Anatoly Kulomzin, whom Witte had put in charge of managing the Committee and was also responsible for 'auxiliary enterprises', all the other tasks which the Committee had taken on, of which included the emigration process. Like Witte, Kulomzin came from a minor provincial aristocratic family and was a capable administrator, eager to modernize Russia, while retaining the system of absolute monarchy, and also like Witte, he had a long period at the heart of Russian government. Officially, he was the administrative secretary of the Committee of ministers, equivalent in modern British politics to the post of cabinet secretary. If Witte can be considered the architect of the railway, then Kulomzin was equally the guiding mind behind the resettlement programme.

The difficulties of developing a coherent policy in the context of such a conservative regime were legendary. Kulomzin did not always have it his own way. One potentially large group of emigrants was the family members of Old Believers, an austere and devout breakaway from an arcane schism in the Orthodox Church and so called because it opposed changes to sacred texts promoted by the mainstream church on the basis that inaccuracies in transcription had crept in over the years. Such differences inevitably led to accusations of heresy and sin, resulting in persecution. As a consequence, many Old Believers fled to far-distant corners of the Russian Empire in the late seventeenth century, where they formed the biggest religious groups in many parts of Siberia. Kulomzin wanted to give them the freedom to bring in their co-religionists from across the nation, but the ever-reactionary Orthodox Church managed to block the initiative.

Kulomzin saw peasant resettlement as the key to binding Siberia with European Russia. Vast amounts were spent on subsidizing the travel of the emigrants, providing them with wood and basic equipment to build homes and on ensuring their welfare. This encouragement of settlement was not born of generosity on the part of the Russian government, but rather was motivated by a desire to see off what was perceived as the 'yellow peril', the invasion of Russian territory by China or Japan. To some extent, the 'peril' was already there. Various native peoples considered themselves as being under the yoke of the Chinese – rather than the Russian – emperor and about a third of the population of the two most distant provinces was of Chinese or Korean origin. And just over the border to the South there were 300 million Chinese. Therefore, bringing in vast numbers of Russian-speaking newcomers loyal to their Fatherland was the key to Russification. As Steven Marks concludes, 'The underlying purpose of Kulomzin's civilizing mission was to strengthen the Russian state's political control over its territory.'[3]

There was a fierce debate in the Committee on what terms the emigrants would be allowed to take over land. While in European Russia the peasants had been emancipated a mere generation before, in Siberia there never had been a serf system. Before the advent of the railway Siberia was peopled largely by nomadic tribes and those who settled were considered 'state peasants', since all the land was government-owned. There were consequently no large landowners or nobility, because the rulers – unlike their counterparts in European Russia – had never needed to protect themselves from invaders, and therefore had no need to impose servitude on those who worked the land. Therefore Siberia was, theoretically, a freer society. The aristocrats sitting on the Committee for the Siberian Railway did not exactly relish the prospect of millions of peasants heading for Siberia, where they could lead more independent lives, freed from the shackles of the commune system that effectively kept the peasantry in order throughout Russia. However, the Committee members were desperate to see the land in Siberia populated and took a very detailed interest in the settlement process, both to ensure its success but also to impose their authority. As an aside, the burgeoning but repressed Left, including the Bolsheviks, disliked this move away from the communal system, partly because they were against anything that the tsarist government did, but mainly because they feared it would lead to property relationships and attitudes that would prevent the attainment of some variety of socialism. Indeed, when the Communists came to power, it was the peasants who had done best, establishing the largest holdings, known as kulaks, who were the target of Soviet repression and extermination.

The Committee saw the migration process as solving two problems simultaneously. There was a widespread, though wholly misguided, perception that there were simply too many people to live off the available land in European Russia, a feeling reinforced by the famine of 1891–2, which ignored the obvious fact that more equitable distribution of agricultural produce, greater efficiency and less emphasis on exports would have allowed the population to be perfectly adequately fed. The Committee therefore saw migration along the railway as a way of reducing the population of 'overcrowded' European Russia and populating the vast lands of Siberia. This was not America, however, where migrants were encouraged and basically there had been a free-for-all once the railways started snaking across the West. There was no equivalent to the Wild West and the frontier spirit accompanied by the massacre of native peoples. Siberia had no cowboys, since cows were used mainly for dairy and slaughtered for local consumption rather than being driven hundreds of miles across prairies. The settlers were far poorer, and because they came from a peasantry that had only recently been freed from centuries of serfdom, they were not imbued with the same entrepreneurial spirit as their American counterparts. They mostly behaved better, too, as they came as families, unlike in America, where the majority of new arrivals were bachelors without womenfolk to damp down their wild spirits. The land, too, was much less fertile and there was little scope for private enterprise, though Kulomzin dreamed of creating in southern Siberia a series of 'little Americas', huge areas of grain production akin to those in the American Midwest. He even suggested clearing out the Kazakhs – a people who depended on nomadic grazing – from their land, which he felt was underused, and populating it with settlers, but such visions were impractical and were not eventually attempted.

Russia was a police state where to take a long train journey required an internal passport (it still does) and consequently there was no question of allowing in all-comers. There was a fear among the major landowners in European Russia that if Siberia mopped up all the available labour, there would be none available to till and harvest their fields. Kulomzin and Witte recognized, however, that, despite restrictions, many peasants would come to Siberia in the hope of bettering themselves on the newly opened-up lands. Although they had been released from serfdom in 1861, the Russian peasantry in the late nineteenth century still led a very restricted life, being attached to a local commune made up of elders who dictated most aspects of their lives, such as allocating land and administering the law. The more adventurous, therefore, saw Siberia not only as an opportunity to make new lives for themselves, but to break free from this oppressive communal system that had prevailed in rural Russia since time immemorial. It was the quest for land and freedom which drove this vast army of emigrants, and they found both. As Treadgold sums it up, 'For millions of peasants, freedom was not to be found in their native village, and the opportunity to seek it even thousands of miles away compelled them to uproot themselves and risk everything for its sake.'[4]

Prior to the building of the railway, migration was a haphazard process not controlled by the authorities. Despite the requirement that every rail traveller had to obtain not only their internal passport but specific permission to travel from the local police, in practice many simply upped sticks without permission. Technically, too, the arrivals were supposed to register with their new settlements, but their attempts to do so were often lost in the bureaucracy and they simply did not bother, although that left them in fear of their legal status. Concerned at the prospect of hordes of landless peasants roaming around the Siberian countryside, the Committee decided to try to regulate the emigration process and effectively became a kind of welfare organization by providing comprehensive support both before and after the migrants' arrival in order to help them travel and settle. Each family was allocated forty acres of land with access to the forest and pasture. Around 100 such plots formed an enclosure and the housing tended to be concentrated in the centre to form a closely knit village. An extra incentive for the migrants was that their earnings for the first decade would be tax-free. In order to boost the supply of land, extensive and expensive projects were undertaken to drain swamps and to irrigate dry areas of steppe. Vast swathes of land were expropriated from the traditional nomadic people and allocated for peasant resettlement.

Millions of brochures extolling the advantages of life in Siberia were distributed to attract families to the region. Kulomzin, though, also ensured that the information given to emigrants – who, of course, were mostly illiterate and would need literature to be read to them – dispelled various myths of the 'streets paved with gold' type. There was, of course, plenty of gold and silver in the hills, but the emigrants were unlikely to get their hands on it. Rumours, too, abounded of the fantastic fertility of the Siberian soil, so Kulomzin's pamphlets presented a more realistic view of what productivity could be achieved. The material was, in fact, not unlike the publicity put out by the more responsible train companies in the United States, seeking to attract the right type of migrant following the completion of the rival transcontinental lines.

In order to make it easier for families to settle – indeed, sometimes whole villages moved en bloc – the Committee organized transport for family scouts to come to Siberia on their own to decide on a location and to make advance preparations, before returning to fetch their families. Such was the eagerness of the authorities to populate Siberia that the flow of migrants actually started intensifying while the first section of the railway was being constructed. They arrived at the end of the existing line at Tyumen, where they awaited river transport further east. The Committee did everything to help them, organizing transport on rafts for the river journey for both the settlers and their farm animals. The start of the construction of the railway immediately stimulated the expected sharp increase in migration and until the end of the century there was no let-up, either, in the numbers of exiles and prisoners being sent to Siberia. While previously the emigration had not been controlled, since the internal-passport requirements were difficult to enforce in the vast lands of Siberia, the building of the railway had the effect of regularizing the emigration process. The attempts to regulate the flow did not always work. Peasants were, quite literally, clamouring to come to Siberia and the slow, grinding Russian bureaucracy could not keep pace, with the result that many families, and even at times whole villages, simply upped sticks and headed east, after hastily selling their animals and any chattels they could not take with them.

When the railway was completed, the Committee provided subsidies for people to reach Chelyabinsk, where there was a camp for prospective migrants, and then grants of up to fifty roubles – and 100 roubles for those travelling beyond Lake Baikal – to purchase their train tickets. In fact, later the rules were changed so the whole family was given a discount instead of receiving a grant and, consequently, by the end of the century migrants were paying just fifteen roubles (around £1.50) for their fare, which partly explains why the railway required substantial subsidy during the early years. The scouts, sent by families and communes, paid only a quarter of the regular third-class fare. As support during the journey, the Committee set up a network of posts offering medical facilities and the inevitable samovar dispensing hot tea. Food was provided cheaply to adults and free for children. The only attraction lacking was the Empress Maria Feodorovna (Nicholas II's mother) herself dispensing tea – a rumour about her presence at a feeding station was widespread among the migrants.

However, some early migrants, attracted by the rather premature opening of the West Siberian Railway in 1896, suffered from the line's inadequacies. An early traveller, James Simpson, describes how the lack of capacity on the line led to vast numbers of migrants being stuck in boxcars so long that they had to be detrained into hastily erected camps. He found 'cholera, typhus and other loathsome enemies of mankind had walked – were walking – at their ease amongst them – thirty per cent had died'. The poor migrants lived in crude tents next to water-filled trenches, which bred the clouds of mosquitoes that filled the air. Simpson, however, was moved by the late-evening singing 'of one of those soft, weird, minor melodies that are the priceless possession of the Russian folk. And when the dying strains of the song soared to a high-pitched note held by the female voices, while the men prolonged it an octave lower, it seemed like some sad musical interrogation. Why had they left Poltava [their village] to die on the Siberian steppe?'[5]

Travelling itself could, indeed, be perilous. Apart from the numerous accidents and derailments in the early years, the migrants often failed to understand the dangers of train travel. Russian wagons are higher than in Europe with more space underneath and when, as happened frequently (and still does), they were parked on a track in the middle of a station, the travellers would think nothing of crawling underneath to save walking the long way round the front or back of the train. Numerous unlucky individuals perished when the train unexpectedly started. Others died when they tried to clamber up on to moving freight trains, like the hoboes of the United States, or travelled on the roof of passenger coaches for a free – if cold and perilous – ride.

Later, as the urgent improvements to the line instigated by Prince Khilkov took effect, the journey became smoother. Kulomzin ensured that the facilities provided to the migrants were rapidly improved, too. The work on the ground was carried out by a dedicated series of enlightened administrators, who belied the general view in the West of Russians as a harsh and uncaring race with little concern for the lower orders. Jules Legras, a French observer of the migration, for example, singled out Peter Arkhipov, the official in charge of the Chelyabinsk and Tyumen migration points (a function he carried out for fifteen years) for particular praise: 'One only has to listen to him talking for a few minutes to understand that he devotes himself to his difficult tasks as a work of charity and devotion.'[6] Treadgold describes the multi-tasking role of one of Arkhipov's colleagues, Andrei Stankevich, who supervised the passage of migrants as they arrived at the western staging points: 'He was always on the road, inspecting migrant points . . . [His] daily routine required him to give instructions to subordinates, plan the furnishing of land, water, wood and grain, act as architect, agronomist, surveyor of provisions to the settlers, [and] get along with the provincial governors.'[7] Clearly these officials went well beyond their remit of simply administering the migration and made great efforts to reduce the suffering of huge numbers of people who had embarked on this journey in to the unknown.

The completion of sections of the railway provoked the expected rush. In four of the five years following the opening of the first section in 1896 at least 200,000 migrants came to Siberia, an average of 5,500 per day, a quite astonishing influx and both a logistical and practical nightmare. The railways, with their very limited capacity of a handful of trains per day, as well as the rest of the transport infrastructure, struggled to cope. Another observer, Richard Penrose, travelling in 1901, described how 'the emigration is now going on faster than ever; all the trains and boats are crowded, and along the rivers many emigrants are seen on rafts floating down to their new homes, with families, horses, hogs and household possessions.'[8]

Before the advent of the railway, migration had been a slow and perilous process. Generally, the migrants had travelled with their own horses and carts, often loaded with unnecessary belongings, which were retained for sentimental reasons. At night they slept in the open, irrespective of the rain and cold. Despite the establishment of welfare stations, which offered them loans to buy food and provided limited medical facilities, migration was a perilous process. Given the lack of proper equipment and unaware of how far they needed to travel, migrants died in droves, mortality reaching thirty per cent among children and averaging around ten per cent for adults. Many of the survivors – up to a quarter in bad years – found the conditions too harsh and returned.

The railway not only made migration far quicker, but also safer. Mortality fell to one per cent as travelling conditions were so much easier and the migrants' passage was helped by the establishment of distribution centres for food and medicine at the main stations. It also, ironically, made it easier for 'returners', as they were called, to come back to European Russia, whose numbers peaked at 90,000 in 1900, but then the total dropped as Siberian settlements became established and amenities were developed.

Once arrived, the migrants received considerable financial assistance to help establish themselves. New state-run shops provided building materials at cheap rates (oddly, this became one of the few profitable enterprises run by the Committee) and even, in the distant Amur region, livestock and grain to new arrivals. Settlers could also apply for interest-free loans of up to 150 roubles and nearly all took advantage of this facility. As Penrose suggested, 'the settlers are probably better treated and better cared for than any colonists that ever entered a new country'[9] and this was thanks to Kulomzin: 'Safeguarding the health of migrants en route became Kulomzin's most persistent concern.'[10] The emigrants certainly needed a bit of mollycoddling, since most came with nothing. They tended to sell up quickly, because they were generally in a hurry to leave their previous homes and therefore rarely obtained the full value for their animals and chattels. Most, in any case, had been landless and close to destitution. As Treadgold puts it, 'the majority of migrants simply took a deep breath and plunged across the Urals.'[11] This was another difference with America, where, by and large, it was the more affluent rural migrants who made it out to the West.

While comparisons with the United States are inevitably simplistic, the changes were nevertheless radical and 'Siberian migration produced a society much more like that of America than was the Russian society from which it stemmed.'[12] Moreover, the migration afforded by the railway not only transformed Siberia but had repercussions throughout Russia: 'Siberian migration resulted in the creation of a new Siberian society, which had a higher level of prosperity and a greater degree of social flexibility than European Russia.'[13] The migration led to a new type of peasant who owned a smallholding, a different model from the communal one they left behind. This apparent liberalization by the monarchist regime was a response to the failed 1905 revolution. The relatively progressive politician Pyotr Stolypin, who became prime minister the following year, was anxious to win over the discontented peasantry. Land reforms directed at the remaining peasants in European Russia provided them with more freedom and created for the first time legally independent farmers living on their own land.

Oddly, despite these improvements to the peasants' conditions in European Russia and the gradual move away from the oppressive and inefficient commune system, the end of the Russo-Japanese War (during which there had been a steady flow of around 800 migrants per week to Siberia) led to a remarkable increase in the rate of migration. A further 3 million emigrants arrived between 1906 and the outbreak of the First World War in 1914, a rate which peaked in 1908 when an average of 15,000 travelled weekly.[14] While most of the migrants throughout this era settled in western and central Siberia, a higher proportion of the later ones settled in the east, as many as a fifth in the peak years.

Not surprisingly, this stream of people led to the transformation of the region; the very look and feel of Siberia changed forever through rapid urbanization and widespread settlement near the railway. This was inevitable given that settlement, with few exceptions, was confined to a swathe of land about 125 miles either side of the tracks. The urban population grew even faster than the overall rate of increase and more than doubled in towns as far apart as Omsk, Chita, Krasnoyarsk and Irkutsk in the two decades after the opening of the first section of the line in 1896. The population of Tomsk province increased nearly tenfold in this period. Other towns simply developed spontaneously. Jules Legras found himself in Tayga, a junction town east of Tomsk, which, thanks to its location on the line, had sprung up from nothing (with no buildings recorded before 1896) into a bustling settlement of 2,000 souls within a few years of the opening of the railway. Even a sympathetic observer like Legras could not disguise his horror at the squalid and anarchic nature of Tayga, which demonstrated the difficulty of trying to co-ordinate settlement from a capital thousands of miles away: 'Alcohol is a friend from which the Russian people can never be separated. Naturally, there is neither police nor administration; the town only exists officially since the previous autumn's census and no order has yet arrived from St Petersburg to organize this ant heap. Meanwhile, theft, debauchery, even murders are regular occurrences in the town of Tayga, which may, in a quarter of a century, overtake Tomsk.'[15] He was wrong on that last point, as in 2010 Tayga's population had only struggled up to 25,000, while Tomsk boasted twenty times that number.

Haphazard developments like Tayga were commonplace, given the inability of the authorities to control the growth of settlements in Siberia, but in other towns, particularly the large ones, there was an element of planning. Several garden cities or areas designed to similar standards were built, based on the movement pioneered around the same time by Ebenezer Howard in the United Kingdom. Howard believed in well-laid-out towns with gardens for everyone and green space around the residential area, together with industry for the workers. At Kuznetsk, on a branch line, a garden city was laid out to a clearly defined plan with nine different types of one-storey houses for railway employees, two-storey dwellings for bachelors, a brick factory and a four-storey building for railway management. Other garden cities were built in Omsk and Tomsk based on Howard's ideas, which also had a profound impact on later developments in Siberian town planning in Novosibirsk and Kemorovo, which is on a branch line near Novosibirsk.

No fewer than twenty-three settlements were officially declared towns in the first decade after the line was completed and the original towns expanded rapidly, even though, for the most part, the stations were often some distance away from the line, because of the policy of keeping costs down by not building right up to them if that required expensive embankments or bridges. The fastest-growing was Novonikolayevsk (now Novosibirsk), which expanded from a population of just 764 in 1893, to 26,000 by 1905 and more than 100,000 at the time of the Revolution. No less than a third of the land in the town, which, as we have seen, owed its very existence to the line, was taken up by railway facilities. Most of it was destroyed by fire in 1909, partly because the railway blocked the way to the river, the main source of water to douse the flames. Dubbed the 'American City', because it was laid out in blocks like US cities, after the fire Novonikolayevsk was designed to a fixed plan with, for example, two-storey primary schools at every junction of main roads.

The nature of other towns changed, too. In the large ones, the first multi-storey buildings appeared, often built as offices for the railway management or for the technical schools that were essential to train people to work on the railway. The railway resulted in the introduction of a new style of architecture, based more on plainer Russian designs than the more ornate traditional Siberian vernacular. Siberia was undoubtedly becoming more like the rest of Russia, as William Oliver Greener described: 'The neat railway settlements, composed of large immigrant homes, schools, picturesque churches – built out of the Alexander III memorial fund [created in honour of the tsar's father] – substantial and commodious dwellings, the mills, stores and station buildings are not properly representative of Siberia but of the new better free colonies the Russian State is doing its utmost to plant all over the fertile regions of Northern Asia.'[16]

Because of their distance from the towns and the importance of the line to the local economy, the railway effectively pulled the towns towards the tracks. Generally, the railway occupied huge amounts of land at the periphery of these cities where it was cheap, and as this became developed it meant many towns were split between two separate centres. In the new towns, housing and offices for the railway workers set the pattern for future development. In some places, town planning did suffer somewhat because of the demands of the railway, which, given it had the backing of the government and the tsar, were not negotiable. Vast swathes of land, up to 750 acres, were designated for railway purposes, preventing other facilities from being built near the station.

There was, too, military intent in the way that developments built up around the stations, since, as we see in the next chapter, the generals realized that the railway was the key to controlling the wider region. Near the major stations an area would be zoned for barracks, which were built on a grand scale, far larger than would be necessary on a day-to-day basis. If the railway brought in the military, it also ensured God was present. Kulomzin allocated 150,000 roubles to build chapels and churches at the main stations and this was supplemented by the Alexander III memorial fund. By 1903 nearly 200 churches had been built or were under construction, as well as almost as many parish schools. Settlements on the railway without a place of worship could benefit from the church carriages introduced on the line from 1896, which were large enough to hold seventy worshippers. That was a use of the railway which the Communists would later imitate for their own form of propaganda. All these facilities were provided so readily by a normally parsimonious government because Kulomzin believed they were essential to the project to Russify and, indeed civilize, Siberia. On his visits to the region before the completion of the railway he had found a lack of schools and churches, which he felt contributed to what he saw as the absence of civilization and culture in the region.

Overall, Kulomzin's view that the railway was the key to transforming Siberia was borne out, because by the beginning of the First World War the region had changed irreversibly. At the risk of sounding like a Soviet propaganda team boasting about its five-year plan, the numbers were impressive. Thanks to the influx of the five million migrants in the twenty years running up to the war, the area of land under cultivation more than doubled, the number of livestock more than tripled to reach thirty-eight million, and both wheat and rye production were booming. The amount of butter produced in the region increased fivefold in the ten years to 1904, reaching two million puds (the Russian unit which weighs just over 36 lb), which created a profitable export market to Britain, Denmark and Germany.

Butter trains became one of the regular features of the line. The butter was transported in refrigerator cars, distinctive because they were painted white, and whole trains could be seen running up and down the line. The trade was huge: 'In the early summer peak period about a dozen trains, each of 25 cars, were despatched each week.'[17] This vast agricultural produce of Siberia was not only for export. Soon, the whole of Russia was enjoying the fruits of Siberia's greater productivity. By 1911 half the meat eaten in the two biggest cities, Moscow and St Petersburg, was delivered by rail from Siberia. It was not only food. Huge mineral wealth, such as coal, oil, silver and gold, was beginning to be tapped, although much of it was not discovered until the later stages of the Soviet era.

While the decision to build the railway had been controversial, now, of course, there was no doubt that it had become essential to the well-being of the region. By facilitating the mass emigration, the Trans-Siberian had created its own demand. It was not profitable, especially since millions of roubles would be spent on completing its tracks through Russian soil (as we shall see in the next chapter), but it was heavily used and the hugely increased population of Siberia was utterly dependent on its efficient functioning. The railway brought them all the supplies that could not be found locally and distributed their excess produce to the rest of Russia. While eastern Siberia was still dependent on imported grain supplies from further west, western and central Siberia began to send produce for western Russia. In fact, this caused concerns among producers there and they had to be protected by a mechanism known as the Chelyabinsk tariff break, which artificially raised the price of transporting grain on the line for long distances between Siberia and western Russia.[18]

The Trans-Siberian laid the foundations for the economic and industrial development of the region. From being a dumping ground for exiles and penal colonies, Siberia now became part of Russia with the Urals no longer representing a barrier between two different worlds, although industrial development was slower than Witte had hoped. The line, though, definitely did not live up to the hype portrayed in the *Guide to the Great Siberian Railway* given to tourists, which also would not have been out of place in a Soviet propaganda sheet: 'The rapid increase in the profits of the Great Siberian Railway, connected with the general economic growth of Siberia, strikingly illustrates the effect produced upon civilization and commerce by this great work, which will serve as a monument to the reign of the Tsar Pacificator and to the Russian Slavonic nation, which is destined to propagate Christianity and civilization in the east of Asia.'[19] There were, of course, no profits, even if takings exceeded early expectations, because the constant need for repairs and investment meant the railway represented a continuous drain on government resources. However, as mentioned before, no clear accounts were ever available, since the railways' finances were blended into overall government figures. Quietly, in November 1905, the Committee for the Siberian Railway was abolished, its work done. There was still, however, the task of completing the all-Russian route and bringing the line up to a standard to cope with ever-increasing demand.

# EIGHT

# RUSSIA ALL THE WAY

While ostensibly the Trans-Siberian opened fully in 1903 with the completion of the Circum-Baikal Railway which meant the iron road finally linked Moscow with the Pacific Ocean, in reality it was still work in progress. As we have seen, improvements went hand in hand with the construction process and did not cease when a section of line opened. Indeed, with the demands first of war and then of the huge numbers of migrants, the need to boost capacity was all too obvious, and there was, too, the thorny issue of trying to avoid having to go through Manchuria.

Therefore, within a couple of years of the end of the disastrous Russo-Japanese War, work began on a project to double the tracks on the busiest section of the railway, from Omsk to just beyond Chita, which encompassed virtually all the Russian part of the railway. The scheme almost entailed the construction of a new railway, given that the original embankments and cuttings had been so narrow, and a few bridges remained single-track until much later. The work took eight years and was completed just after the outbreak of the First World War in the summer of 1914. By then, the timetable for the journey from Moscow to Vladivostok on the fastest train – still via the Chinese Eastern Railway – had been speeded up to nine days. Tokyo, therefore, which was connected by a fast steamer service, was just twelve days away from St Petersburg (which was hastily renamed Petrograd at the start of the First World War, as its original name sounded too German). It was not only the main line that saw improvements. The impact of the Trans-Siberian was far more limited than the government had envisaged, being confined to a swathe stretching for the most part barely 125 miles either side of the line. In order to extend its usefulness, branch lines were constructed, mostly by private companies, principally to service mines, but also to carry agricultural produce from the hinterland. Nevertheless, by and large, the impact of the railway did not extend far into the steppe.

The need for such a major expansion in capacity reflected not only the heavy use of the line by both freight and passenger traffic, but also one of its indirect effects: the efforts to improve the road across Siberia – a project that had been mooted in the late nineteenth century – had been abandoned once the decision to construct the line was taken. Consequently everything had to go by rail. The lack of a road was highlighted by the most bizarre use ever made of the trackbed: to help an Italian aristocrat win the Peking to Paris road race.

Prince Scipione Borghese was one of the competitors in the race organized in 1907 by France's *Le Matin* newspaper to prove that cars could go anywhere. When he and his driver, Ettore Guizzardi, reached the eastern shores of Lake Baikal they considered the road to be impassable and were therefore granted permission by the governor general of Irkutsk to use the track bed of the Circum-Baikal, despite the fact that trains would continue running. Fortunately, the sleepers had been laid flush to the surface, rather than protruding upwards, so the track bed actually gave his monstrous car, a 7.4 litre Itala, a reasonable ride. In fact, it was a lot better than he had encountered previously and was testimony to the skill of the railway builders, as he later recorded: 'The sensation of this motor journey was at first delightful. That superb, even, level, clear road was full of attraction after the ruts, the woods and the ditches of the other.'[1] It was, however, perilous: 'We went across numerous little bridges of the same breadth as the sleepers, without parapets, slung over deep ravines, in the depths of which we could see foaming water through the large spaces between one sleeper and another . . . The car advanced with its left wheels between the rails, and the right wheels on the outside – over the few inches of sleepers.'

In fact, apart from a near encounter with a goods train, he fared better on the railway than on the road, where a bridge collapsed under his car's weight, plunging it into a torrent. However, after enlisting local help he managed to rescue the vehicle, which was unscathed, and he survived to triumph in the race, which had only four other competitors, reaching Paris on 10 August, precisely two months after leaving Peking (Beijing).

Normal service on the Trans-Siberian resumed two years after the Russo-Japanese War and by the summer of 1907 there were three fast trains every week between Moscow and Vladivostok. The best one was operated by the Compagnie Internationale des Wagons-Lits created by Nagelmackers (who had died in 1905) and, while the rolling stock never matched those at the show in Paris, it was far better than on the other two state-run *trains de luxe*. There was, therefore, a brief golden age of travel on the Trans-Siberian between the two wars when it became the route of choice for diplomats heading for China and merchants travelling to Japan. The company, according to Harmon Tupper, 'diverted some of its second-best cars to the Siberian run; staffed them with solicitous attendants speaking Russian, French, German and English, provided good foods and wine; and widely publicized the fact that, via the rail route, one could travel from London or Paris to the Extreme Orient in less than half the time and cost of the sea voyage by way of the Suez Canal.'² That was a crucial point. The Trans-Siberian, for all its faults, offered a far quicker and easier journey than the long boat rides, especially in the summer with the hot tropical sun of the Indian Ocean.

While the Wagons-Lits Company had higher prices than the state trains, it was still a bargain. A Mrs John Clarence Lee, a Philadelphia clergyman's wife, travelling in 1913, wrote a wonderfully witty account of her journey westwards, reported that the fare for the train from Shanghai to Moscow via a ship from Dalny (Dalian) and Harbin on the Chinese Eastern Railway was £44 8 shillings (£44.40) first class and £32 4 shillings (£32.20) in second class, compared with £30 and £20 on the Russian state train. Her three meals a day in the dining car cost just £1.75. She had been advised by her travel agent not to get off 'as there was nothing there', but she ignored him and enjoyed Irkutsk and Lake Baikal.

On the South Manchurian Railway en route to Harbin she found 'a spotless new Pullman — made in Illinois — with "Sleeping Car" painted in English on the outside. The car is divided into compartments for two, with an individual washbasin of the latest type and hot and cold water. At night one locks the door and opens the window, and it is wonderfully comfortable.'³ At the South Manchurian terminus at Changchun, south of Harbin, where ownership passed from the Japanese to the Russians, she changed to the carriages that would take her through to Moscow on the Trans-Siberian itself. She found the accommodation equally pleasant, with cars upholstered in velvet and a toilet for every two compartments, which each accommodated two people. The railway discipline, too, that had been so lax in the past on the Trans-Siberian seemed to have been sorted out with a clear method of signalling departure, which ensured the unwary were not left behind: 'Five minutes before departure the bell rings twice, and just before the train starts it rings three times.'⁴

The fact that most of the passengers on the Trans-Siberian, like

Mrs Lee, went to or from China rather than Vladivostok prompted the Russian government to re-examine the possibility of building the Amur Railway. The Russians were rather piqued when *The Times* suggested that the Trans-Siberian was not a main line to Vladivostok, but rather a trunk line to the China Sea with a branch to Vladivostok. This increased public pressure in eastern Siberia to build the Amur line to redirect enterprise and capital from Manchuria to Siberia. The people of eastern Siberia felt the Chinese Eastern Railway was taking away their livelihood, having become the main form of transport linking Vladivostok with the rest of the world. Rather than coming to eastern Siberia, Russian peasants were settling in Manchuria or remaining on the more accessible land west of Lake Baikal.

The previously thriving steamers on the Amur river had lost much of their business and the local merchants complained that most of their trade had gone to Manchuria. Therefore, the overall economic impact of the Trans-Siberian on eastern Siberia had not lived up to its billing, and, in fact, could even be considered as negative. Vladivostok itself, which was supposed to have been the great beneficiary of the railway, was suffering, too. Despite the defeat by Japan, the Russians had retained their naval base at Port Arthur rather than moving it to Vladivostok and it was Harbin, at the junction of the two railways, that became the boom town. In fact, it had developed into the nearest equivalent of a frontier town in the American West, a veritable melting pot of races and cultures. Little more than a village before the arrival of the railway, it was now a bustling Russian town in Manchuria. A pair of visitors after the Russo-Japanese War were amazed that Harbin appeared to have been taken over by the Russians, despite the fact that it was technically still part of China: 'The police are largely Russian. Harbin is so Russian that they dare to hang printed notices in hotels telling you to lodge your Russian passport for inspection at the Russian police station before you have unpacked your trunks. The colossal impertinence of the thing.'[5] Harbin was not only the administrative headquarters of the Chinese Eastern Railway, but also housed numerous other enterprises which employed vast numbers of Russians, including various mills, military barracks and a distillery that produced three million gallons of vodka a year (or, as Tupper elaborates, thirty gallons for every inhabitant, although one hopes that much was for export). Another visitor, Daniel de Menocal, a banker, recalled his visit to Harbin in 1909, where, in the hotel, he found a scene that he describes as being out of a Western with 'a milling gang of bearded, husky, half-drunken and fully drunken, noisy Russians in circulation from the bar to the billiard table . . . There were Buryats who were half-Russian, half-Mongol, some Japanese and mixing with these frenetic groups some women, big tough creatures.'[6] The railway and its associated development had brought prosperity, however, and the streets were full of well-dressed wealthy people from across Asia, along with native men and women, equally well turned out in their local costume. Although clearly under Russian control, there was a cosmopolitan air of affluence and self confidence in the crowds that thronged the centre of Harbin.

The Russification of Manchuria and Harbin, rather than Siberia and Vladivostok, was not only galling for the eastern Siberians, but also presented a risk to the Russian government. The peace with Japan was fragile. A trio of treaties were signed with Japan in the years following the Russo-Japanese War, largely in an attempt to establish the ground rules for their respective imperial ambitions, but it was an uneasy relationship with mistrust on both sides, and the need to avoid antagonizing the Japanese was the keystone to Russia's Asian policy. As Witte wryly put it, 'In the far east, it is no longer we who play first violin but Japan.'[7] Reducing dependence on the Chinese Eastern Railway, which always threatened to be a catalyst for trouble in Russo-Japanese relations, was therefore essential for Russian foreign policy. Moreover, given that the Trans-Siberian had been built partly for military purposes, it could no longer fulfil that role unless it ran through all the way on Russian soil. Under the peace treaty, signed in Portsmouth, to end the Russo-Japanese War, the Russians were banned from using the Chinese Eastern Railway to carry their army. Just to make matters worse, the Chinese were beginning to flex their muscles over the Russians' continued presence in Manchuria, calling it, with no little accuracy, an invasion.

Yet again, the construction of a railway became a military goal. The issue of whether to build it became a huge political controversy in the (slightly) more democratic corridors of power in St Petersburg. The supporters of the railway won the argument and the construction of the Amur Railway became the centrepiece of a more aggressive policy in the east. It would allow the construction of military bases in Transbaikalia, the strengthening of the Pacific Fleet with better support facilities at Vladivostok and the establishment of a fleet to patrol the Amur river, which forms the border with China.

Witte, out of government now, saw the building of the railway as yet another act of aggression and suggested instead that the defence of the Chinese Eastern Railway should be strengthened, although, of course, that reflected his own role in the initial decision to go through Manchuria. He was ignored by what he called the 'war party', in which he included the tsar as well as other senior government figures. It was, therefore, the political and military imperative dictated by these concerns, rather than any consideration of the needs of local merchants, that determined the decision to build the Amur Railway. And it proved to be an expensive one.

The assessment by the men who had surveyed the route in the 1890s had been correct. This would not be an easy railway to build. The route was determined by the need to be sufficiently far from the border to afford protection from potential attack from the Manchurian side of the Amur river, whose path the tracks largely followed, but also, on the other hand, the desire to remain in the south, where conditions were more likely to stimulate economic development and population growth. Formal approval was given by the Duma in 1907 and work started the following spring under the control of Nikolai K. Schaffhausen-Schönberg och Schaufuss, who, despite his remarkable German aristocratic name, was nevertheless Russian. The new line branched off the Transbaikal thirty miles west of Sretensk and followed a curve parallel to the river for 1,200 miles, reaching Khabarovsk and crossing the Amur over the longest bridge, stretching nearly a mile and a half, of the whole Trans-Siberian.

It was another epic achievement. The usual problems of labour shortage, harsh conditions and difficult terrain were exacerbated by the fact that most of the line had to be built on permafrost, as the original surveyors in the 1890s had predicted. The problem with permafrost is that, despite its name, it is not actually permanent. While a few feet or yards down there is, indeed, a layer of permanently frozen soil, the immediate surface thaws in summer just enough to cause problems with the track. Consequently embankments collapsed and landslides filled cuttings, and like on the Transbaikal, water was a permanent problem. In the summer, floods washed away the track bed and ballast, while in winter the shortage of water meant there was great difficulty in keeping locomotives functioning.

Just to make the project even more difficult for the engineers, this was the least populated and coldest part of Siberia, and the route went through an unforgiving series of forests, swamps, marshy plains and mountains. Although the line was to be built as a single-track railway, the lessons of the need for increased capacity had been learnt and sufficient space was allowed on the bridges and tunnels to allow for double-tracking the line in the future. While the greater part of the other sections of the railway in eastern Siberia had been built by Asian labour, this time the government insisted on a virtually all-Russian workforce, because it was seeking to ensure the vast resources it was putting into the project stayed in the country. Therefore, more than 15,000 labourers were brought in from European Russia and western Siberia to supplement the smaller number of available locals and convicts, while, as an exception, the mountainous terrain required the employment of expert tunnellers from Italy. This emphasis on Russian labour did not arise solely from economic considerations, but was part of the rationale for building the line in the first place with the idea of using it to strengthen Russia's control over Siberia. Despite the failings of the Trans-Siberian – or, rather, precisely because of them – there was an even greater desire to see off the threat from the Chinese once and for all through this final link of an entirely Russian railway to the Pacific.

Therefore, it was a much more overtly colonial project than the construction of the previous sections. The labourers themselves, brought in from the rest of Russia, were seen as potential settlers, and in order to attract new arrivals facilities were built simultaneously with the railway, rather than cobbled together later as an afterthought. By the time the line was completed in 1916, 'stretch after stretch of hitherto unusable terrain had been cleared for new settlers. In arid areas, wellholes had been sunk through perennially frozen layers of bedrock, gravel, sand, silt, clay organic material and ice, not infrequently to a depth of more than 350 feet before reaching water beneath the permafrost floor.'[8] Construction was somewhat more mechanized than for previous sections and steam-powered excavators were used to drain vast swathes of marshes and turn them into arable fields. Nevertheless, the bulk of the work was still carried out by navvies wielding pickaxes and shovels, helped by the occasional use of dynamite. Even before the railway was completed, villages had sprung up in forest clearings and carefully planned towns had been laid out. Supply roads were built to permanent – rather than temporary – standards, postal services were established and churches were provided, an ornate mobile carriage serving those communities without one. J. N. Westwood, the historian of Russian railways, rather cynically notes: 'Much publicity was given to the building of the churches for the railwaymen; the new gaols were probably a better investment, although less advertised.'[9] That was not entirely fair, because the facilities created along with the railway were built to a high standard and were intended to ensure that settlers were attracted to eastern Siberia. The polar explorer Fridtjof Nansen, who visited the line in 1913, was impressed to find a series of hospitals and clinics erected along the railway and found 'the wards, operating rooms, baths, etc., . . . light, clean and well arranged', while the schoolrooms were 'large and airy [and] the children looked happy; it could not be seen that the climate had done them any harm'.[10] This was, therefore, not so much a railway construction project as the creation of a new part of Russia, and there is no little irony in the fact that it was precisely this sort of social engineering that was at the heart of Soviet thinking after the Revolution.

Other than tunnel and bridge work, progress on the railway was only possible for the four months from June to October, and consequently the labourers brought in from the rest of Russia were despatched back home in the autumn to save money. Nevertheless, the total cost of the railway exceeded 400 million roubles (£40 million), although, once again, money seemed to be no barrier. The higher cost per mile (£30,000) in comparison with the other sections of the Trans-Siberian was due not only to the difficult conditions in this remotest part of Russia, but also to the decision to build an alignment formation suitable for subsequent doubling of the tracks as well as the provision of a wide range of extra facilities that were included in the budget.

Once the government had decided to go ahead, there was no stopping the project, whatever the cost or the difficulties of construction. It was, proportionately, the worst drain on government resources of all the various projects that made up the Trans-Siberian, given that, at the time, the total annual budget of the Russian government was around three billion roubles. In other words, a seventh of one year's annual income was spent on building a line that was at the furthest end of the Russian Empire and which had little economic use at a time when the country was constantly teetering on the edge of revolution. As Steven Marks puts it, 'St Petersburg fixed its attention on building this railroad without regard for local conditions, costs or predictions of its negligible impact, because of the perception that it was a matter of safeguarding the Empire.'[11]

The enormous sums of money spent on these Far East ventures certainly contributed to opposition to the tsarist regime. It is not mere idle speculation to suggest that had these vast resources been put to a more practical use in an effort to head off the revolutionary mood by offering the masses at least some hope of improving their lot, the history of Russia – and, indeed, the world in the twentieth century – might have been very different. Even if that is fanciful, the Trans-Siberian certainly was about to play a significant role in the civil war that followed the Revolution, and, in different circumstances, could have led to a completely different outcome. As Tupper notes with acuity, 'The Trans-Siberian is inseparable from the history of this bloodshed.'[12]

# NINE

# THE BATTLE
# FOR THE TRANS-
# SIBERIAN

Almost as soon as the Amur Railway was completed Siberia was thrown into chaos by the 1917 Revolution and its aftermath. The Trans-Siberian had not covered itself in glory during the First World War, which Russia was caught up in right from the beginning in 1914. Or rather, those managing the railway had yet again failed to exploit its potential in wartime. The Allies, keen to keep the Germans and Austro-Hungarians engaged in the east, had sought to resupply the Russians through Vladivostok and the Trans-Siberian, since sending goods through the Western Front, which stretched from Belgium to Switzerland, was obviously impossible and the Baltic was patrolled by German submarines. However, in one of its final acts of monumental incompetence, the tsarist government had failed to ensure that the railway was able to carry these supplies. Apart from the overall lack of capacity, the main problem was caused by a blockage at Tomsk in western Siberia, where production had vastly increased at a coal mine, resulting in fifteen extra coal trains a day, leaving few paths for trains coming from the east. Moreover, the Trans-Siberian was still operated by primitive methods that limited the potential to put on extra trains.

Unlike in most of Europe, locomotives were still fuelled by hand – in other words, coal was shovelled up from the ground into their tenders, rather than fed by gravity from hoppers above – and they also took a long time to take in water because of the standard design of Russian locomotives, which were fitted with small-bore pipes. These kinds of details were vital to improve the efficiency, and therefore capacity, of the line.

No one in the government had thought to prioritize the delivery of this vast store of goods and, consequently, Vladivostok had become the largest warehouse in the world, with goods clogging up the port and lying unguarded on the fields and beaches for miles around the town. It was a remarkable cornucopia of weapons, together with raw materials and luxury items, such as a thousand cars that had not even been removed from their crates. According to the historian of the American intervention, 'these supplies, a monument to the inefficiency of the Czarist regime, which had never paid for them, lay strewn along docks and stacked in open fields [and included] a mountain of cotton bales, millions of rounds of ammunition, 37,000 train wheels, enough steel rails to build a third track from Vladivostok to Petrograd and enough barbed wire to fence Siberia.'[1] The *pièce de résistance* was a submarine, presumably for use in patrolling the Sea of Japan. The total was valued, in contemporary money, at between $750 million and $1 billion, a quite staggering sum. Not only was this vast stockpile rotting in the relatively mild but damp climate of Vladivostok, but, worse, the Bolsheviks were beginning to take an interest in it, although they did not yet control Vladivostok.

This Aladdin's cave played a crucial role in the involvement of the Trans-Siberian during the civil war that followed Russia's revolution because it became part of the excuse for a series of foreign interventions by armies from, amongst others, Britain, the United States, Japan and France, all of which were characterized by uncertainty about their purpose and considerable dithering. Following the October Revolution of 1917, when the Bolsheviks took over from the Provisional Government that had ousted the monarchy in March that year in the initial uprising, within a few months a peace agreement was negotiated with the Germans at Brest-Litovsk in western Russia.[2] While the Bolsheviks were able to consolidate their control in most of European Russia, establishing themselves in the further reaches of the nation proved more difficult.

The wider context was that the Allies held on to a vague notion that perhaps with the right intervention, and a bit of luck, the Bolshevik Revolution could be reversed. It was, though, an incoherent idea and no one had worked out a way of achieving this goal. There was little understanding within the governments of these varied nations about the nature or causes of the Russian Revolution and the strength of support it enjoyed among the masses was greatly underestimated. Or more accurately, they did not realize the depth of hatred towards the old tsarist regime. The Siberian intervention was one of several attempts to support the Whites against the Reds. In the north a British-led force, with some American support, was sent to land at Murmansk in the Arctic Circle to safeguard war matériel stockpiled at Archangelsk (where the port is frozen in winter). In the Baltic states, too, there were hopes of an uprising by various anti-Bolshevik elements. Finland, meanwhile, was also fighting for its freedom. On the other hand, in Baku, now the capital the Azerbaijan, the British fought side by side with Armenian revolutionaries in a vain attempt to stop the city falling to the Turks in order to protect the oil supplies. While this made sense locally, it demonstrated the confusion of the period, the British unable to decide who to support, given their main enemy remained (until the November 1918 Armistice) the Germans. British policy was, in fact, a muddle, since the

Foreign Office really wanted Soviet Russia to take up arms against Germany, but was simultaneously supporting the most rabid anti-Bolshevik forces, which was hardly the way to achieve this aim. Almost anyone who claimed to be able to build up an army against the Reds soon found themselves flush with British government money.

Therefore, in the three years following the Revolution, Siberia became an uncontrollable maelstrom of political factions, freelance armies and criminal elements. It was the key battleground between White and Red forces in the later stages of the civil war and became the arena for the final struggle for control of Russia.

Even before the October Revolution the Allies had taken an interest in the region and, in particular, the functioning of the railway. The Americans (with the agreement of the Kerensky regime) had sent a specially created 300-strong force of experienced railway engineers to oversee operations on the railway and ensure it did not collapse. They landed in Vladivostok and concluded, after an inspection, that the line was the only viable link to Europe, although they recognized the difficulties being caused by the bottleneck at Tomsk. In order to support operations, they broke up into fourteen units – scattered along both the Chinese Eastern Railway and the main Trans-Siberian – to help the operations of the railway, but did not act in a military role. Once the Brest-Litovsk Treaty had been signed in March, the Allies were intent on persuading the Americans to send a military force to Siberia. The idea was that if America were prepared to commit itself to a military assault, nearby Japan – which had supported the Allies during the conflict, but had been involved in very little military engagement – would be able to provide considerable numbers of troops. To encourage the idea of intervention, rumours emanated from secret-service sources that there were large numbers of German and Austrian prisoners who had been enlisted in support of the Bolsheviks. R. H. Bruce Lockhart, the British diplomat who headed the mission to the Bolshevik regime during the civil war, observed in his memoirs that 'according to the reports it [the British secret service] received, Siberia was teeming with German regiments composed of war prisoners who had been armed by the Bolsheviks. They were in control of a vast area.'³ This was another case of British intelligence providing a dodgy dossier. The assistant despatched by Bruce Lockhart to investigate informed him after a six-week tour of Siberia that there was no sign of any German army, a finding that the British government did not welcome since it destroyed a potential pretext for intervention.

The American President, Woodrow Wilson, who had only agreed to send troops to the Western Front in 1917 after considerable provocation from the Germans with the sinking of several US merchant ships based on a policy of unrestricted submarine warfare, was reluctant to become embroiled in a second front, despite the fact that 'allied pressure on Wilson to intervene was strong and continuous'.⁴ Then came one of those seemingly insignificant incidents that change the course of history: a minor fracas between Czech and Hungarian soldiers at Chelyabinsk at the foot of the Urals led to American involvement in Siberia, the only time in history that US troops have set foot on Russian soil.

A group of 70,000 Czech soldiers had found themselves stranded in Siberia by the Revolution. Czechoslovakia was at the time part of the Austro-Hungarian Empire and most of the men had been captured in combat alongside the Austrian forces against the Russians. They were, in truth, reluctant fighters against the Russians and, in fact, after the Revolution the Czechs were quickly made part of the Russian army, fighting enthusiastically and successfully for Kerensky's Provisional Government in July 1917 at Zborov in Ukraine against their former masters in order to further their ultimate cause of an independent Czechoslovakia.

However, when the Bolshevik regime signed the armistice with the Germans, the very effective and well-regarded Czechs found themselves in a difficult position. They did not want to make peace with the Germans and consequently pledged loyalty to the French, who were still fighting on the Western Front and took on the name Legion, a tribute to the famous French Foreign Legion. Although Stalin, then boasting the grand title of People's Commissar for Nationalities' Affairs, offered them free safe passage back to the West, the Czechs were understandably concerned that they would end up in German hands and be massacred as traitors, since they were effectively deserters from the Austro-Hungarian army which had fought alongside the Germans. The only option was to return the long way round, travelling by train to Vladivostok, followed by a boat journey halfway across the world. They had obtained the agreement of the Soviet authorities to do this, but gradually the trust between the Czechs and the Bolsheviks broke down, and, as Orlando Figes, author of an epic history of the Russian Revolution and its aftermath, suggests, 'Had this agreement been adhered to by both sides, the civil war would have taken a very different course.'[5]

Clearly, given the poor state of the heavily used railway, this huge movement of Czech troops would have taken several weeks, but the vanguard was already well on the way to Vladivostok when the Legion's progress was halted as a result of the incident at Chelyabinsk Station on 17 May 1918. A group of Czech Legionnaires happened to arrive at the station at the same time as a trainload of Hungarian prisoners, who were being returned to their homeland by the more direct westerly route. Although both countries were part of the Austro-Hungarian Empire, the two nationalities had traditionally been antagonistic, in the way that neighbours often are, but all passed off relatively smoothly with a bit of banter until the Hungarian train was moving off. A foolish hothead hurled a heavy piece of cast iron from a broken stove at a group of Czech soldiers and one fell injured, bleeding from his head.[6] The Czechs chased after the slow-moving train, forced the driver to stop it and, after having persuaded the Hungarians to identify the culprit through threats of violence, killed him in retaliation.

The train carrying the Hungarians was then allowed to leave, but there then followed a playground-style tit-for-tat escalation between the Russians and the Czechs that led to three years of chaotic and bloody conflict and could ultimately have altered the result of both the civil war and the Revolution. Local Soviet officials arrived with a detachment of Red Army soldiers, who promptly arrested several of the Legionnaires and whisked them off to the town prison. An officer and several men who went as a delegation to find out their fate were also thrown into jail. The Czechs were having none of it and two battalions marched into Chelyabinsk, taking over the town until the prisoners were released. The Czechs helped themselves to arms and ammunition and withdrew.

This would have been the end of the episode, but for Bolshevik pride and arrogance. The Reds were now infuriated and an order was issued by the ever bellicose Leon Trotsky, the commander of the Red Army, that all Czech units along the Trans-Siberian be detained and that the Czech legions be broken up and placed in units of the Red Army. Any Czech soldier found armed on the railway was to be shot. This was the classic mistake of a tyro military commander giving orders that were impossible to carry out. While the Bolsheviks had taken over the towns along the Trans-Siberian, with the exception of Vladivostok, their tenure was weak, given the sheer logistics of controlling the vast region of Siberia and the fact that the Red Army at this stage was still an untrained and ill-disciplined militia principally made up of local workers sympathetic to Bolshevik ideals. Rural Siberia, in any case, where there had been no serfs or arrogant aristocratic landowners, was not fertile ground for revolutionary fervour. The weak Soviets – the local communist committees who controlled the towns – were no match for the much better-organized Czechs, who spread out rapidly along the Trans-Siberian, helped by their control of the telegraph system to communicate between stations. Using improvised armoured trains to great effect, they sped along the line, taking over towns from the Bolsheviks mostly with consummate ease. When Lenin, in retaliation, sent an armoured train, hauled by a famous armoured locomotive called *Zaamurets*, to fight the Czechs in July 1918, it was quickly captured and the Legionnaires used it extensively to control and then patrol the line. Within a few weeks of the Chelyabinsk incident, the Czechs, fighting alongside the anti-Bolshevik Whites, who suddenly found themselves with effective allies, had overcome Bolshevik resistance throughout the Western section of the Trans-Siberian and, indeed, much of western Siberia.

The Czech takeover of the line caused what one historian of the Intervention called 'a world-wide sensation'[7] and President Wilson came under further sustained pressure from the Allies to intervene, since the summer of 1918 was a low point in the war. The Germans had broken through the Western Front with their Spring Offensive in March, resulting in the first significant breach of the lines since 1914, and, consequently, reopening a front in the East to make up for the collapse of Russian resistance was a tempting prospect for the allies. According to the author of a book on the Americans' Siberian adventure, 'In Wilson's mind, the re-creation of an Eastern Front by Russian forces, even on a relatively modest scale, would not only revive Allied morale . . . but would compel the Germans to retain crucial divisions in the East, which might well be the difference between victory and defeat in the war.'[8] There was, too, little downside, since the diversion to the east of a few thousand soldiers would make little difference to the millions on the Western Front. The Allies hoped the Czech success could be part of the wider movement of anti-Bolshevik forces in Ukraine, the Caucusus and the Arctic that would overthrow the Bolsheviks and consequently get Russia back in the war against the Germans. Overhanging all this, there was what Peter Fleming (brother of James Bond author Ian and author of a history of the intervention) called 'a nebulous project which envisaged the creation, somewhere in South Russia, of a sort of bastion or bridgehead upon which would converge, or round which would coalesce, the Rumanian Army, the Ukrainians, the Transcaucasians and anyone else who might be supposed to [be] our friends in Russia'.[9]

By mid-June the Czechs had started arriving at Vladivostok, although there were no ships to take them back home, and now, with the support of local counter-revolutionary forces, they controlled virtually all 3,000 miles of the railway from Penza to Irkutsk, while the Bolsheviks held the Amur and Ussuri sections. Throughout the fighting the Czechs suffered very few casualties and had been victorious in every town where they launched a major assault. They had shown themselves to be a formidable force, but clearly, spread out over such a vast area, they could not hope to remain dominant. They needed help and support, but the Allies were confused about precisely how they should get involved.

Despite this chaotic situation, the railway still operated, with the Reds and the Whites surprisingly cooperating to allow railway staff to go about their jobs normally. The Czechs' success, however, had one highly significant side effect that was to send shockwaves around the world. Their proximity to Yekaterinburg, where the tsar was being held, had prompted the local Bolsheviks, under the orders of Lenin, to murder the royal family and their retainers on 17 July, although this might have been just a useful pretext for the execution of the family.

Wilson, after much procrastination, eventually acquiesced to despatching a force of 8,500 men. An aide-memoire to the commanding officer, Major General William S. Graves, offered three reasons for the intervention: to help the Czechs evacuate from Siberia, to guard and recover the supplies sent by the Allies to Vladivostok and to 'help the Russians organize their new government'. This last reason needed further elaboration to explain what government was to be helped, because, at the time, the Whites had various headquarters around Russia where they were still fighting, while the Reds were established in Moscow, their new capital. However, no such clarification was offered. Not surprisingly, the man handing the memo to Graves, the Secretary of State for War, Newton Baker, warned him: 'Watch your step; you will be walking on eggs loaded with dynamite.'[10]

The British, French and Italians all sent small contingents, but the Americans' main partner in the intervention was Japan, which promised to send a similar number of men in response to a specific invitation by Wilson sent to Tokyo, but soon built up a far greater force, reaching 72,000 at its peak in eastern Siberia and Manchuria. Their machinations were complex and quite uncertain, too, given there was considerable public reluctance to get involved. Up to this point the Japanese had enjoyed an excellent war at little cost, either financially or in terms of casualties. They had joined early, in 1914, on the side of the Allies, but had despatched few men, losing a mere 1,000 in battle, and had benefitted economically from taking over the German colonies in Asia and the Pacific. Now it seemed they might become embroiled in a far bloodier conflict, which domestically elicited widespread opposition. However, there were huge potential advantages in intervention, given Japan's longstanding designs on establishing itself as the dominant power in the Far East, as it would enable the Japanese to consolidate their control of the Chinese Eastern Railway and consequently northern Manchuria. The Japanese were not interested in the fate of the Czechs or in staying permanently in Siberia, but they did have vague, long-term designs on Mongolia. They agreed with the Americans not to go any further west than Irkutsk, but there remained continued mistrust between the providers of the two biggest forces during the whole of the Siberian intervention.

The Japanese rather betrayed their unstated motive through their strong support for the worst elements fighting in Siberia: the freelance armies led by violent Cossack officers, whom they showered with money, arms and practical support. The two most significant, and bloodthirsty, were led respectively by self-styled generals, Gregori Semyonov and Ivan Kalmykov, who seemed to be in an ugly contest to demonstrate which was the most reprehensible. Semyonov, with his huge head and his brilliant eyes, was described as a 'Heathcliff of the steppes' by Peter Fleming, but was called a 'murderer, robber and dissolute scoundrel' by Graves. Semyonov fancied himself as a bit of a Napoleon, always carrying in his pocket the great French general's book on warfare, *Maxims*, though it was unclear whether he ever read it, and tucking his arm, ridiculously, into his jacket in true Bonaparte style. As the civil war unfolded, Semyonov managed to raise an army of around 2,000 local Cossacks and other mercenaries, and briefly grabbed a section of the Trans-Siberian, the junction with the Chinese Eastern Railway, and based himself at Manchouli, the border town. He was rewarded for his efforts with £10,000 of British money from the Foreign Office, which was eager to support any potential uprising against the Bolsheviks, but soon realized that they were supporting a bloodthirsty bandit. The Japanese, however, were not so picky and Semyonov benefitted enormously from their largesse, since 'the chaos he created in eastern Siberia suited the Japanese, whose intention was to prevent Russia from uniting under any government that might restore its place as a rival to Japan in the Far East'.[11] This highlighted the difference with the British, who did want to see a strong Russian force come together in Siberia in order to fight the Bolsheviks. The French, meanwhile, still dreamed of creating an Eastern Front to divert German resources away from the Western battle zone. Figes sums up the confusion among the Allies in one neat sentence: 'None of the Western powers knew what their aims were in Siberia; but neither did any of them want to be left out.'[12]

When Japanese funds dried up Semyonov simply went on raids, robbing banks and Chinese merchants, but mostly the Japanese always seemed ready to replenish his coffers. He used his fleet of nine armoured trains, captured from the tsarist Russian army, to patrol and control a lengthy section of line around his base. These trains were given deliberately awesome but rather puerile names, such as *The Merciless*, *The Terrible* and *The Destroyer*, which was the most formidable, shielded by steel plate and eighteen inches of reinforced concrete and equipped with four mounted cannons and numerous machine guns.

Kalmykov, who based himself further east around Khabarovsk, had become the leader of the Ussuri Cossacks after murdering the legitimate heir to that position. Graves was even harsher in his estimate of Kalmykov than of Semyonov: 'He was the worst scoundrel I ever saw or heard of . . . Kalmykov murdered with his own hands, where Semyonov ordered others to kill, and therein lies the difference between Kalmykov and Semyonov.'[13] He terrorized the local population and held up trains almost at will.

The Americans hated the murderous Cossacks, not least because they could do nothing to lessen their barbarity. The dislike was mutual. Kalmykov took to throwing dead horses from his trains at American encampments in the vain expectation they would stay away because of the stench. The Americans were prevented from launching attacks on the Cossacks by their terms of engagement, which were supposed to be simply to protect the Czechs and the Vladivostok booty. Consequently, they suffered these indignities without retaliation. Moreover, when the Americans tried to persuade the Japanese to clamp down on the two Cossack generals, they were told that this was out of the question as it would be interfering in Russian affairs. In his memoirs, Graves was unequivocal that supporting the Cossack generals had been a massive mistake: 'It should be remembered that Semyonov and Kalmykov were brigands and murderers. They had no character which would deter them from committing any kind of offence.' The two men's main activity was to disrupt the railway, which their sponsors, the Japanese, were supposed to protect: 'Within their areas of operation, Semyonov in the Trans-Baikal and Kalmykov around Khabarovsk, these two men routinely interrupted traffic on the railway, harassed Allied railway engineers, held up trains, hijacked weapon shipments and other valuable goods destined for the Omsk government [the Whites' unified headquarters], and pursued brutal anti-partisan activities against local populations, even where no partisan forces were present.'[14]

It is almost impossible to exaggerate the cruel and murderous activities of these two renegade commanders, who had the support of the eventual leader of the Whites, Admiral Aleksandr Kolchak. (A measure of the bloodthirstiness of the Whites is revealed by the experience of my father, Boris Kougoulsky. A former army officer who deserted and fled to Odessa after the Revolution, he visited White headquarters in Ekaterinadar (now Krasnodar) in 1918 as a potential recruit, but was deterred when he was shown men hanging from every telegraph pole along the road, some of whom had their penises cut off and stuffed into their mouths. His old commander, Colonel Livitsky, who had invited him there for a week told him: 'They are all Communists, they tried to take over one of our ships and we stopped them.' My father, who hated the Bolsheviks with a passion to the end of his days, nevertheless was disgusted at these men's treatment and found himself being moved by the courage of the remaining prisoners who cussed loudly at their executioners, but showed no sign of fear, despite knowing their imminent fate. He refused to sign up, returning to Odessa, fortunately for me, and later fled to Marseilles and Paris.) Indeed, this sort of behaviour was also noted by Graves, who wrote: 'The general belief is that a mere statement that a man is a Bolshevik is enough to cause him to disappear.'[15]

Semyonov, who boasted that he could not sleep at night if he had not killed someone that day, set up a series of killing stations where his enemies were taken daily for execution and on one day in August 1919 a trainload of 350 prisoners were machine-gunned at one of these stations. At the end of the war, US Army Intelligence estimated that Semyonov was responsible for 30,000 executions in that year alone. Kalmykov was less prolific, but even less discriminating. He is reckoned to have killed at least 1,500 people without trial, and, most notoriously, he murdered two members of the Swedish Red Cross and stole their aid money. According to one historian, Kalmykov 'boasted that killing never became monotonous to him because he varied his execution methods'[16].

These two were the worst, but not the only, White war criminals. General Boris Annenkov, for example, who led a group known as the Semipalatinsk Cossacks, massacred 2,200 Jews in a pogrom in Yekaterinburg in July 1919. The Cossacks, of course, claimed that they were merely responding to similar massacres in the Red Terror, but that hardly justifies their action. Kolchak was directly implicated in his own reign of terror. Desperate to enlist as many local Siberian peasants as possible, his officers went to villages to pressgang any men of the right age. If they hid, the local older men were tortured and killed: 'Some were beaten so badly that their blood splattered on the walls. Others had their arms broken and their teeth knocked out . . . some were partially hanged and then let down . . . After being tortured in this fashion, the old men in these villages were then shot to death, generally feet first and then up along the rest of the body. Sometimes six or more bullets were used to kill one victim.'[17] Sergei Rosanov, Kolchak's commander in the Far East, instructed his men to kill every tenth person in a village whose inhabitants refused to reveal the location of partisan leaders. Rosanov later went on a killing spree in Vladivostok, murdering at least 500 people in the dying days of the Kolchak regime. As Fleming elegantly sums up the various massacres and outrages on both sides, 'All one can say is that the pot was black, and so was the kettle.'[18] Indeed, the Allied support for these war criminals would prove to be counter-productive. General Graves felt that local people realized that it was the presence of foreign troops that allowed these murderous Cossacks a free rein and that made them far more sympathetic to the Reds: 'The acts of these Cossacks and other Kolchak leaders under the protection of foreign troops were the greatest asset to Bolshevism that could have been devised by man.'[19]

The various Allied forces arrived during the summer of 1918 and created a chaotic situation in Vladivostok, where military men in all kinds of uniform milled around, unclear of their role. The British sent an almost farcically ill-suited group, the Middlesex Regiment,[20] led by the Labour MP for Stoke-on-Trent, Colonel John Ward, an active trade unionist, who, interestingly, had been the founder and first general secretary of the wonderfully named Navvies, Bricklayers' Labourers and General Labourers' Union. According to Peter Fleming the regiment was 'composed of men graded B1 (i.e., unfit for active service in a theatre of war) and this imperialist spearhead was affectionately known as the "Hernia Battalion".'[21] Moreover, sent hastily from nearby Hong Kong, they arrived in early August without basic necessary equipment, such as tents or mosquito nets, a serious omission in the Siberian summer, and with black fur coats and hats to use in the winter, not a sensible choice for fighting in the snow – although, of course, they were not supposed to fight, but merely to help the Czechs, whatever that meant.

With the arrival of the Americans in September, responsibility for guarding the eastern section of the Trans-Siberian was divided between the Americans and the Japanese, since the Czechs, supported by various White groups, controlled all the section west of Lake Baikal. By this time the resourceful Czechs had overthrown the local Soviets and the Japanese were well established, having ousted the Communists from their stronghold around Khabarovsk. The Trans-Siberian Railway, therefore, was now entirely in Allied hands. The American forces were concentrated at the Eastern end on the Ussuri Railway, and also given the task of guarding the Suchan coal mines west of Vladivostok, which supplied much of the railway, and the rest of the line remained in Czech hands.

By the time these Allied forces had assembled in Siberia, the situation in Europe had changed radically with the Germans on the run and clearly heading for defeat. Now President Wilson was even less keen on the US troops becoming involved in any military action, which left poor Graves bemused, his dynamited eggshells even more fragile, given he had no clear remit on what precisely he was supposed to be doing; he decided on a policy of non-intervention which at times infuriated the other Allied forces. He disappointed the Japanese, as he adamantly refused to submit to their command, and the relationship between the two main forces was fraught with tension. When the Armistice was announced in November 1918 the situation became even more complicated, as Admiral Kolchak, who had been sponsored by the British, was persuaded to support a coup d'état in Omsk, at the western end of the line, 4,000 miles from Vladivostok. Rather strangely, as conspiracy theorists have subsequently pointed out, the takeover was announced by Kolchak just after the Middlesex battalion and General Alfred Knox, the head of the British Military Mission in Russia, arrived in the town.

Knox was a Russia expert who had been the military attaché in Petrograd and a fervent anti-Communist who had previously gone to Tokyo to meet Kolchak and enlist him in the Intervention. Knox had form, too, in terms of political interference, having worked to try to overthrow the Kerensky regime, and he had actively supported various White senior figures. The fact that Kolchak's action took place a week after the Armistice suggests, too, that there was British involvement in the decision. A second battalion of British troops, the 1st/9th Hampshires,[22] arrived in Omsk soon after the coup, as did the advance guard of a Canadian force; however, the rest of what was to have been 5,000 men were never sent by Ottawa because the Canadian government was worried about their discipline, which had deteriorated markedly after the Armistice. That episode, showing that there was no appetite for another war, demonstrates precisely why the Czechs never received the mass support they had desperately sought.

The different attitudes to the Kolchak coup by the various forces brought together to fight the Bolsheviks and maintain the operation of the Trans-Siberian revealed its weakness and instability. While the British welcomed the coup, the American soldiers were largely unhappy about it and Graves noted that the very presence of US troops seemed to signal support for a regime that was autocratic and unpopular among local people. The Czechs were unequivocally opposed to it and became deeply resentful. They disliked Kolchak's extreme right-wing and anti-Semitic politics, as they were largely sympathetic to the left-wing socialist revolutionaries, who were a mix of democratic socialists and Bolshevik sympathizers rather than communists, and had been their main allies during much of the battle over the Trans-Siberian. The summer months had been the high point of Czech control of the railway, when they had still been optimistic about being relieved by the Allies. Their force of 40,000 men scattered along the line would never be enough to hold

After the completion of the line, the Russian government made considerable efforts to attract affluent Western passengers by providing luxurious facilities, such as this saloon car seen in 1903.

Buryat people at Talbaga station in eastern Siberia, where they form a considerable proportion of several districts.

A waiting room for third-class passengers, like this one in Krasnoyarsk pictured in 1905, were designed to a standard spartan style.

Vladivostok station where future Tsar Nicholas II inaugurated construction of the line.

Passengers on a platform 1915.

Yaroslavsky station in Moscow, the terminus of the line in 1908...

...and in 1974.

A railwayman stands beside snow-covered tracks in 1978.

A team of volunteers, members of the Young Communist League, at the Yaroslavsky Railway Terminal in Moscow prior to their departure to construction sites of the Baikal-Amur Mainline.

The completion of the Baikal-Amur Mainline was announced several times by the Russian government, including on this occasion in October 1984 but, in fact, it was not completed until 1991 – and even then required much remedial work.

Plaque at Vladivostok station commemorating 100 years of service on the line.

Novosibirsk station, the grandest in Russia, designed by Nikolai Voloshinov in a classical style and containing several huge waiting halls lined with Soviet paintings, including one depicting the 1960 U-2 spying incident.

The Circum-Baikal railway near Angasolka, which no longer forms part of the mainline but is retained to serve local villages and tourists.

The *Rossiya* Trans-Siberian train arriving at Ulan-Ude en route to Vladivostok, November 2007.

Ulan-Ude station, dawn in November 2012. The smoke is from the coal used to heat the inside of the train.

Christian Wolmar and Deborah Maby with a sleeping car attendant.

on to 4,500 miles of railway in the long term and they had started to lose ground in the weeks running up to the Kolchak coup. As it dawned on the Czechs that no one was coming over the hill to rescue them, they refused to fight the Bolsheviks in Kolchak's name, and they began preparations to head eastwards and go home. Kolchak dismissed the Czechs as insignificant and was rude to their leaders, foolishly failing to realize that he owed them huge respect for having taken over the Trans-Siberian, and set about raising a big enough army to head for Moscow. He would come to regret his haughty dismissal of the Czechs.

Kolchak, never one for modesty, called himself the Supreme Ruler of All the Russias, and proved to be a totally unsuitable candidate for high political office. One of his contemporaries described him as 'neurotic, quick to lose his temper, [with] no idea of the hard realities of life . . . no plans of his own, no system, no will; like soft wax from which his advisers and intimates can fashion whatever they like'.[23]

The Allies may have been reluctant to support the Whites with troops, but they did not shy away from financial and material aid. In the first six months of 1919 Kolchak received enormous support from the Allies. Vladivostok again became a staging post for a remarkable flow of supplies. Figes lists it as 'one million rifles, 15,000 machine guns, 700 field guns, 800 million rounds of ammunition, and clothing and equipment for half a million men'.[24] Enough for a sizeable army, but through incompetence and corruption Kolchak never managed to make proper use of the Allies' munificence

Kolchak's worst failing was his knack of alienating much of his potential support. He and his officers strutted about in their epaulettes, expressing haughty contempt for the people around them and exhibiting exactly the same kind of arrogance that had led to the demise of the tsar. Siberia's history meant it was not fertile ground for the Bolshevik cause, but nor did its people want the kind of oppressive regime that Kolchak seemed to offer. The peasants, in particular, hated him and joined the partisans fighting against the Whites – though not necessarily for the Reds – in droves. The Siberians in general had widely supported the socialist revolutionaries in elections, and they were dismayed by Kolchak's arrogance and his brand of right-wing politics. They, too, proved to be reluctant recruits. Kolchak's inability to mobilize the population contrasted with the Reds' knack of attracting local people to their cause. He also failed to exploit the goodwill of the Allies, stupidly alienating the US forces by pouring out fatuous propaganda against their troops, one pro-Kolchak newspaper suggesting that they were all 'Bolshevik Jews', when most, in fact, came from the very goyish state of Illinois.

The harsh truth was that Kolchak was never going to deliver the hoped-for counter-revolution, because he was an incompetent commander leading a disparate group of mostly corrupt, self-interested and arrogant officers. Probably nothing is more revealing than the situation at Omsk, when Kolchak embarked on his main offensive towards Orenburg. He left behind a city in which 2,000 of his 'staff' officers spent leisurely days sitting in cafés or shuffling paper in offices to administer an army that at its peak had 100,000 men. Omsk, according to Fleming, 'was an Augean stables, but it soon became obvious that Kolchak was no Hercules'.[25] Corruption was endemic; vendettas flared up between different groups and revenge, in the form of murder and executions, was all too common. Nevertheless, there was still fun to be had: 'Cafés, casinos and brothels worked around the clock.' Kolchak also neglected his own men. When Graves travelled to Omsk in the summer of 1919 he came upon a trainload of Kolchak's sick and wounded troops, perishing in wagons, seemingly abandoned on the line to their fate. 'Many of these men were too ill to help themselves and there was only one nurse to five or six hundred men. We looked into the first boxcar and found two dead men and a third was dying, while a sick comrade held his head and tried to give him a drink of water.'[26] Some of the men had crawled out of the wagons and lay on the ground, exhausted from the effort. Yet a few hundred yards away there was a 'gay crowd' of a thousand people enjoying a concert in a park.

The Trans-Siberian itself was in a poor state of repair, given its overuse and neglect during the war. Bridges, depots, water towers and other railway equipment had been wrecked by fighting and sabotage. Tunnels had been damaged, and rolling stock and locomotives had deteriorated due to the lack of routine maintenance. To remedy this, in January 1919 the Allies created a joint committee – the Inter-Allied Railway Agreement – to operate and maintain both the Trans-Siberian and the Chinese Eastern Railway. The committee, composed of representatives of every nation with troops in Siberia, was well funded by the Allies. The main four countries – the United States, Japan, Britain and France – each contributed $5 million and undertook vast amounts of work to repair war and weather damage. The Technical Board that carried out the work was based at Harbin and headed by an American, John F. Stevens, and the division of responsibility for the sections of the railway was formalized. The Americans were responsible for around 500 miles and the Czechs all of the Western section, while the Japanese retained control of 2,300 miles, and the Chinese looked after the Chinese Eastern Railway with some Japanese oversight. All this suggested that the Allies expected to be in it for the long haul, although their intense activity raised some big questions: given that the war in the west was over, and the Czechs whom they were supposed to be 'protecting' wanted to get back home, especially after the Treaty of Versailles, signed in June 1919, granted them statehood, what on earth were all of these occupying troops still doing in Siberia? And why were these foreigners running the railway? The explanation differed between the various parties in the Alliance. The Japanese, who refused to accept the authority of the Board over their military activities, continued to be involved in attacks on the local partisans who supported the Bolsheviks, while the Americans remained steadfastly – painfully even – neutral and argued that guarding the railway was their sole purpose. The Japanese also refused to withdraw from the Chinese Eastern Railway, even though the line was supposed to be the responsibility of the Chinese.

That question about the presence of foreign troops in Siberia became all the more embarrassing as the Kolchak regime disintegrated. Kolchak's high point was in the spring of 1919, when his three armies had advanced to a maximum of 250 miles. The Whites had taken Perm soon after the coup, but then faced with the vast emptiness that could not be covered in winter, their advance was stalled. In the meantime, however, Kolchak's supply lines were disintegrating and his support base dwindling. The vast supplies sent to Vladivostok were not reaching him as the Trans-Siberian was all too easy to ambush. Partisans and the Reds, too, were both attacking the line wherever they could. According to Figes, 'The partisans' destruction of miles of track and their constant ambushes of trains virtually halted the transportation of vital supplies along the Trans-Siberian Railway to Kolchak's armies for much of the offensive.'[27] Even Kolchak's supposed allies, the two evil Cossack generals Semyonov and Kalmykov, expended more energy attacking and plundering trains than in furthering the White cause. The trains that did get through unscathed only managed to do so at great cost of bribes, which had to be paid to railway workers and bandits alike. Much of the equipment fell into the hands of the Bolsheviks, prompting Leon Trotsky to display his sense of humour by telegraphing Knox to express his gratitude.

According to Graves, 'One hundred thousand men clothed, armed and equipped by the British had joined the anti-Kolchak forces by December 1919 and the Bolsheviks wired General Knox thanking him for supplying clothing and equipment for the Soviet forces.'[28]

Trotsky was, in fact, running the war from an armoured train, the real-life version, of course, of the terrifying Commissar Strelnikov in *Doctor Zhivago*, the book based on Boris Pasternak's experiences in Siberia. In two and a half years, from the summer of 1918, Trotsky made no fewer than thirty-six trips, totalling precisely 65,660 miles (he was a bit of a trainspotter and kept a detailed record), many of them on the Trans-Siberian, in a well-equipped armoured train that became his headquarters and a rallying point for the Red Army. The train of the *Predrevoyensovie* – Chairman of the Revolutionary Military Council (Trotsky's title) – was part armoured train, part car carrier and part office, from which Trotsky ran the civil war. Although its contents and make-up changed over time, the train always included 'a secretariat, a printing press, a telegraph station, a radio station, an electric-power station, a library, a garage and a bath'.[29] It was so heavy that it needed two locomotives to haul it and later it was split into two.

In his carriage Trotsky 'received those who brought reports, held conferences with local military and civil authorities, studied telegraphic despatches, dictated orders and articles'.[30] When the train stopped, Trotsky would then use the motor cars carried on the train, which were heavily protected by machine-gunners, to drive to the front line or to local army barracks. He reported how his visits galvanized local support and boosted morale for several weeks afterwards: 'The work of the train was all bound up with the building-up of the army, with its education, its administration, and its supply.'[31] The train was a mobile support base for units which were scattered, at one point, across sixteen different battle zones. Not only did it carry a good supply of equipment, such as boots, underwear, leather jackets, medicaments, machine guns, field glasses, maps, watches and all sorts of gifts, but also, according to Trotsky, 'we always had in reserve a few zealous communists to fill in the breaches [and] a hundred or so of good fighting men . . . They all wore leather uniforms, which always make men look heavily imposing.'[32]

Trotsky was in constant communication with Moscow through the telegraph wires, sending out demands for supplies and battle orders, and he boasted that 'We could receive radio messages from the Eiffel Tower, from Nauen [a major German transmission station west of Berlin], and from other stations, thirteen in all, with Moscow, of course, foremost.'[33] Thanks to this technically advanced feature, the train received constant news about events in the rest of the world, which were conveyed to the passengers through a train newspaper.

Kolchak had no such sophisticated back-up. He was ultimately defeated not only by his own incompetence and the strength of the Red Army, but also the sheer logistics of trying to take over such a vast nation backed by just one thin railway line. The Reds had the whole of European Russia behind them. It would have taken a far greater leader, with much more local support, to sweep through Russia; and many before and after him, such as Napoleon and Hitler, similarly failed. The hopes in early 1919 that an all-out White assault from the four points of the compass would triumph over the Reds proved unrealistic and soon began to unravel. As Kolchak met fierce resistance when he headed west, the other White attacks started to disintegrate, hampered by the failure of the various forces to communicate with one another and co-ordinate their efforts. They were riven by fighting factions and politics, since they ranged from left-wing supporters of Kerensky to traditional supporters of absolute monarchy, who sought to avenge the murder of the royal family. By the end of March 1919 Allied forces had been driven out of Ukraine. The following month they started withdrawing from Central Asia and soon the various assaults in Transcaucasia, Baku and Archangelsk petered out. Kolchak was soon left on his own. Nevertheless, the civil war was still raging across Russia and it was not until the autumn that the issue was no longer in doubt. By then Kolchak was already in retreat.

The whole idea of a White counter-revolution spearheaded from Siberia was to prove utterly unrealistic and delusional, dreamt up by optimistic armchair generals and politicians thousands of miles away from the theatre of war. Numerous promises had been broken. At one point the British had committed themselves to support Kolchak 'up to any figure necessary', but dumping lots of expensive equipment in Vladivostok could not make up for the lack of boots on the ground. In truth, the British and the other Allies could never had mustered sufficient numbers from their war-weary forces to mount a serious offensive via Vladivostok. Their soldiers were not only sick of war, but many had left-wing leanings and consequently would have baulked at taking up arms against the Bolsheviks on a mission to overthrow the Revolution. The railway, in any case, was far too vulnerable and long to be used as a supply line to wage war in European Russia. It was, indeed, the lack of men rather than money that was to prove decisive.

By July the Red Army was heading along the Trans-Siberian, having recaptured Perm and Yekaterinburg. The writing was on the wall. Panic set in at Omsk, where the Whites were regrouping and waves of refugees, fleeing the Reds' advance, were arriving in droves. Yet all would not have been lost had the Whites been better organized. According to Fleming, 'The Red Army's spearheads were weak, over-extended and largely dependent on the railway.'[34] However, Kolchak's forces were in disarray and he was not in a position to take advantage of the Reds' weakness. Supplies were running out as the Trans-Siberian had stopped functioning westwards. Kolchak decided to flee in a fleet of seven trains, one of which carried the hoard of the tsar's gold,[35] whose worth was variously estimated between £50 million and £80 million, that he had foolishly been sitting on for more than a year despite his government's shortage of money, which meant that soldiers went unpaid and lacked supplies; even the railway workers had not received their wages, which was to make Kolchak's escape eastwards more difficult.

With barely a fight the Reds took over Omsk on 14 November 1919, almost precisely a year after Kolchak's declaration of becoming Supreme Leader and just a few hours after his retinue had left. The White leaders, more intent on saving their skins than fighting for the cause, had departed hastily and left behind a veritable cornucopia in the city. The Bolsheviks found enough equipment to keep them going for months, including 2,000 machine guns, one million rifles, three million shells, sixteen armoured trains as well as 1,000 American-made armoured trucks. They captured 35,000 troops, including 1,000 officers, and found enough uniforms to clothe 30,000 men, a measure of the White officials' preference for storing equipment to sell at a profit, rather than distributing it to the troops.

While the Trans-Siberian had already seen terrible instances of human suffering and cruelty during the war, those that ensued during the retreat would be far more horrific. The retreat was an ugly, bloody episode that resulted in thousands of deaths and untold human suffering in the face of extreme callousness from the military on all sides. As the line was now double-tracked throughout and there was no traffic heading westwards, the southern rails became the slow line and the northern ones, normally used by Moscow-bound trains, the fast reserved for the likes of Kolchak and his retinue, which included many of the officers' wives and Kolchak's mistress, Anna Timireva. In reality 'fast' was a misnomer since progress even for those with priority was painfully slow, given the condition of the railway, the war damage and the shortage of coal. On the other track a tragedy was unfolding as thousands of panic-stricken refugees sought to flee from the advancing Reds. The trains moved slowly, if at all, given the lack of fuel, and once steam could no longer be produced, the locomotives became paralysed as pipes froze and snapped in the cold. Pumps at watering stations ran out and passengers had to form human chains to fill the boiler with snow, a laborious and slow process. Food and fuel to keep warm were scarce. Even those with money could not buy supplies as the Omsk paper currency was no longer accepted by the local peasants, who only wanted coins or valuables.

There were equally terrible scenes on the Trakt, the old, much-neglected post road, which often ran parallel to the railway, on which a stream of bedraggled humanity, both soldiers and civilians, trudged slowly eastwards, on foot or on horseback. They were the poorest of the refugees, peasants with a few scrawny cattle, deserters, orphans and the destitute, who could not afford a rail ticket or whose train had given up the ghost: 'The travellers on the Trakt looked up at the trains as shipwrecked men on a raft might look up at a passing liner, which they know will not stop to pick them up.'[36]

The worst suffering was in the 'typhus trains'. Once the epidemic broke out it sowed panic along the line. When a hospital train suspected of having typhus victims aboard arrived at a station, 'the railway authorities did their utmost to pass them through without a halt, in total disregard of the occupants' need for succour or supplies. Often a whole truckload of human beings, boycotted by their fellow travellers, perished.'[37] Corpses were stripped and, becoming quickly frozen stiff, were piled like logs to be left for burial when the soil softened in the spring. Red troops entering Novonikolayevsk (Novosibirsk) found 30,000 dead alone. One estimate suggests that as many as a million people died in the exodus along the Trans-Siberian, the vast majority from typhus.

While Kolchak managed to travel past these terrible scenes, it did not do him any good It was his failure to get on with the Czechs, who still controlled the Western sections of the line, that proved his undoing. A month into his journey, having reached Mariinsk, a mere 600 miles east of Omsk, Kolchak was instructed by a Czech officer – a mere second lieutenant in the transportation corps but acting on orders from his high command – to direct the Supreme Ruler's trains on to the slow line. The Czechs, who ensured their own troops had access to the fast line, were becoming unpopular with local people as they headed east, and they wanted to publicly dissociate themselves from the deeply reviled Supreme Ruler. The fact that Kolchak needed seven trains, each so heavy they were hauled by two locomotives, whereas even the tsar had travelled in just one, and Trotsky two, did not help his cause. After stuttering forward at the rate of a few miles a day for a week, Kolchak then really blew it, sending a telegrammed instruction to Semyonov to block the Czech progress towards Vladivostok by blowing up tunnels and bridges in Transbaikalia. Quite apart from the fact that this was effectively a declaration of war on the Czechs, it was a kamikaze-style suggestion, since it would have prevented Kolchak from making any further progress eastwards. Worse, the instruction, though coded, was intercepted by the Czechs.

After being held up at Nizhneudinsk, 300 miles short of Irkutsk for a couple of weeks, Kolchak's coach was allowed to proceed eastwards, but gradually it became clear that all the stations were in the hands of partisans; eventually, too, the train drivers were replaced by men wearing red rosettes. It looked ominous for Kolchak, who remained guarded by Czechs, and so it proved. He was taken off the train and driven to Irkutsk, where he was handed over to the Bolsheviks, who had just gained control of the city. After being interrogated for three weeks and providing much fascinating insight for historians, he was supposed to be sent for trial in Moscow, but a brief counter-insurgency by the Whites led to fears that he would be captured. Instead he was hastily executed on the frozen waters of the Angara river and thrown into a hole created precisely for the easy disposal of bodies. His gold hoard fell into the hands of the Reds, too.

The Allies realized that with the collapse of the Kolchak regime there was nothing to keep them in Siberia. Ironically, though, all except the Japanese left before the Czechs, whom they had supposed to be protecting. The British troops were apparently deeply upset at having to leave behind numerous dogs they had adopted during their stay, but the Americans, clearly more hot-blooded, had paid greater attention to the womenfolk than the local canines, and consequently took with them eighty wives, married en masse by the local American chaplain just before departure. At least the Hampshires on their return to Britain were given sixty-two days' paid leave to compensate for the awful conditions they had endured. The British left by January, the Americans by April, but together they provided shipping for the Czechs, who numbered around 57,000, to leave by September.

The Japanese, however, lingered. And lingered. They retained a small area around Vladivostok and later took over the southern half of the island of Sakhalin off the coast. In the south, the main White army, with little foreign support, fought a vain campaign against the Reds, gaining considerable territory at first. It was eventually beaten back 250 miles from Moscow and was finally defeated in Crimea in 1920. The other Allied forces had by then withdrawn, and eastern Siberia remained, therefore, the last part of Russia not directly under the control of what the Bolsheviks now called the Russian Soviet Federative Socialist Republic. The Far Eastern Republic, created a couple of months after Kolchak's death, was conceived by the Bolsheviks as a buffer state between the new communist state, the RSFSR, and the remaining territory held by the Japanese, creating a breathing space in an area ravaged by the war that would allow it to recover economically; its capital was initially at Verkhneudinsk (now Ulan-Ude) and later at Chita. The Far Eastern Republic was not actually run by the Bolsheviks, but rather by the remnants of the old democratic left groups; the area remained unstable, however, because the remaining White forces, concentrated in Vladivostok, still considered anything except right-wing dictatorship unacceptable.

The fledgling republic had democratic ambitions, voting in a constitution based on the American model in January 1921, but it was a hopeless enterprise. In May there was a White coup, but when Semyonov arrived in Vladivostok to take over as commander-in-chief, the Japanese, who had backed the takeover, finally lost patience with him and sent him away, installing their own puppet leaders instead. Semyonov fled to Europe and then fought alongside the Japanese in the Second World War, but was captured by the Soviets in 1945 and was hanged the following year. His fellow murderous Cossack, Kalmykov, made the mistake in 1921 of fleeing to China, a bad choice given the raids he had carried out on Chinese citizens, and he was quickly killed.

After the Allies left, the Japanese had remained on the pretext that they needed to protect Japanese residents in the area. This was the result of the Japanese having been victims of the worst attack on any of the Allied forces in March 1920. In Nikolaevsk, at the mouth of the Amur, Yakov Triapitsyn, a particularly violent anarchist vaguely allied to the Reds, massacred 700 Japanese soldiers and residents, as well as up to 6,000 local Russians in revenge for a failed Japanese attack. The massacre became a cause célèbre in Japan and enabled the troops to stay another two years.

With the Japanese eventually leaving the country in the summer of 1922, panic swept the White Russian community. As the Red Army approached, thinly disguised as the army of the Far Eastern Republic, thousands of Russians fled abroad to escape the new regime. These troops retook Vladivostok on 25 October 1922, effectively bringing the Russian Civil War to a close and the Far Eastern Republic was quickly absorbed by Soviet Russia. Japan retained the formerly Russian northern half of Sakhalin Island until 1925, ostensibly as compensation for the massacre at Nikolaevsk. All in all the Japanese lost just under 1,500 men in Siberia, far more than the rest of the Allies put together and more than had been killed in the First World War.

The civil war had left the Trans-Siberian in a terrible state. The partisans had destroyed more than 800 bridges, and as the various Allied troops departed, the railway had been badly neglected. Fleming, as ever, found the words to describe its fallen state, transformed from a remarkable engineering triumph and source of national pride to a scene of tragedy and despair: 'Nobody could deny that the Trans-Siberian Railway had a certain greatness, a certain exotic nobility of conception, a touch almost of Jules Verne. Now, less than twenty years after its completion, this main artery of progress, this symbol of Imperial vigour and vision had lost its purpose and its dignity. The proud railway had become a Via Dolorosa, a long narrow stage on which countless tragedies were enacted . . . misery and squalor and cowardice, pain and fear and cold, carrion and excrement.'[38]

The Soviets, however, were not going to leave it like that. This 'artery of progress' was a key part of their plans for the future and they recognized that the Trans-Siberian was their greatest railway.

# TEN

# THE BIG RED
# RAILWAY

The greatest irony of the Trans-Siberian Railway is that while it was built at the instigation of an absolute monarch to help consolidate his hold on the Russian Empire, it was in many ways far more in keeping with the type of project upon which his successors, the Bolsheviks, would have embarked. The railway fitted in well with the Communists' love of *grands projets* as a way of illustrating their power and competence; and the existence of the Trans-Siberian allowed them to indulge in this habit, with Siberia becoming the location of their main big inter-war schemes. The Bolsheviks made good use of the Trans-Siberian, realizing its importance in exploiting the wealth of Siberia, and they set about both improving the main line and adding numerous branches, as well as later building a second line to the north deep into the Siberian steppe.

The civil war had demonstrated to the Bolsheviks the Trans-Siberian's military importance, but they soon found that trains could be used in a rather more subtle way to establish themselves over the furthest corners of the nation they were now trying to control. The enormous size and underdeveloped nature of the country gave rise to great difficulties in trying to spread the message of revolution. The Bolsheviks needed a mobile and reliable system of communication between the centre and the regions, and railways offered an adaptable and relatively cheap solution.

Following Trotsky's successful use of an armoured train as a highly mobile military headquarters-cum-rallying point for supporters, the Bolsheviks made widespread use of the railway to promote their propaganda through the medium of agitprop trains (*agitpoezda* – short for 'agitational propaganda train'). The idea started with the conversion of a compartment on troop trains into a centre for the distribution of propaganda, such as leaflets, newspapers and posters, and from there the concept of the agit train was born. Instead of just one compartment or even carriage, a whole train was devoted to spreading the Communist message. The first agit train, the *V. I. Lenin* (its full name was the *V. I. Lenin Mobile Military Front Train*), which made a trial run from Moscow to Kazan in August 1918, consisted of nine coaches; these included a bookshop, a library, office space and living quarters, with the aim of taking literature, posters, ideas and revolutionary fervour deep into the provinces.

The train spent two weeks distributing material to units of the Red Army, which were at the time beginning to fight back against Kolchak's forces. The success of this experiment encouraged Trotsky to immediately order five more agit trains, along with an agitprop steamer for the River Volga, a series of agit lorries for regions without railways, and (for those really hard to reach places in winter) agit sledges. A whole series of agit points (*agitpunkty*), initially mostly sited at railway junctions, which were both propaganda distribution centres and community halls, were also created, but it was the trains which were 'altogether more dramatic and, in the short term, more important'.[1]

The five new trains developed the original concept even further, often having as many as eighteen coaches, brightly decorated by artists and covered with slogans. They had all the latest mod cons, because the Communists liked to show they were up to date; the carriages were therefore linked by an internal phone system and equipped with a radio for direct contact with Moscow. The trains were also accompanied by the usual bureaucratic baggage, including a political department, an information department and, rather strangely, a complaints office to show that the comrades were listening to the people. One carriage contained a fully functioning printing press, which could quickly produce newspapers covering local news and events. The author of the standard work on early Soviet cinema, Richard Taylor, stresses the vital nature of agit trains in helping the Communists establish themselves across the country, as they were a way of reaching the people directly, avoiding the inefficient old machinery of government: 'Agit trains were a fast, flexible, more direct and dynamic method of communication with the masses.'[2] They had other advantages, too: they created an immediate and powerful government presence in the most remote parts of the nation, since they were staffed by a large crew of more than 100 enthusiastic party workers including specialists who could address particular regional issues, such as improving agricultural production or building cheap housing. Their very mobility, too, was an advantage, as they were seen by the people as 'direct representatives of supreme power',[3] a novel idea in communities that might not have seen an official presence – other than the police and military – for years or even decades.

Ever eager to side with modernism, the Bolsheviks soon added a film department to the trains, and these showed agit films (*agitki*) and newsreels. It was a two-way process as the train's crew produced their own newsreels from the provinces to go back to the centre, which could then be screened nationally to show the best examples of what was happening across the country. The *agitki* were short, not least because of the lack of blank film, and each had a key message presented in a strongly visual and simple manner.

Lenin himself laid great stress on the importance of newsreel and documentary films to disseminate Bolshevik propaganda; and, given the lack of cinemas in rural areas, the agit trains were a key method of spreading the message.

Films with agricultural themes were particularly popular. Peasants would stare in awe at how the Revolution could bring relief from the back-breaking toil in their lives, through such innovations as mechanical cream-making machines and hydraulic peat-lifters. Mostly, the films were shown on huge screens in the open air, the images projected through a window in the side of a specially adapted carriage, but there was also a cinema seating 150 people on the train for use in bad weather or for children's shows. We can get an idea of the vast potential reach of these agit films thanks to the Bolsheviks' obsession with precise statistics (not always reliable, of course): 22,800 children watched films on the *V. I. Lenin* in the three months running up to March 1919.

Most of the films were political, with a clear message, portraying graphically the horrors of the tsarist era or the liberating effects of Bolshevism. Some catered for children and general educational topics were also popular. Although the trains travelled round the whole country, Siberia was a particularly frequent recipient of their visits given the remoteness of the region from Moscow. For example, in October 1919, after Kolchak had started retreating, the *V. I. Lenin* went on a three-month trip along the Western Siberia sector with the specific aim of encouraging the peasants to boost the flow of grain from the region to the cities of European Russia at a time of near famine, caused by the conflict in Ukraine, the nation's principal bread basket.

The arrival of the train, signalled in advance by telegraph, became an event of great anticipation and excitement. The local Soviet would plaster the area with posters announcing film shows, meetings and details of the various exhibitions on the train. The trains, like Trotsky's armoured HQ, would carry motor cars, which went to villages up to twenty-five miles either side of the line, with a stock of books and posters to sell. In many areas of Siberia peasants would never have seen a film before and they suddenly found themselves witnessing realistic moving images of their 'great leaders', an experience that must have felt akin to meeting them. For some of the programmes an admission charge was levied, but in parts of Siberia the lack of a cash economy meant that a ticket might be paid for in eggs or other produce.

For the Bolsheviks the agit trains became a learning process on how to communicate with the masses. When the new regime first sent out the trains, the carriage exteriors had been painted by artists who had – with zealous, revolutionary fervour – produced symbolic motifs in the Futuristic style, which the peasants found baffling. Arthur Ransome, the British author and journalist who was one of the few to be allowed to stay in Russia throughout the Revolution, saw the *V. I. Lenin* and found that 'every carriage is decorated with most striking but not very comprehensible pictures in the brightest colours, and the proletariat was called upon to enjoy what the pre-revolutionary artistic public had for the most part failed to understand. Its pictures are "art for art's sake", and cannot have done more than astonish, and perhaps terrify, the peasants and the workmen of the country towns.'[4] They showed scenes of White outrages and the Reds' love for the people, but the uninitiated peasant would have found it difficult to take away the intended message, not necessarily being able to distinguish the goodies from the baddies. Soon, however, more realistic and simple imagery replaced the efforts of the Futuristic artists.

By their nature, agit trains were a transitional measure and the need for them diminished as more permanent workers' centres sprang up across the country. Their heyday was the 1920s and 1930s, although, astonishingly, some were still being used on a limited scale in Siberia as late as the 1970s, and their importance in ensuring the spread of the Revolution should not be underestimated, as Taylor suggests: 'The agit trains represented one of the earliest attempts at the creation and manipulation of a mass communications medium for political purposes.'[5] Ransome concurred, writing, 'I doubt if a more effective instrument of propaganda has ever been devised.'[6]

Apart from sending propaganda trains up and down the line, there was the rather more serious business of restoring the war-damaged Trans-Siberian back to its peacetime state and then further improving it. Stalin was intent on transforming Russia from an agrarian backwater to an emblematic socialist state that would demonstrate the superiority of communism over capitalism, and Siberia was to play a key role in this ambition. While some mines had operated in Siberia in pre-revolutionary days, the Communists sent in numerous teams of geologists and surveyors to assess what else lay beneath the Siberian steppe, and their discoveries attracted great interest. Siberia seemed to have everything, from relatively obscure metals to vast quantities of basic minerals, such as iron ore and coal. It was ripe for exploitation. Despite the completion of the Trans-Siberian and the vast immigration that ensued, the region remained an economic backwater, contributing less than one per cent of the nation's output. Its raw materials – and, to a much lesser extent, agricultural produce – were now seen as vital for the Soviets' wider economic development programme. Given the lack of roads and the difficulties of river transport in the winter, the Trans-Siberian was the only way of moving these minerals and food, which ensured priority was given to repairing and upgrading the line.

The line was patched up quickly after the war, but cleverly Trotsky, who was given responsibility for the railways in the immediate post-war period (a demonstration of how important they were considered to be by Russia's new rulers), arranged for improvements to be carried out simultaneously. The numerous damaged bridges, for example, were replaced by stronger and bigger ones, depots were enlarged and a programme of station rebuilding began. Although money was always scarce, the Soviet government ensured substantial resources were invested into the Trans-Siberian to ensure its efficient functioning, but evidence of the war damage remained apparent for many years. Two American women passengers on the Trans-Siberian, Helen Wilson and Elsie Mitchell, travelling in 1927 – five years after the end of the civil war – noted that all the bridges had been repaired, but that while some new rolling stock had been introduced on to the line, there was still a shortage of locomotives and carriages: 'On the sidings and in the repair yards of every large town may still be seen such a collection of battered and war-damaged engines and freight and passenger cars, broken, splintered, burned, shot to pieces, as fairly baffles description.'[7]

Apart from repairing the line and the railway structures, the Soviet regime needed to re-establish rules for travellers. During the war the Trans-Siberian had effectively become a free railway, with guards often not bothering to collect fares, but pocketing a bribe instead, and passengers travelling illegally: sitting on the buffers or on the roof (since most sections had no tunnels) was a frequent method of obtaining a free ride. In fact, one passenger as late as the 1960s saw people still travelling on the buffers of the steam locomotives that had not yet been phased out.

The Communists imposed new rules to ensure that fares began to be collected again. All the takings, however, were paid into the transport ministry's accounts, which meant that the railway's economics were obscure, to say the least, and its losses could not be assessed. Train services stuttered back into life after the civil war, although passenger traffic, which had virtually ceased during the conflict, was restored at a much less frequent level than in 1913. By 1924 there were just three trains weekly between Moscow and Vladivostok, which went via Perm and the Chinese Eastern Railway (as partisans had blown up two of the spans of the bridge at Khabarovsk) and took 12 days – far longer than before the war. By 1927 that was reduced to just two weekly passenger journeys between the two ends of the line, one via the Amur Railway and Khabarovsk (the bridge having been repaired), the other via Harbin, although there were more trains running on intermediate routes, connecting the main cities of Siberia. The coaches operated by the Compagnie Internationale des Wagons-Lits had been confiscated, but were still running on the line, although Junius B. Wood, the European correspondent of the *Chicago Daily News*, who crossed Siberia on the train in the summer of 1926, found them to be in a poor state with cracked windows, broken wood panels and torn carpets. The dining car fare was grim, too: 'At 3.30 p.m. a plate of soup appeared – greasy hot water poured over cold pieces of fish that had been cooked earlier in bulk. The next course was pre-cooked cauliflower warmed with a sauce of unknown texture. Roast veal, cooked weeks earlier and now dry and hard, smothered in warm brown gravy, without vegetables, was the main course.'[8] (It was not that much different on some of the trains when I travelled on the line in 2012.) At least there was a dining car, though Wood might have been better without it. Another traveller, Malcolm Burr, who went on the Trans-Siberian a couple of years later, found that he could purchase far more appetizing food at the stations from peasant sellers, whose small businesses had not yet been made illegal by the Communists. Indeed, Burr was surprised by the extent of this enterprise and his description is not dissimilar to the list of fare available on the pre-war *wagons-lits*, but now on sale off the train: 'The station markets were allotted a substantial area on the platforms, arranged in crescent-shaped buildings open at the front; behind the counter were peasants selling their goods classified in groups; at one end large stacks of bread, black, brown and white, *kolachi* or rolls and great loaves in abundance and variety and all excellent; another group would be selling bottles carefully labelled "boiled milk",' although a fellow passenger, a doctor, counselled against drinking it, because of the risk of typhus. Yet more sellers offered honey in jugs made from birch bark; others had a range of fish, including 'smoked sterlet [sturgeon], perch, pike and ide or burbot, the latter a rich and juicy fish, also *keta*, the dog salmon of the Pacific'. Finally, there were 'great cauldrons . . . with cutlets, tongues, whole chickens and ducks and game, as hazel hen, hares, blackcock and capercaillie', as well as eggs, fruit and enormous water melons. As Burr suggests, 'all this abundance seemed strange and unexpected in the land of famine',[9] where, just a few years previously, crop failure and government sequestration had led to millions of deaths through hunger in Ukraine and the Volga region.

Ordinary Russian travellers struggled to obtain a ticket for the trains, since there were very few services, because of the priority given to freight and the overall lack of capacity due to war damage. Wood describes how 'half an hour before the train arrives, the ticket office opens, usually a round hole in the wall no larger than a saucer and the riot starts'. (This strange custom of opening a ticket office only briefly before the arrival of the train was actually the norm at the time across much of Continental Europe and still prevails in some areas.) Wood noted at one station there were 200 people who wanted to travel, many of whom had slept overnight in the station in the hope of being ahead of the queue, but there were perhaps a maximum of forty places on the train. Worse, all but a handful of these were allocated to passengers with a government pass or who had paid a bribe: 'The first five who have stood patiently in line for hours get the surplus places, and the cashier slams his window and turns down the others as coldly as a pay-car passes a wayside tramp.'[10] At least, according to the two American women, the fortunate ticket holders invariably squeezed on to the trains: 'The trains are inevitably jammed . . . and in due course everybody – or nearly everybody – succeeds in getting on, breathless, exhausted but triumphant.'[11]

The crowding on the trains of the Trans-Siberian, and indeed elsewhere on the rail network, was a direct result of the Soviet regime's emphasis on freight, rather than passenger traffic, since it was the railway's ability to carry massive amounts of goods that was seen as its value to the economy. Stalin, who came to power following Lenin's death in 1924 (after being in de facto control for much of the period since Lenin's stroke in the spring of 1922), embarked on a crash programme to develop the country, focussing on making the nation militarily, industrially and financially self-sufficient. The economic policy was delivered through five-year plans, setting out production targets for every area of the economy. The emphasis of the first plan, launched in 1928, was on heavy industrial, rather than consumer, goods – a policy that would last until well after the Second World War. The passengers on the Trans-Siberian were no different from any other consumers in Soviet Russia and to buy a ticket they had to join a queue, which, of course, was a custom that became characteristic of the Communist system. As Harmon Tupper puts it, 'It was obvious that the Soviet government cared nothing then about the betterment of passenger service.'[12] For the Trans-Siberian itself, however, the emphasis on heavy industry was unequivocally beneficial, since Stalin realized it needed considerable investment to fulfil its function as the catalyst for Siberian development.

Class distinctions had been officially done away with by the Communists. Well, sort of. There were, in fact, two distinct levels of comfort, 'hard' and 'soft', but the communist ideology would not allow them to be called 'first' and 'second' (the same is true of twenty-first-century Britain with its 'first' and 'standard'!). And as the Communists became more dictatorial and lost any sense of their original purpose, a classic example of elitism was established. The *Lux Blue Express*, an unpublicized fast train, was introduced in May 1933 – on May Day itself, Workers' Day in the Soviet Union, an irony surely lost on the Soviet leaders – and it was reserved exclusively for the nomenklatura: party leaders, senior politicians, military commanders and, of course, their spouses. The facilities made the luxury of the Compagnie Internationale des Wagons-Lits appear second rate, as they were decidedly seven star, rather than five. On Stalin's explicit orders the carriages had been soundproofed, using special insulation involving layers of felt, lead and wood, in order that the noise of the wheels could not be heard; while before every trip the conductor passed through the train spraying eau de cologne and putting flowers on the tables. Luxuries unavailable to the masses were laid out for free on the tables, including American cigarettes, expensive chocolates, the best caviar and fruit. Stalin's mahogany-lined carriage had two bedrooms, and behind it was an identical dummy car for his bodyguards, so that no one knew in which one he slept. Every station was closed when the train went through and priority was always given to the *Lux Blue Express* (a decidedly odd choice of name for Communist leaders); ordinary citizens were not even allowed near the station when the train was due. It was used throughout the year, except in winter, and travelled between various summer resorts, and occasionally to Moscow, but its existence was never officially recognized.

Even though the Amur Bridge at Khabarovsk was restored by 1925, many trains continued to use the Chinese Eastern Railway. That route remained, of course, a shorter way of reaching Vladivostok, but the railway continued to be a source of trouble for Russia. There were constant disputes between the various parties involved, which included not just Japan and China, as well as Russia, but various warlords and bandits who were not controlled by Beijing. The Japanese had never really accepted Russia's right to share the railway with the Chinese, following the 1904–5 war, but Russia managed to continue to exploit the weakness of Chinese central government to maintain its hold over the line. In fact, it had done more than that. Despite its defeat in that conflict, the tsarist government had blatantly used the Chinese Eastern Railway as a way of creating a mini-state in Manchuria. The railway administration had effectively become the government of Manchuria. The remit of its 'Civil Administration Department' extended far beyond what might normally be expected of a railway management. It was responsible not only for local land taxes, but also levies on alcohol and tobacco, and controlled the police, law courts and local municipal councils. The department spent millions of roubles on churches and schools, and even issued passports and employed diplomatic agents. It was, in short, a state within a state. As the former head of the railway, Chin-Chun Wang later wrote, 'The General Manager of the railway appeared to the people much more like a viceroy of the province than a railway executive.'[13] He quoted an English visitor who felt the officials were so focussed on the political and strategic aspects of the railway that they had neglected its commercial potential.

Since all this expenditure, together with the original cost of the railway, remained on the railway's books, it had built up a quite staggering debt of 850 million roubles by the time of the Revolution. The overthrow of the monarchy meant this subsidy had dried up and the railway took to issuing its own currency to pay suppliers and its workers. However, since these were denoted in the rouble, which was plunging rapidly due to the hyperinflation caused by the Revolution, there were numerous protests and strikes against the railway administration. In early 1919, to ensure the line kept running, because it was the only through route to Vladivostok while the bridge was out of action, the railway, like the Trans-Siberian, became the responsibility of the Allies under the Inter-Railway Agreement, with the Chinese overseeing its operation and security. During this period the Allies' Technical Board, which had been granted considerable sums, spent an estimated \$5 million dollars on maintaining and improving the line. When the Board was dissolved following the departure of the Allied forces, an agreement was signed in October 1920 between Russia and China to create a new board, half Russian and half Chinese, to run the railway. The currency for the railway was changed to the more stable Chinese silver dollar, which immediately damped down the unrest and hostility towards the railway. Nevertheless, the situation remained unstable, a feature, indeed, of the whole lifetime of the Chinese Eastern Railway until after the Second World War. The Japanese still had designs on it. Under the Treaty of Portsmouth, signed after the Russo-Japanese War, they had retained control of the South Manchuria Railway up to Changchun, a point halfway between Mukden and Harbin, and had also built a branch line through to Korea. The importance of these lines, combined with the complex diplomatic arrangements between the three nations and the fall-out from the Russian Revolution, meant the situation was never stable and always likely to blow up into a dispute or even a war.

The 1920 agreement, setting out joint control by the Chinese and Russians, was effectively ratified in 1924, following further negotiations, but such an unusual arrangement to run a railway was always going to be questioned by one of the parties involved. Crucially, the arrangement specifically excluded the Japanese, who were concerned that this threatened their interest over South Manchuria, not least because the Soviet government appeared no less imperialist in design than its predecessor. Almost as soon as the ink was dry on the 1924 contract, they set about undermining the Chinese position on the railway – which, incidentally, was a vast enterprise with 16,500 workers, 500 locomotives and 11,000 freight wagons. Russia wanted to retain control of Manchuria, and, as Tupper sums it up, 'Under Soviet Rule, the Chinese Eastern became a Russian state on China's soil.'[14] Except that now, not only did Russia have its own schools, churches and even museums, but there was a political imperative. Communist cells sprang up under the protection of the railway management and were busy spreading the socialist message among the local Chinese population. Although under the 1924 agreement staffing on the railway was supposed to be equally divided between Chinese and Russian workers, gradually the Chinese were being pushed out and Russian dominance was being established.

Matters came to a head when the Japanese, who were intent on extending their sphere of influence beyond Southern Manchuria, assassinated the local warlord, Zhang Zuolin, placing a bomb under his train carriage, and replaced him with his son, Zhang Xueliang, who they thought would be more compliant, but who, in fact, also fought against the Japanese takeover of Manchuria. Zhang Xueliang was also resentful of the Russian presence in Manchuria and effectively confiscated the railway in July 1929 and arrested many Russian officials. Stalin, in response, sent large numbers of troops to the Chinese border and Zhang Xueliang buckled under the pressure, reinstating the joint running of the railway.

However, when two years later the Japanese launched a successful attack against the Chinese that culminated in the creation of the puppet state of Manchukuo, which incorporated Manchuria and some other Chinese territory, it became clear that the arrangement was unworkable. The Russians still ran the trains and managed the railway, but there were frequent raids by bandits, who had both criminal and political motives, which resulted in several Western travellers being kidnapped or robbed. The Japanese were increasingly putting pressure on the Russians to cede control of the line, and demanded, for example, free transport for their troops and the freedom to determine train movements for their convenience. An attempt by the League of Nations to bring the line under the control of a multinational body, comprised of the main European powers, was rejected by Japan, which clearly had only one objective in mind: the total control of the region.

By 1934 there seemed only two possible choices for the Kremlin: either Russia would have to launch a war against Japan or sell the railway. Stalin, who did not want a war, given the weakness of Russian forces and his desire to concentrate resources on rapid industrialization, decided to negotiate a sale with the Japanese. Eventually a price of nearly $50 million was agreed. It was quite a windfall for the Soviets for a line that had been problematic for Russia ever since its conception and would remain so for its new owners, until its takeover by the Chinese following their revolution in 1949. Moreover, the Russians once again started causing trouble over the railway almost as soon as the sale was carried through, and the fraught relationship between Japan and Russia continued until the outbreak of the Second World War when they were on opposite sides.

Given the troubles on the Chinese Eastern Railway, in 1933 Stalin ordered the doubling of the track on the 1,700 miles of the Amur Railway between Ulan-Ude (literally Red Uda, previously called Verkhneudinsk) and Khabarovsk, employing a massive workforce of more than 10,000.

Indeed, the Trans-Siberian was the beneficiary of much investment in the interwar period. The emphasis on heavy industry in western Siberia was at the heart of the strategy for the first five-year plan. The region had everything Stalin wanted and combined his two obsessions: a fear that the Soviet Union would be invaded from the west, and the need for rapid industrialization. Western Siberia possessed 'the best known reserves of non-ferrous metals in the country, the best and most accessible reserves of coking coal outside the Donbas [the Donets Basin in Ukraine], many other useful minerals, good agricultural land, and plentiful waterpower resources'.[15] Best of all, unlike Ukraine where steel production had been concentrated before, all these factories were far away from Russia's vulnerable border with the West, where all kinds of potential capitalist enemies lurked. The very remoteness of western Siberia was a great asset, but inevitably put an enormous strain on the Trans-Siberian Railway.

The plan required the construction of enormous steel and iron plants in the Urals, which would be fed by coal from the Kuznetsk basin (also known as Kuzbas), near the present city of Novokuznetsk (which was renamed Stalinsk in the 1930s), just under 300 miles south of Tomsk. The mineral wealth uncovered by the Soviet geologists in the Urals was indeed staggering, with a vast array of ores, including iron, copper and bauxite; however, the coal to fire the huge blast furnaces built by the Soviets had to come from the basin 1,300 miles away, with only the Trans-Siberian as a realistic connection between the two. No matter. Stalin had decreed it and it would happen, even though throughout the 1930s the railway struggled to cope. Moreover, the pressure on the line was intensified by the Soviets' dislike of railways wasting resources by carrying empty wagons; and the other aspect of Stalin's scheme, the construction of the enormous iron and steel works at Magnitogorsk, near Chelyabinsk, solved this dilemma. The town was the site of the biggest known iron deposits in the world, the Magnitnaya Mountain, parts of which were almost pure iron; and consequently the Trans-Siberian hopper wagons carried iron ore from the Urals east to Novokuznetsk, while returning to the Urals with coking coal for the plant at Magnitogorsk. This required the construction of a 250-mile branch line to connect

Magnitogorsk with Chelyabinsk; and later a new line was built to reduce the distance between the Urals and the Kuznetsk Basin. To add to the increased loads being carried on the railway, a massive tractor plant was built at Chelyabinsk that would play a key role in the Second World War. Moreover, the Trans-Siberian hauled coal from a new field at Karaganda in what is now Kazakhstan, which was also connected by a branch line in the early 1930s. Given the intense use of the line, the Soviets had considered the idea of building a second line parallel to the existing one, but in the end decided on a programme of improvements, upgrading the Western section of the Trans-Siberian into a *Sverhmagistralizatsia* – a super trunk line. Thanks to these improvements the capacity of the line was tripled in this period, with better signalling, the doubling of sections of the track, faster line speeds and heavier rails. Electrification, too, was begun, a process that would take thirty years to reach Irkutsk, 2,600 miles away from Moscow. While this investment certainly helped, the sheer volume of traffic inevitably resulted in hold-ups and delays, especially during the winter.

The biggest railway project of the period was the construction of a line linking Siberia with Turkestan, known as Turksib, which inevitably put yet further pressure on the Western part of the Trans-Siberian. This was another grandiose project, a near thousand-mile railway that had been started under the last tsar, but work had been halted by the First World War. A section had opened in 1915 between Novosibirsk and Semipalatinsk and then in 1926 the Communists restarted construction on the Turksib, which was completed through to Tashkent four years later. The Turksib was built to allow the export of grain and wood from Siberia, but it also enabled the region to be turned over to cotton production, as part of the Soviet obsession with concentrating particular crops or industries in a specific area.

To sum up all this rapid Soviet enterprise, focussed on industrialization of this part of Siberia, the Trans-Siberian – and particularly the West Siberian Railway – assumed the role that Witte had envisaged for it as the catalyst for the development of the region. As well as shuttling coal and iron ore between the Urals and the Kuznets Basin, the railway carried petroleum, industrial and agricultural machinery, grain and timber, and all kinds of foodstuffs intended for European Russia. Most available money for transport investment had been channelled towards the railways and consequently the roads were still inadequate to transport these heavy loads.

Not surprisingly, given all this activity, the population of the region soared; and its very character was transformed further with a huge increase in the urban population, mostly by immigration from rural areas of Siberia to the jobs created in the vast factory and mining complexes, but also with a considerable influx from European Russia. In the dozen years running up to the outbreak of the Second World War, the population tripled in Novosibirsk (previously Novonikolayevsk) and Sverdlovsk (previously Yekaterinburg), while Novokuznetsk went from being a tiny town of just 3,900 souls to a city of 170,000. Even further east, the numbers living in the major cities such as Irkutsk, Ulan-Ude and Khabarovsk also increased dramatically.

These population rises, together with the lack of passenger services, explain the huge queues of people struggling to get on the trains at ticket offices. At least in some towns they were better catered for as they waited. Despite the obvious disregard for passenger services, much emphasis was placed on improving stations, perhaps as a kind of unconscious recognition that queues and waiting were going to be the lot of rail travellers for a long time. More likely, they were yet another opportunity for the Communists to show off how much they cared for the people with architecture designed to demonstrate their power, in the same way, ironically, that private train companies had done across the world since the mid-nineteenth century. The most splendid of these stations was at Novosibirsk, the boom town of Siberia, beside the massive Ob river and almost precisely a third of the way along the line to Vladivostok. It was at the heart of the industrialization of Siberia and consequently needed a grand station – the biggest in the country – to match the vision. Designed by Nikolai Voloshinov, it is a traditional classical building with a huge arch, slightly off-centre, over the main entrance, which is reached by a wide bridge that is at a level above the platforms, allowing passengers to descend stairs to reach their trains. In the front is a huge piazza that enables the building, painted in traditional Siberian light blue, to be viewed in its full splendour from afar.

Towards the end of the 1920s and throughout the 1930s there was, however, one major source of increase in passenger numbers: unwilling ones, carried in freight wagons and guarded heavily. These were the vast numbers of prisoners being sent to Siberia being punished by Stalin's increasingly repressive regime. The exile system had been abandoned when the Trans-Siberian was originally completed, since Siberia was being populated with willing immigrants. However, it was restarted on a far bigger scale under the Communists, because Stalin's push for rapid development required a vast pool of cheap or free labour; the creation of labour camps – Gulags (*Glavnoe Upravlenie ispravitel'no-trudovykh* **Lagerei** or Main Administration of Corrective Labour Camps) – suited his purpose. They were located at the extreme ends of the nation, the Arctic Circle, the Central Asian south and, mostly, Siberia. Stalin's increasing intolerance of any opposition and his constant purges ensured there was a constant flow of new prisoners – the lucky ones (although many considered themselves the unlucky ones) who escaped firing squads. The Gulags therefore served a joint purpose, as both a tool of repression of any elements hostile to the regime and as a pool of labour to produce the heavy industrial goods that Stalin saw as the key to rapid development. It was, effectively, a slave-labour system and it did not take much to end up in the camps. While initially there was some intention to send only criminals and anti-revolutionaries to the Gulags, by the mid-1930s criminality was no longer relevant to the possibility of being sent there. The authors of a book on the forced-labour camps cite a few examples: 'A woman cook failed to salt the dinner; she was prosecuted . . . A kolkhoz [collective farm] worker took a horse and went about his business; the horse was stolen; the kolkhoz worker was prosecuted . . . A one-eyed foal was born in a kolkhoz and was killed and eaten; the chairman of the kolkhoz was prosecuted for "failure to protect" the young horse',[16] and so on. And they conclude: 'The overwhelming majority of the camp inmates was composed of national and social elements which in the usual sense of the word could never be considered offenders.'[17] Mortality rates in the terrible conditions of the Gulags were usually between twenty and thirty per cent annually, although they reached fifty per cent. The level of terror intensified across Russia in the mid-1930s. Whereas arbitrary arrests, executions and exile to labour camps had been a feature of post-revolutionary society right from the beginning, in the years running up to the Second World War they became so commonplace that victims were normally quite unsurprised when it was their turn to get the knock on the door.

The congestion and backlogs on the Trans-Siberian, as well the rising number of accidents, led to accusations against railway workers of sabotage and incompetence, even though the fault lay with the planners in not devoting enough extra resources to the railway. The appointment in 1935 of Stalin's chief troubleshooter, Lazar Kaganovich (who had overseen the construction of the

Moscow Metro and was nicknamed 'The Locomotive'), as the Communication Commissar was a demonstration of the importance that the railways were accorded throughout this period, but it also spelt trouble for many workers in the industry. Transport delays – particularly on the Trans-Siberian, which was now expected to carry a much heavier load than previously – were an all too visible reflection of the society's inefficiency, and as J. N. Westwood, the Russian railway historian, suggests, 'Government and Party remained unconvinced that the railways were working anywhere near their real limit, a conflict that was almost inevitable . . . the two weapons [in government hands] were the purge and the Stakhanovite movement.'[18]

Kaganovich had more blood on his hands than almost any other of his contemporary Communist leaders, having organized forced grain confiscations during the starvation deliberately brought on by the regime in the early 1930s in Ukraine as a punishment. He was one of those who took the hardest line against the slightly better-off peasants characterized as kulaks (rich peasants, but often misused as a way of identifying those reluctant to hand over grain) by the regime, a group that was almost exterminated under Stalin's forced collectivization of agriculture. Tupper rather disingenuously suggests Kaganovich was good for the Trans-Siberian, because he 'augmented the rolling-stock fleet with more powerful locomotives, large, four-axle freight cars and all-metal passenger coaches',[19] built a huge locomotive repair facility at Novokuznetsk and ensured that workers were better trained, but that is rather in the 'Mussolini got the trains running on time' mould. In fact, under Kaganovich (who, incidentally, lived to see the end of communism in 1991 and was subsequently posthumously found guilty of genocide in a court in Kiev) railway workers lived in terror as he organized the arrest of thousands of railway administrators and managers as supposed 'saboteurs'; they were either executed or sent to the Gulags. Of course, to some extent this had the desired effect, because railway managers were terrified of delaying trains unnecessarily in case they received a knock on the door in the middle of the night, so they strove to keep the system going. Not surprisingly, as a result, the accident rate rose; and even minor mishaps could easily result in the hapless local manager being accused of being a 'wrecker' bent on destroying socialist society, the worst possible accusation. Under Kaganovich, too, Stakhanovite efforts were encouraged to improve productivity. Named after a miner who supposedly carved out more than 100 tons of coal in a single shift, which was, in fact, an obvious charade, Stakhanovite efforts were imposed on the railways, but to terrible effect. Specially selected train drivers were set up to ensure their locomotives pulled greater loads, or used less coal per verst, but as Westwood suggests, this usually meant that all the engineer did was 'drive his engine badly, "thrashing" it so it produced a third more steam per hour'; but while this did increase the speed, it simply meant it 'raised fuel consumption per horsepower to a much higher rate and brought his fireman [who had to shovel the coal into the fire box] to a state of collapse'.[20]

Even the relatively neglected passenger services improved in the 1930s, thanks to the investment on the line. By 1936 the Moscow–Vladivostok journey was eight and a half days, a reduction of seventy-two hours on the immediate period after the civil war (and only about forty-eight hours slower than today's fastest trains on the all-electric line). Freight remained the priority, although in the war the railway was heavily used for troop and prisoner transport, as well as goods.

The Second World War is, in fact, reckoned by some historians to have started not with the German invasion of Poland in September 1939, but a few months earlier with a battle in Mongolia, 400 miles south of the Trans-Siberian, and a continuation of the Russo-Japanese struggle over Manchuria. Since the Japanese takeover of Manchuria there had been mounting tension on the Mongolian border between the Japanese Kwantung Army, which occupied Manchuria, and Red Army frontier units. In the summer of 1938 there had been a major skirmish between the Red Army and the Japanese, resulting in a total of 750 deaths at Lake Khasan, near Vladivostok, which the Japanese had lost; but this time, with the tacit backing of the Japanese government, this initial minor confrontation became the far more significant Battle of Khalkhin Gol.

Though notionally independent, Mongolia was effectively a client state of the Soviet Union – just as Manchuria (Manchukuo as it had become) was under the control of Japan – and in May 1939 a border dispute between the two erupted into a brief, full-scale war. A group of Mongolian cavalry roamed into what the Japanese considered Manchurian territory and were attacked by the Kwantung Army. The Red Army responded strongly and created a massive force of 58,000 men under Marshal Georgy Zhukov, backed by 500 tanks and 250 aircraft ready to counter-attack. This took a couple of months to assemble because of the distance from the railhead and, amazingly, the Japanese were unaware of this big build-up. When the main attack was launched in late August, the Russians quickly overcame the Japanese and scored a decisive victory. This had a wider significance and altered the likely course of the Second World War, since the Japanese realized that the Red Army was stronger than they had thought, and this meant they did not attack Russia in conjunction with the German invasion on 22 June 1941. Instead, the Japanese turned their attention south rather than north, which ultimately led to the raid on Pearl Harbor.

In 1941, Stalin reacted remarkably quickly by moving troops from the east to the west to face the Germans. He got wind of the attack ten days before and began moving the Red Army on the Trans-Siberian in what Simon Sebag Montefiore called 'one of the decisive logistical miracles of the war', with the redeployment of '400,000 fresh troops, 1,000 tanks and 1,000 planes across the Eurasian wastes on non-stop trains'.[21] The last train left the east on the 17th and the troops deployed behind Moscow secretly.

The Trans-Siberian Railway had a good war. It enjoyed a more peaceful time than in the First World War, since, as a result of the Japanese restraint, it was not subject to any direct military action, but the line was incredibly busy. As Stalin had predicted, the Germans invaded Ukraine, putting the Donbas coal out of reach of the Russians. Therefore, coal had to be supplied from the Kuznets Basin and the coalfields in Kazakhstan at Karaganda, which, fortunately, had been connected with a new line that enabled a large part of the Trans-Siberian to be avoided.

As a result of all this activity on the railway, there was a constant programme of upgrading and continued increases in capacity were achieved by the addition of more loop lines, better signalling and new sections of parallel routes. The purges also stopped, allowing the railway managers to relax, rather than living in constant fear, although many perfectly competent officials had been executed.

Following the German attack in 1941 there was an immediate evacuation of industry in the threatened areas to the east on a series of hundreds of special trains. In a quite remarkable manoeuvre, whole factories were packed up into wagons that were transported to pre-planned locations with great haste. Most of the industry was shifted to western Siberia and Chelyabinsk became the centre for tank production, based on its tractor factory, but some factories were relocated further east. According to one historian, 'It was arguably the most important feat the Soviets achieved in the Second World War in the sense that it facilitated their eventual victory over Germany. The factories were re-established in a matter of weeks and immediately began to produce vast quantities of war material.'[22]

The Trans-Siberian was also Stalin's potential escape route. Extensive preparations were made for the dictator and his leading ministers and officials to evacuate to Kuibyshev (Samara), and trains, with locomotives permanently in steam, were standing ready to take them from Moscow throughout the period when Germany appeared to be about to overrun the capital.

Another, crucial, role of the Trans-Siberian was bringing troops from the Urals and Asia, as well as supplies landed by the Americans at Vladivostok, which did actually get through, unlike those in the First World War, the Soviets proving themselves more efficient at running the railway than their tsarist predecessors. The trains would often return with yet more unfortunates heading for the Gulags, such as those who, according to Tupper,[23] were termed 'socially hostile' Poles, 'unreliable' people from the Baltic states or 'traitorous' ethnic minorities who had allegedly collaborated with the Germans. There were, too, hundreds of thousands of German and Japanese prisoners of war, who were sent to the labour camps, of which there were more than one hundred, with some having a less than ten per cent survival rate by the end of the war. Essentially, only those prisoners able to get some type of clerical or administrative job survived – the rest who undertook heavy labour invariably perished of starvation or disease. The way they were treated was actually akin to a form of slow murder, since the prisoners who did not fulfil their quotas were given reduced rations, which in turn made them too weak to carry out their required tasks. Being sent to Siberia under Stalin was a far worse fate than under the tsars. Although the numbers in the Gulags declined after the end of the war and conditions improved slightly, it was not until Stalin's death in 1953 that most would be closed down and some remained until Gorbachev's era.

The Second World War had demonstrated yet again the vital nature of the Trans-Siberian to Russia's Asian interests, and to its overall defence needs. As well as continuing improvements to the railway (most notably electrification), in the immediate post-war period consideration turned again to building a parallel line and that project would offer challenges that were even greater than those faced by the line's original builders.

# ELEVEN

# THE OTHER
# TRANS-SIBERIAN

Even at times of war, the Trans-Siberian has been work in progress, always needing improvements, major repairs and extra capacity. Therefore, as Russia was waging a war for its very existence in the east, ways of improving the worst bottlenecks on the Trans-Siberian were being developed. Consequently, in western Siberia there was continued investment to reduce journey times and upgrade the track in recognition of the importance of keeping the line working to full capacity to serve the industry that had been relocated there. Even further east improvements were being made, notably on the difficult 110-mile-long Circum-Baikal Railway around the lake, where work began to improve the track in 1940. The line had been doubled just before the First World War, but remained a slow railway because of the sharp curves, the ever-present risk of landslides and the primitive nature of the equipment. The war led to delays in this improvement scheme and then a change in plan. Rather than trying to improve the existing line, it was decided to by-pass it by building a new alignment further away from the lake. A shorter route, which already had a single-track line, was developed into a double-track electric railway through the mountains between Irkutsk and Slyudyanka. When this was completed in 1949 it was used by all the Trans-Siberian trains, and the section of the old line from Irkutsk to the lake along the Angara was dismantled in conjunction with a hydro-electric project, which led to a rise in the river level. The lakeside route was retained but with only one train per day and consequently the villages along the railway, which mostly could be reached only by the line and had been developed for railway workers, deteriorated markedly. The second track was removed in the 1980s, but because of the interest from tourists the line was saved, much to the relief of the villagers, and it has become a key local attraction.

A far bigger construction project – the longest individual scheme of the whole railway – was also being developed in the immediate post-war period. After their defeat at the hands of the joint Mongol and Soviet forces at the outset of the conflict in the summer of 1939, the Japanese avoided conflict with Russia during the course of the Second World War. In fact, it turned out to be the other way around when Russia – knowing that Japan's imminent defeat was likely, as Stalin had been tipped off about the dropping of the Hiroshima atomic bomb on 6 August 1945 – launched an attack on Manchuria, eager to regain its hold on that part of China. Therefore, bizarrely, both the first and last battles of the war played out in and around the Trans-Siberian Railway. The attacks against the dispirited Japanese forces in the brief war which ended in early September allowed the Russians to regain control of the Chinese Eastern Railway and to help the Chinese Communist and Nationalist (the Kuomintang) armies rid China of the Japanese invaders. After the defeat of Japan, the Communists' People's Liberation Army used Manchuria as a safe haven from which to launch the revolution, which eventually succeeded in 1949 when the Nationalists were forced to flee to the island of Taiwan.

The Chinese Eastern Railway, incidentally, was handed over by the Russians free of charge to their then allies, the new communist regime in China, allowing Russia to divest itself of a railway that had caused its various rulers nothing but trouble for half a century. Now known as the Trans-Manchurian, it continues via Harbin through to Beijing, and is well used as a link between China and Russia for passengers including many Western tourists, few of whom will be aware of its troubled history and freight. The route is popular as it avoids going through Mongolia, the other route to Beijing from Moscow. There is still, however, the need for a change of gauge at the border between the two countries.

Despite their 1945 victory the Soviet regime remained wary of Japanese strength. What if the Japanese launched an attack on the Amur section of the Trans-Siberian, as well as establishing control of the Chinese Eastern Railway? Vladivostok would be cut off and Russia could find itself chased out of Siberia. This paranoid thought process led the Soviets to look at the construction of a new line well north of the existing Trans-Siberian, where it would be not only less vulnerable to attack (always a consideration in Stalin's mind), but would also open further vast swathes of Siberia and its natural resources that were previously too far from the railway to be exploited.[1]

That was the strategy behind the start of construction of the 2,300-mile-long[2] Baikal Amur Railway, known always by its acronym BAM (*Baikal Amur Magistral* or Baikal Amur Mainline), a project that dwarfed any of the sections of the existing Trans-Siberian in both difficulty and cost. It was in the long line of Soviet megaprojects, such as the industrial combines mentioned in the previous chapter, and other schemes like the successful space programme, the Virgin Lands Campaign to boost the use of land (another failure), and the madcap idea (fortunately abandoned) to reverse the flow of several Siberian rivers. The BAM, though a mere railway line using tried-and-tested technology, was actually more ambitious in scale than any of these other projects because of the difficulties and inaccessibility of the terrain, which proved to be a far greater obstacle than for the earlier sections of the Trans-Siberian. The authors of a guide to the BAM are not exaggerating when they say 'constructing the BAM and the BAM zone was the largest civil engineering project ever undertaken by the Soviet Union and probably by any country in the world. It devoured the same gigantic amount of resources as were used to conquer space in the 1950s and 1960s.'[3] Indeed, it took three attempts and more than half a century to complete a line that became emblematic of Soviet aspirations, but which has forever been mired in controversy and played no little part in the widespread disillusion in the communist ideal of the younger generation of Soviet citizens.

The idea behind the scheme was to provide an alternative route to the Pacific to the existing Trans-Siberian, running parallel between 400 and 600 miles to the north, leaving the main line at Tayshet, a town created by the railway and famous only for its role as a transit camp for Gulag prisoners and for its deadly creosote factory, described in detail by Alexander Solzhenitsyn in *The Gulag Archipelago*. The route crosses the Angara river on a dam at Bratsk, runs north of lake Baikal through the town of Severobaikalsk, a mountainous region that required several lengthy tunnels, traverses the Amur at Komsomolsk-na-Amure and reaches the ocean at Sovetskaya Gavan, more than 500 miles north of Vladivostok.

The first attempt to build the line was made in the 1930s when the Soviet Government, worried about events in Manchuria, passed a secret decree to construct a new line, but contained no details of the route other than the two termini, Tayshet and Sovetskaya Gavan. An extensive survey was undertaken and plans for the railway were announced in the second five-year plan, which covered 1933 to 1937. It was 'streets paved with gold' propaganda. The Plan concentrated on the economic rather than military advantages, saying the BAM 'will traverse little investigated regions of eastern Siberia and bring to life an enormous new territory and its colossal riches – amber, gold, coal – and also make possible the cultivation of great tracts of land suitable for agriculture'.[4] A major survey was embarked upon, but many of the poor geologists soon became victims of a purge when the authorities decided that the work had not been carried out properly; several were executed, while others ended up in the construction gangs.

In the second half of the 1930s a series of Gulags was created along the proposed route known as BAMLag (BAM Corrective Labour Camps). For most of the estimated 400,000 prisoners sent there between 1932 and 1941 (when Russia was attacked by Germany and the internal deportations ended for a while) this was a death sentence. Russians knew that being sent to the BAM meant they were unlikely to ever return. BAMLag, the organization which ran these camps, was created specifically to ensure there was a constant pool of labour to build the line. It grew rapidly to run dozens of camps, but ironically, and perhaps inevitably, its leadership was purged in 1940 (and sent to work on the railway) and it was absorbed into the wider Gulag administration. As mentioned in the previous chapter, the prisoners received insufficient rations to carry out the hard labour they were expected to undertake and therefore they were systematically starved. In the BAMLag camps a particularly sadistic form of five different types of 'cauldron' was operated, ranging from a meal three times a day to thin soup and 300g of bread daily. Good workers started on the top rations, but since these were insufficient for them to carry out their allotted task, they would gradually be allocated to the cauldrons providing less and less food, yet still expected to work as hard. There was only one likely result.

Progress was slow for several reasons. The main difficulty was the permafrost on which virtually the whole line needed to be laid – unlike the Trans-Siberian where only sections, mostly on the Amur Railway, were permanently frozen. Therefore the difficulties of laying tracks on permafrost were far greater, because there were hundreds of miles of it, and the very haste with which the line was being built, under the terrible conditions imposed by the Soviet authorities, exacerbated the problem. The permafrost is not a consequence of the current low temperatures in Siberia which are not quite cold enough, believe it or not, to create permanently frozen ground. Rather, it is a leftover of the Ice Age, which hasn't thawed because it never gets warm enough. However, once the railway workers started digging into the soil of the permafrost, which varies between a few and several hundred metres deep, it thaws and does not refreeze in the same way in the winter. Instead a swamp is formed and laying a track before it settles is problematic, since it is impossible to know to what extent the roadbed will sink. In recent years China has found better ways to build railways on permafrost when constructing the line up to Tibet, using heat exchangers to ensure that the permafrost remained frozen, but this is extremely expensive.

There were other difficulties, too. The Western sections of the BAM are in a zone of constant seismic activity. There have been three major earthquakes in the region since work started on the line, but more seriously in some parts there are almost constant tremors whose effect is dampened by the permafrost. Once this is removed, the impact can be much greater. Therefore building tunnels in such conditions can be both foolhardy and impractical, and, indeed, several were to be the cause of enduring problems.

By the time the Second World War broke out, the prisoners had completed parts of the BAM at each end: in the west from Tayshet to Bratsk, where a massive hydroelectric project was being developed, and in the east from Komsomolsk-na-Amure to Postyshevo, 120 miles away, as well as a couple of branch lines. Work was then stopped, except on the section between Komsomolsk and the Pacific Ocean at Sovetskaya Gavan, where construction continued with the use of prisoners of war and a few Russian Gulag inmates because the line was seen as having potential importance for the war effort; and, in fact, it was used as a supply route for troops and equipment in the brief war between Japan and the Soviet Union in 1945.

Remarkably, as soon as the war ended, work restarted on other parts of the line, this time largely undertaken by Japanese and German prisoners of war, forced labour in contravention of the Geneva Convention. If the treatment of the domestic prisoners had been harsh, these foreigners fared even worse. One estimate suggests that only ten per cent of the German prisoners of war who worked in the Ozerlag camp complex near Lake Baikal survived to be repatriated. The Japanese prisoners suffered a similar mortality rate, and a conservative estimate of the death toll of the two groups is 150,000. Some progress was made, such as the completion of the track to Bratsk and, later, to Ust-Kut, the most westernmost section, a total of 450 miles from the start of the line at Tayshet, but progress was slow. The dam at Bratsk had not been completed and therefore tracks were laid on the ice across the Angara river in the way that they had been on Lake Baikal before the completion of the Circum-Baikal.

Following Stalin's death in 1953 all work on the BAM ceased, because his successor, Nikita Khrushchev, was not convinced of the worth of the project. The surviving prisoners of war were sent home and the Gulags began to be closed. Ironically, the Western intelligence services did not learn of the cessation of work. They were fooled by the radio silence in the official press into thinking the scheme had become a secret military project. In fact, the idea of the BAM was quietly forgotten during the early part of the Khrushchev era. The reconstruction of European Russia was seen as more important and, in a way, there was a repeat of the arguments between pro- and anti-Siberian groups that had preceded the construction of the original Trans-Siberian before Witte made his decisive intervention. Those arguing that it was more important for Russia to build up its strength and consolidate its industry where most of the population lived held sway during the 1960s.

Russia's railway projects have always depended on politics and, inevitably, the BAM was no exception. However, the idea for the BAM never quite went away, because the railway had supporters in the top echelons of Soviet government. Gradually support for the line coalesced with a very different model of construction, given that the Gulags had closed. There were lots of ostensibly good reasons. The new line would relieve congestion on the Trans-Siberian; it would open up the western Siberian gas fields to the United States and Japanese markets; and it would be used for container traffic between Asia and Europe. Suddenly, the Soviet leadership, now under Leonid Brezhnev, became caught up in the enthusiasm. This was the early 1970s, when there were rapid price rises in oil and later in raw materials. The Soviet Union, which had the largest reserves in the world of many key raw materials, seemed to be on the point of a boom, and the BAM would help it to exploit these resources. There was, too, the continued military justification, although this did not stand up, given that modern long-range bombers would be able to reach any part of Siberia, however far north.

The most immediate economic justification was that massive copper deposits at Udokan – halfway between Tynda, which became the administrative headquarters of the BAM, and Severobaikalsk, on Lake Baikal – had been discovered during Stalin's dictatorship. Once support for the project took hold in the Soviet Union, the naysayers would tend to hold their fire, ever aware of what happened to dissenting voices under Stalin. Moreover, Brezhnev gave the scheme a brilliant ideological gloss. The core idea (which could have only been dreamt up by dictators with an overblown sense of their own popularity) was to make use of the support for socialist ideals among the population, especially young people. So it was not the transport or interior ministry which was given responsibility for the project, but the Komsomol (an acronym for the All-Union Leninist Youth League), the youth division of the Communist Party.

The reasoning was clever. The BAM was seen by party officials as a way of restoring national pride and showing the world that the Soviet Union was a major force able to carry out big schemes and, in effect, 'conquer nature': 'Unlike its predecessor, the tsarist-era Trans-Siberian, BAM would be laid down with "Leninist enthusiasm" through the barren taiga towards the promised land of Communism.'[5] It would, in effect, be a better version of the Trans-Siberian because it was built under socialism – the watchword was 'developed socialism', a convoluted expression to explain away why communism had not yet been achieved. The Soviet leadership was always informing the population that 'communism' would be reached in a few years, a moving target that drifted forever forward, and the BAM became caught up in that search for the Holy Grail.

For Brezhnev, the project offered a peaceful rallying cry for socialist propaganda, a war against nature and the elements, and also a 'path to the future'. It was a battle that did not require the use of military force. That, of course, made it a struggle that had to be won; as a consequence, the project to build the BAM started with a lot riding on it. That meant, on the one hand, that almost infinite resources could be thrown at it, but on the other that the project constantly faced unrealistic timetables and deadlines.

After much behind-the-scenes preparation, the Komsomol announced its plan to build the line in just ten years with a completion date of 1982 – later changed to 1984 (Orwell was probably not on Brezhnev's reading list, so the irony would have been lost). It was deemed a 'shock project', which ensured it received priority and the Komsomol was given responsibility for mobilizing the nation's youth to work for the BAM. The Komsomol issued a nationwide appeal on TV and in newspapers for young volunteers to work for three-year stints on building the railway.

While undoubtedly many young people did turn up for idealistic reasons, the offer of vouchers to get priority for cars and new apartments rather contradicted the notion that their patriotic fervour was the main driving force. There were other advantages, too. Having the experience of volunteering for a 'shock project' looked good on the CV of those interested in a political career in the Communist Party; and for others the opportunity of being promoted to a foreman at the tender age of twenty-six (not uncommon on 'shock projects') was another lure.

Even the Soviets' own publications recognized the inherent contradiction. An article in *Soviet Sociology* published in the spring of 1983 warned of the risks: 'Offering people the privilege of receiving scarce goods as a way of attracting a workforce to the BAM region cannot be considered an adequate method . . . it stimulates consumerist attitudes among young people, paving the way for various kinds of speculation and intrigue, and damage is done to the patriotic spirit which should prevail on an urgent construction project.'[6] Moreover, those who did join for idealistic reasons were soon disillusioned: 'While interviews with a number of BAM participants reveal that although many of them initially possessed genuine enthusiasm for building BAM, they soon lost that sentiment after seeing the project in the flesh.'[7]

There were other groups of labourers. Many older workers were attracted by the high pay – treble the normal level for such work in the Soviet Union – and the vouchers for new apartments and cars. Holidays, too, were longer than the norm and free train or plane tickets to and from Siberia were provided. No prison labour was to be used – Brezhnev promised it was to be built with 'clean hands' – and groups of young people from countries friendly to the Soviet Union, such as the Warsaw Pact nations (most came from Poland, Czechoslovakia and East Germany) and client states like Angola and Cuba, also worked on the line. There was a third group: railway troops, consisting of conscripts who made up as much as 25 per cent of the workforce on parts of the project; essentially a form of forced labour, they barely feature in the official propaganda.

The difficulties the workers faced may have been less life-threatening than their predecessors experienced, but they were nonetheless daunting. As the author of an analysis of the BAM project puts it, 'the area presented geologic, seismic, climatic and epidemiological challenges to its would-be conquerors, as much of the region is composed of taiga.'[8] In short, building the line was not a good idea in the first place, but Soviet incompetence and corruption made it even harder.

The Soviet Union may have been a 'planned economy', but oddly planning was not one of its strong points. Therefore, when the first BAMers (as the workers were known) were sent to work on the line in 1974, neither a detailed survey of the route nor a clear plan of the construction schedule had been completed. Even *Izvestiya*, the Soviet government mouthpiece, admitted in May 1974 that 'at this point it is difficult to say with precision how many stations, settlements and cities will spring up on both sides of the BAM'.[9] It was three years into the construction programme that a full, detailed plan with the final route was finally set out. The lack of proper training for many of the young volunteers was a constant problem, too, and it was only in the latter stages of the work that the skills shortages were recognized. Large-scale training programmes were devised, which had the side effect of further delaying work.

The route involved about 400 miles of marshes, more than twice that length of taiga, the virgin forest, and then most challenging, around 75 miles of terrain at risk of being hit by landslides. The temperatures in the middle of winter were routinely –20°C to –30°C and when they reached –45°C without wind (or –35°C with wind) the workers were allowed to down tools and stay inside. However, even at –20°C bulldozers often seized up and axes would shatter, preventing further work. While huge amounts of resources were thrown at the project, the machinery provided was often not up to the task of working in the Siberian conditions or was underpowered for the huge lifting work required. Bulldozers, for example, were mostly converted tractors, which were unable to work continuously in the harsh conditions. There were frequent supply problems, too, especially with sleepers, which further held up work.

The planning and labour issues were dwarfed, however, by the technical problems. When work was restarted by the BAMers in the 1970s, the experience of the past difficulties with the permafrost seemed to have been forgotten. To ensure buildings and other structures do not start sinking into the ground or sagging, it is essential to wait a couple of years after digging out the foundations to allow the soil to settle, since the amount of subsidence depends on how much of the subsoil melts after being disturbed. Ice takes up more volume than water, and consequently it will leave gaps under the building, causing subsidence. In the haste to finish the line, such precautions were widely ignored. Therefore, when the track was laid down too quickly without allowing the ground to settle, it risked subsiding and causing derailments and required speed restrictions. In time, a new bed would have to be created and the track relaid. As a result, long before the BAM was completed, sections had to be rebuilt. At the western end, between Tynda and the connection with the main Trans-Siberian at Tayshet, the use of poor materials together with subsidence caused by permafrost melting meant that there were permanent speed restrictions.

According to the guide to the BAM, 'Originally the line was laid with low-quality rails on a mixed sand-gravel ballast. This resulted in the 187 km [117 miles] taking eight hours and during four months in 1987 line subsidence and ballast washouts caused three train wrecks.'[10] Eventually, the whole section was relaid, but still necessitated a 30 mph speed restriction.

It was not only the track but the buildings in the towns that were being constructed along the BAM which suffered as a result of the failure to properly account for the effects of permafrost melting. Consequently, by the early 1980s, at various stations along the line, more than seventy buildings were affected by subsidence and many had to be demolished. The worst hit was Mogot, on a branch line, where all the 1970s buildings were, within a few years, collapsing because they had been laid on insufficient foundations. Throughout the line many quite major structures, such as hospitals and administrative headquarters, were affected, and even today there are several abandoned buildings quietly sinking into the ground.

If the permafrost was a major issue, the tunnels were, as the guide put it, 'the bane of the BAM'.[11] The line crosses several mountain ranges and at one point reaches 4,000 feet above sea level. Unlike the Western sections of the Trans-Siberian, numerous tunnels were required to reduce the need to clamber slowly up and down the mountains. The half-dozen major tunnels – with a total length of over twenty miles – accounted for a remarkable one third of the overall cost of the line; and their construction faced unprecedented difficulties, because they go through geological fault lines and, worst, underground waterways. According to the BAM guide, 'A number of new tunnelling techniques had to be developed which further slowed construction,' and many of the required skills were not available in the existing workforce. It adds: 'In retrospect, several of the tunnels should never have been built, as a more cost effective route could have been found had more time been spent on survey work.'[12]

The most difficult tunnel was the near ten-mile-long Severomuysky, 200 miles east of Severobaikalsk, on which work started in 1978 with an estimate that it would take six years. In the event, it would be two decades late. There were two principal difficulties: the local seismic activity which results in around 400 minor tremors per year, and, even more seriously, the presence of various water channels and underground lakes. Consequently work was held up for years in the face of almost insuperable problems.

The worst incident happened in September 1979 when a drilling team unwittingly broke through into a huge underground lake and water flooded the tunnel. The disaster highlighted the inadequate nature of the geological surveys, a feature of the whole construction process. Because of communist censorship, this incident was not reported until four years later and the death toll is not known. The builders sought advice from Western tunnelling experts, but the problems of the Severomuysky Tunnel were so complex and unique that they were unable to help. To stem the flow, the workers devised the clever idea of injecting liquid nitrogen into the granite to freeze the water and stop the seepage, giving enough time for a permanent seal of concrete to set. Eventually, with the draining of the lake through underground pipes, the creation of a safety passage in the event of an earthquake or flood, and the lining of the whole structure with seismic sensors, the tunnel was opened for traffic in December 2003.

In the meantime, not one but two bypasses had been built, offering the workers who had to ride on the trains rather perilous journeys along temporary tracks laid over the mountain. The first, completed in 1987, was supposed to last only until 1992 and had a very steep 1 in 25 gradient. The BAM guide's description suggests it was a perilous journey: 'Two or three electric locomotives pull the cars. The grades and the drops are so steep that, when the cars are heading downhill, the drivers literally ride on the locomotive running boards, so they'll be able to jump off in time if there's an accident.'[13] Actually, jumping off a moving train did not seem necessarily a better option. That temporary bypass was replaced by another one which, at thirty-four miles, was twice as long allowing for gentler gradients. Again, the BAM guide was not encouraging: 'Although it is safe for light-weight passenger trains, there are regular derailments of the heavily laden goods trains.'[14] Dervla Murphy, the feisty Irish travel writer, was in her seventies when she went along the BAM in 2001 with a bicycle before the tunnel opened, and, after travelling on this section, she reported that all the passengers went quiet as the train crawled up and down the mountain: 'For quite a distance that edge not only seems, but is, a mere yard from the train's wheels. And the drop is a long one.'[15] However, she preferred it to the prospect of a ten-mile tunnel in an earthquake zone.

The original BAM scheme was to have included a connection to Sakhalin Island with a five-mile undersea tunnel, and a 300-mile railway running from Komsomolsk-na-Amure, but while part of the line was built, and a start was made on the tunnel, the scheme was abandoned after Stalin's death.

All the problems of building the BAM would merely have been rather unfortunate and expensive, but for the fact that there was a much wider issue, the catastrophic environmental effects. The very ethos behind the building of the project mitigated against attention being paid to the environmental effects: 'These developers [journalists and high-level administrators] maintained that any obstacle put forward by nature could be conquered by humankind through the use of technology. Showing little regard for environmental concerns, these individuals served as a mouthpiece of one perspective of official rhetoric.'[16] According to this argument, the BAM zone was essentially an endless virgin territory with such vast resources that they could not be damaged by human intervention.

Unfortunately, this was not the case. As Dervla Murphy put it, 'Because of its extreme ecological fragility all industrial developments – oil wells, dam-building, paper and pulp combines, logging, mining for coal diamonds, gold, copper – can only be cataclysmic, though the map may show them as mere flea bites on a mammoth.'[17] All of these activities were, of course, encouraged by the construction of the railway.

One of the odd and unexpected consequences of the construction of the railway was the vast number of fires that swept through the taiga far beyond what might have been considered as the area affected by the BAM. Siberia, being inland and protected by mountains in the south, has a dry climate and the draining of swamps leaves an environment vulnerable to fires. According to one former BAMer scientist, there were more than 400 fires in the Irkutsk *oblast* (county) in 1979 alone and the number grew in the 1980s. The situation was exacerbated by a desperate lack of forest rangers to monitor and control the fires. Parts of the area were beginning to resemble a lunar landscape. Fire damage in southern Siberia takes only fifty years to recover, whereas in the northern parts it is nearer 200 years, because of slower growth in the colder climate. Deforestation was the other major issue, with satellite imagery suggesting there was a '40 per cent loss of trees in the BAM Zone from 1960 to 2000'.[18] Trees are not only lost when they are cut down for use on the railway or associated structures, but they die, too, when the permafrost melts, creating a swamp.

The pristine Lake Baikal suffered, too, from BAM activity and in 1979 two factories associated with the railway were accused of polluting it with various metals and oil. Along the whole line, oil was a particular environmental concern, as not only did the diesel trains on the tracks leak fuel, but also, during construction, oil supplies had to be imported in drums, which were then left scattered around depots and sidings.

The final irony of the project – laughable if it were not so tragic – was that the completion of the scheme was announced three times by the Russian authorities. In order to meet the schedule ordained by Brezhnev (who died of alcoholism - and prescribed-drug-induced diseases in 1982) a golden spike – in an echo of the ceremony held to mark the completion of the First American Transcontinental line in 1869[19] – was hammered into the ground during a ceremony held in September 1984. No foreign journalists were invited, for the simple reason that it would have been all too obvious to them that the project was nowhere near completed and they would have asked difficult questions. Apart from the fact that just one of the major tunnels was ready for use, only a third of the 2,000 miles of track was fully operational and the condition of much of the line was lamentable, with insufficient ballast, rails that were too light and severe speed restrictions. Some other sections could be used by work trains, but the prospect of a through journey on the whole line was several years ahead. Therefore, seven years later, Mikhail Gorbachev, the Soviet leader, announced once again that the line was complete, and he stressed that it would form a new link with Japan. The Severomuysky Tunnel, however, was nowhere near finished and there were still other sections that could only accommodate work trains. As a result, it was only under the first presidential term of Vladimir Putin that the line was completed, and a third announcement was made in 2001, although the Severomuysky Tunnel still did not open until two years later.

There are many tragedies in the history of the Trans-Siberian Railway, and the BAM, while being perhaps the least well-known, is probably the greatest. It involved the deaths of thousands prisoners and Gulag inmates and the desecration of a region, including threatening the integrity of the world's deepest lake, and largely proved to be a waste of resources. Moreover, it killed off the enthusiasm and fervour of thousands of young people who genuinely believed they were creating a new type of society based on socialism, and damaged the lives of many of those who helped build the BAM. Visitors to the BAM zone today talk of abandoned villages, ghost towns and lasting environmental damage linked by an inadequate single-track railway, where trains rarely exceed 20 mph. Dervla Murphy found she fell in love with the railway, but for reasons which will not have pleased its promoters: 'A train that travels hundreds and hundreds of miles at an average speed of 20 mph, often slowing to 15, surely represents the acme of civilized public transport.'[20] Even today towns designed for large populations remain semi-inhabited, creating desolate townscapes littered with abandoned buildings, collapsing streets and laid out areas that remain empty, rather like those out-of-town developments in the United States made bankrupt by the 2008 collapse in property values.

As a monument to communist failure, the BAM ranks alongside North Korea. The PR puff on the Russian Railways website sounds almost convincing, although its tone reminds us how much communist ways still prevail:

BAM's construction represents an engineering triumph. Stretching nearly 2,000 miles from Lake Baikal in Siberia to Khabarovski Krai on Russia's Pacific coast, BAM negotiates 7 mountain ranges, 11 alpine rivers and areas of high seismic activity. And for almost half of its length, it runs through the permafrost, where winter temperatures can plummet to –60°C. Building BAM through this difficult terrain required 142 bridges over 100 metres long and more than 200 railway stations and sidings, as well eight tunnels, including

Severomuysky, which at 15.3 kilometres is the longest mainline railway tunnel in Russia and the fifth longest in the world. Over 60 towns and townships along the route were established.[21]

Interestingly, there is no mention of the cost and that is because no remotely accurate estimate has ever been made available. The official figure of $11 billion is widely discredited, and one suggestion is that the BAM used up more than one per cent of the whole of the Soviet Union's gross domestic product during every year of the main construction period. That is little more than sophisticated guesswork, given the lack of conventional accounting in the Soviet Union. There is, though, no doubting that it was the most expensive project ever undertaken in the Soviet Union and, probably, anywhere in the world during the twentieth century. Possibly the most ironic footnote on the quality of the work carried out on the line in the Brezhnev era is that, according to the BAM guide, 'From anecdotal evidence, it appears that the Gulag prisoners and POWs in the 1930s and 1950s built the most durable sections.'[22]

In the event, whatever the gloss put on the project by Russian Railways, there can be no shying away from the fact that none of the assumptions that led to the construction of the BAM have stood the test of time. The hope that it would open up new agricultural areas was misplaced. There was a good reason why indigenous settlers had not created farms in the region: the climate, with barely a three-month growing period, is unsuitable except for the hardiest vegetables like cabbage and carrots, while other crops require expensive heated greenhouses. As for relieving pressure on the Trans-Siberian, the opposite is the case. The biggest strain on the Trans-Siberian is in the Western section, west of Tayshet, where BAM traffic actually shares the same tracks and therefore exacerbates congestion. The eastern Siberian oil and gas fields did not live up to their early promise and the BAM is a slow railway that does not really provide an alternative to sea routes between Asia and Europe. Container traffic continues to be carried mostly by sea, but while it has built up on the main Trans-Siberian, the BAM is still considered too slow to carry it, although reliability has now improved thanks to the stabilization, at great expense, of the sections built over permafrost. The BAM may even ultimately lose traffic to the sea route north of Russia if global warming means the sea eventually remains open all the year round. The author of the analysis of the BAM project is unequivocal: 'The project made few positive tangible contributions to the economic development of the Soviet Union.'[23]

At least, though, it caused a few laughs: 'Many Soviet citizens thought of the project as the butt of popular jokes rather than the "project of the century".' Indeed, it may well have contributed to the fall of communism: 'By repeating ad nauseam claims of BAM's economic, social and cultural significance, the Komsomol, the Communist Party and the Soviet government held an unwavering belief that the USSR's youth needed this message to avoid a loss of collective faith. Ironically, however, the realities of the railway helped to intensify such a loss of faith in the Soviet political and economic system in general.'[24]

The widespread disillusion of the young people that the Soviets were trying to inspire was deeply damaging to the communist cause. The post-war generation needed their faith in the system reinforced but, instead, hundreds of thousands of them had experience of a gigantic failure of the system, either by working on it themselves or through socializing with those who had.

Eventually, around half a million Komsomol volunteers and older people worked on the line, and, disillusioned, many turned against the system and became supporters of the opposition to the Communists. Rather than being a 'beacon to our communist future', it soon became obvious that 'there was not much behind the myth, just as the Brezhnev era as a whole was more notable for its window dressing than any substantive accomplishments'.[25] Far from carrying people to the promised land of a twenty-first-century future, as the slogans promised, BAM clearly went nowhere.

Moreover, even those seeking simply individual benefits also lost out. While some BAMers stayed in the area, most returned to European Russia, only to find that the promised extra benefits did not materialize. Many of the vouchers for cars and apartments proved worthless, as the authorities found themselves unable to redeem them because of the huge numbers issued. This resulted in a scandal which stretched into the post-Soviet era, when there were public demonstrations by those affected.

The only bit of leaven in this terrible story is that there are signs that all the effort of building the BAM will not be wasted. After languishing unwanted during the Gorbachev era and the early years of the post-Communist period, there has recently been considerable investment in the BAM with the expectation that the line will fulfil a useful economic purpose. In particular, a new 2.5-mile single-track Kuznetsovsk Tunnel – to bypass an older tunnel and cut out a series of curves – opened in December 2012, greatly improving access to the port at Sovetskaya Gavan. The old tunnel had difficult gradients and the new tunnel relieved a bottleneck on the BAM, but the high cost of the new alignment – nearly $2 billion, which included just 12 miles of new track – shows how expensive it is to build infrastructure in this remote part of Siberia if there is no source of cheap or free labour.

This investment, the first of several proposed improvements to the BAM, was stimulated by the fact that mineral deposits along the line are now being exploited, thanks to high world prices, bringing traffic to the line. Moreover, Russian Railways is promoting the line strongly, as witnessed by its PR puff, and there is even talk of reviving the idea of connecting Sakhalin Island with a tunnel, though the cost would appear to be prohibitive, even if the undersea tunnel proves technically possible. Therefore the two extremities of the BAM may well eventually carry enough traffic to have made their construction worthwhile, if the environmental damage and the high cost are disregarded, but the main middle section, which remains single-track and not electrified, is unlikely ever to justify the vast resources spent on it.

There is also progress on the environmental front. Considerable work has been carried out to reduce the damage caused by the BAM. The water in Lake Baikal, for example, is now once again improving after many nearby plants were either shut down or turned into closed systems and more attention is being paid to the fire risk in areas that have been affected by the railway.

There is, however, another major scheme in the offing, one that would dwarf the BAM. Russia may no longer be communist, but big projects are in its rulers' DNA, whether they are tsars, commissars or presidents. The most outlandish recent idea – first dreamt up by Tsar Nicholas II a century ago and recently revived – is to continue the branch line up to Yakutsk more than 2,000 miles north-east and build a tunnel or a bridge across the Bering Strait to Alaska, which, of course, the Russians sold to the United States in 1867. This grand scheme was notionally given Russian government support in 2011 with a cost estimate of £60 billion, although that is very much a back-of-the-envelope calculation. There were suggestions it would carry three per cent of the world's freight, but the project appears unrealistic (to put it mildly) as well as being a huge environmental threat to the whole region. The heightened interest in environmental concerns would, therefore, arouse great opposition to such an enormous scheme and make it unlikely that it could be built. Finance, too, is likely to be an insuperable barrier.

While the BAM struggled to justify its existence after its completion, the Trans-Siberian was enjoying a boom, as part of a worldwide renaissance of the railways. The focus on freight remained, but the need for hard currency meant that the Communists began opening up the Trans-Siberian to tourists once again, although their travels were strictly controlled.

# TWELVE

# THE GREATEST RAILWAY

Travelling on the Trans-Siberian during the communist era was not much fun. Not only was so much priority allocated to freight trains that delays were common, but the facilities on board were parsimonious; and for Westerners there was the constant presence of the secret police watching every step, as well as bans on getting off the train at many stations in towns which were closed to foreigners. One traveller in the 1980s reported going along the whole route on a train without water, unable to get off because of not having the right visa.

In the immediate post-war period there was a continual process of improvement to the line. By 1956 the Soviet Union had stopped producing steam locomotives (four years earlier than Britain) and five years later the electrification of the Trans-Siberian from Moscow to Irkutsk (3,400 miles) was completed with the help of army labour (the whole line was electrified by 2002 – seventy-three years after the first wires had been installed). Diesels gradually replaced steam engines on the remainder of the line. The diesel and electric trains were faster and cleaner, reducing the time of the Moscow–Vladivostok journey to just under eight days (it is now slightly more than six and a half on the fastest train).

Eager for hard currency from tourism, despite the intensification of the Cold War, the Soviets improved the trains substantially in the post-war period. Harmon Tupper, who travelled in the early 1960s, found them relatively pleasant. The train was huge and offered several 'soft' class coaches with compartments for four people; a diner; a deluxe 'International Class' sleeper; and several third-class, open-plan carriages. The deluxe carriage had a 'distinct Victorian elegance about the compartments that would have surely been familiar to Annette Meakin and her mother, who travelled on the State *train de luxe* in 1900: the glistening mahogany-finished panelling; the massive, highly polished brass door lock and other fittings; the white, semi-transparent window curtains and side drapes of thick blue plush; the weighted table lamp with its fringed silk shade; the upholstered easy chair by the window; the multicolored Oriental carpet',[1] and so on.

It was not quite like Stalin's personal carriage, however: the toilets had rather scruffy roller towels; there was a pungent aroma of burning charcoal when the attendant fired up the samovar; both taps in the washroom ran cold; and there was no air conditioning, only electric fans in every carriage, while the windows were permanently shut. Worst of all, the loudspeakers in every compartment blasted out propaganda and martial music, and the volume control, which did not always work, was tucked away under the compartment table.

The dining car was all white tablecloths and partitions; there was a lounge section with armchairs, but the piano and the library of tsarist times had disappeared. So had the menus in French and the male waiters, replaced by white-bloused aproned women, wearing white paper lace tiaras. Their supervisor warned Tupper 'that the sale of vodka, much less expensive than champagne and brandy, might lead to "uncultured" behaviour on their part'.[2] As for the food, only the soups were edible (which actually I discovered, too, travelling in 2012).

There were always minders. Every Western traveller of the post-war period mentions them, usually smartly dressed men travelling in the next compartment or following their prey around towns. There were, too, detailed restrictions on taking photographs – bridges, stations, railway structures, goods trains, even rivers and lakes, all were the subject of bans ('*Nyet fotograf*' was the constant refrain), although, of course, the Intourist (the state tourist agency) guides who invariably accompanied all Western tourists often turned a blind eye. Individual travel was almost impossible and tourists had to book through Intourist or notionally independent operators such as Progressive Tours, which had permanent advertisements in the Communist Party paper, the *Morning Star*. The high rouble, which was officially on a par with the pound (but was far lower at black-market rates), made everything prohibitively expensive, although there was precious little to buy.

Eric Newby, who travelled in the mid-1970s, played games with his minders, trying to dodge them whenever possible to take photographs and see places where technically he was not allowed to go. He was travelling with a photographer, Otto, who waged a constant war with the authorities. Newby tells the story of one hilarious confrontation at Omsk: 'The big scene, which should have been played in bathing costumes with horizontal stripes, with what was, presumably, the deputy female stationmaster, a person of uncertain age who was wearing a terrible grey skirt, which made her look as if she was embedded in concrete.' A virtual battle ensued and the fierce lady managed to get her hand in front of Otto's camera and 'the other under his chin, shoving his head back for the final neck-break – what she was doing with her knee was not clear.'[3] All to stop the poor fellow taking a picture of the station frontage, which was covered in scaffolding and plastic sheeting. Otto was subsequently arrested a few times, but he led a charmed life and was always released in time to return to the train.

The tours in those days generally included visits to places such as 'the Banner of Lenin collective farm' and (Newby's particular bête noire) wire-making factories, a regional speciality according to him.

The locals themselves could be kindly, nevertheless. Deborah Manley tells a story of a woman in her seventies who got off at a small station, only for the train to move off without warning. While the men she was talking to managed to get back on, she could not. She found a group of babushkas who gave her tea and 'after four hours, many smiles and much tea, a little car came across the vacant Russian landscape. She bade farewell to the babushkas and climbed into the little car with the men.'[4] They drove her to an aerodrome, where a small plane flew her across the steppe; on arrival she was met by another car with two men who put her back on the Trans-Siberian.

The Soviets' paranoia over photography was universal, but was heightened by the fact that the railway was being used to deploy rail-based mobile missile systems, which clearly they did not want photographed. These are relatively ordinary looking trains, which carry a missile that can be deployed quickly. The advantage over silo-based systems is obvious, as trains can travel as much as six hundred and twenty miles in a day, making them very difficult to target. The only tell-tale pointer from the air was that these trains required three locomotives to haul them, because they were so heavy. Several systems were tried from the late 1960s onwards, but it was only in 1987, after several failures, that the Soviets had developed rail-borne launchers for the SS-24 missile. These were nuclear-armed rockets with a payload equivalent to 550,000 tonnes of TNT and capable of reaching the United States from the eastern Trans-Siberian with their range of 6,000 miles. They were not widely tested, however. In *Engines of War*, I wrote: 'Apparently only one test missile was ever fired from a rail-based launcher and, according to Russian news sources, it reached its target in

Kamchatka, in eastern Russia, without the US spy satellites being able to ascertain the whereabouts of the train from which it had been launched.'[5]

At their peak there were thirty-five (some reports suggest fifty-six) of these launchers with each train having up to three, and while many were deployed in Ukraine, some were also hidden along the Trans-Siberian, which, of course, offered the advantage of proximity to the United States. The difficulty was that the line was mostly electrified by the 1980s – except for the Amur Railway – and consequently the overhead wiring made it difficult to allow for the firing of the missiles. That would have had to take place in special sidings, but it was not an insuperable obstacle. With the end of the Cold War, and various missile treaties, the trains were eventually scrapped in 2003 in favour of road-based or silo-fired missiles, but they have not been forgotten. Early in 2013 there was some discussion in military circles that the Russians might restart manufacturing rail-based nuclear missiles, having retained the technology. One of the bases of these trains was at Krasnoyarsk on the Trans-Siberian, but the site was reported to have been in ruins. The likelihood of recommencing such an arms race seems remote, unless there is a remarkable change in the global political scene.

The Khrushchev era was a boom time for the railway. The Russian economy was growing steadily and the line was carrying more agricultural produce and industrial goods. Branches were being spun off to make greater use of the main line. The most significant development, however, was containerization, and the line started carrying containers between Western Europe and the Far East in 1967. This was another sign of desperation from the Soviets. Previously they had been reluctant to trade with the West, but now they were intent on obtaining hard currency to pay for vital imports. In 1971 a highly profitable flow of containers from Japan was devised between Nakhodka and the Baltic states. For a time in the 1970s and 1980s Nakhodka replaced Vladivostok, which was fifty miles west and had been turned over to military use, as the terminus of the Trans-Siberian. By the mid-1980s the railway was carrying more than 100,000 containers per year, an important source of hard currency for the Soviet Union. As ever, though, when examining Soviet achievements, the figures may have been massaged somewhat, because administrators always had to be seen to achieve their targets, under pain of being dismissed – or, worse, accused of sabotage.

Nevertheless, the container traffic on the Trans-Siberian was a boost to the Soviet Union, a crucial link across the Iron Curtain at the height of the Cold War. The railway was able to carry this traffic economically because the railway was not run on conventional commercial grounds. It was heavily subsidized by the regime in order to garner this fruitful source of hard currency. Following the collapse of the Soviet Union, this traffic has increased further.

The story of the Trans-Siberian Railway has been one of continuous change. Conceived initially largely for military purposes, it was the location for many battles in the civil war, resulting in a huge loss of life. The forced industrialization driven by Stalin put an enormous strain on the railway and changed its nature. It was no longer a winding, substandard railway, but rather a modern, heavily used freight line.

That is, indeed, the impression travellers will receive today. It is only by travelling on the line that one becomes aware of the vast scale of both the railway and the nation it serves. When my partner Deborah Maby and I travelled on the line from Vladivostok to Moscow in 2012, the first leg of our journey up to Ulan-Ude took two and a half days, longer than we had ever spent on a single rail journey – and that brought us a mere third of the way.

The railway is big in every sense. The track, of course, is slightly wider than in Europe, which allows for the carriages to be that bit broader, but more importantly, the loading gauge – the overall envelope that the carriages cannot exceed – is bigger, adding to the sense of scale. On every section the goods trains trundle by in the opposite direction every few minutes, far more frequently than those carrying passengers. Every significant station has numerous platforms, many of which have freight trains standing idle which, apart from preventing passengers walking across the tracks, make them feel rather like interlopers.

The railway is predominantly a freight railway, even though it is, of course, the passengers and their needs that give the Trans-Siberian its unique purpose. Make no mistake, the Trans-Siberian remains Siberia's lifeline. Driving across the vast steppe is still too much of a marathon for most, as well as being dangerous, given Russia's huge road death toll (28,000 in 2012). Moreover, the road between Chita and Khabarovsk remained unpaved until recently and parts are still unfinished, despite major improvements carried out since the collapse of communism. As mentioned previously, the very existence of the line squeezed out road development and consequently the railway reinforced its own indispensability. Airports are still relatively few and far between in Siberia, and domestic flights are infrequent and expensive. Therefore, the railway remains the main way for local people to get around, and the trains are heavily used, even in a quiet month like November, when we travelled along the line.

There remain different standards of train. The best is the *Rossiya*, the daily service is train No. 1 from Vladivostok to Moscow, and No. 2 in the other direction. There is TV in every compartment; the beds are softer; the samovars at the end of each coach are more modern; and the toilets do not flush directly onto the tracks. Like the other trains it still has three classes: an open coach (*platskartny*) with around fifty beds for the cheapest tickets; and then two entirely similar compartments for first and second class, the only difference being that first class has two beds (both lower bunks) and second has four.

The other trains, running on part of the line, tend to use older stock and are also generally cheaper than the prestigious *Rossiya*. Just as it always has, the train runs on Moscow time. Clocks in major stations show Moscow time and unwary passengers must be careful to make sure they realize that the departure time is also not given in local time. Fortunately, though, the old habit of serving meals by Moscow time has gone.

Harmon Tupper's 1965 assessment of the Trans-Siberian was fair. It was, he says, 'built by a relatively poor and backward nation under the severest adversities ever encountered in railway construction. For all its frailty, it bound Siberia inseparably to the motherland and kept the eastern regions within a European rather than Oriental Civilization.'[6] That poses an interesting question. Russia was at a crossroads when it belatedly started building railways – did it want to be part of Europe or an Asian power? The vacillations over the construction of the Trans-Siberian (discussed in chapter 2) focussed on this very question. The decision to go ahead set Russia decidedly along a path of looking eastwards, a choice that was to have momentous implications. Without the Trans-Siberian to transport the raw materials needed for its industrialization drive between the wars, Russia might not have been strong enough to resist the Nazi attack that started in June 1941, especially as the line was also vital in enabling much industrial production to be shifted eastwards in the build-up to the conflict and the transfer of the Far-Eastern armies to return to defend Moscow. Then, looking at the post-war period, assuming the outcome of the Second World War had been the same, Russia without the Trans-Siberian – possibly without Siberia, as a result – would have been a very different country, and might, by now, have joined the European Union. The building of the BAM can be seen as a crazy last throw of the dice by a regime still trying to prove that it was great, only to founder on the impossibility of the task. Therefore, while the Trans-Siberian itself helped to bring down the monarchy by stimulating the tsarist regime's Manchurian adventure, the second Trans-Siberian, the BAM, helped to expose the myths of communism.

The Trans-Siberian may have been born of controversy and doubt, but unlike the BAM it has proved its worth, despite the many good reasons not to build it cited in the first paragraph of this book. It has opened up a whole region of Russia and undoubtedly improved the lives of many people in the region, including incomers; and it has attracted millions of visitors to an area whose very name evokes extreme cold and imprisonment in Gulags. The Trans-Siberian is, quite simply, the best thing that ever happened to Siberia, a region that has not been blessed with many other happy events throughout its history.

There have been downsides, too, most notably the role of the Trans-Siberian in various conflicts. It not only stimulated a war, but played vital roles in the two world wars, and even, as mentioned above, featured in the Cold War. This is hardly surprising. The railway was always conceived as having a military purpose and, indeed, that was the prime reason in many of its promoters' eyes for building it in the first place.

The Trans-Siberian has always been a creature of the state. As a result, resources have rarely been skimped because the various regimes – be they tsarist, communist or proto-democratic – have always recognized its importance in holding together this vast nation. Given that the enormous scale of the enterprise means that it is very difficult for the railway to pay its way given the inevitable requirements of maintenance and renewal, state support has been essential and forthcoming. The Trans-Siberian has never suffered the indignities of bankruptcy and penury that was the fate of many of its Victorian equivalents built by the private sector. However, while economically the line has probably never been a paying proposition, it is coming closer to it now, thanks to the carriage of containers. According to a recent report, 'The Trans-Siberian is capable of transporting 100 million tonnes of freight a year, but is almost saturated.'[7] At last, after 110 years, the railway is beginning to fulfil its potential and the section between Omsk and Novosibirsk is reputed to have the greatest flow of freight of any line in the world.

When I started researching this book, I was aware that this was an exceptional railway, because of the amazing engineering that went into building it. I realized that it was the lifeblood of its region and I knew that it had been the focus of numerous wars. However, I was unaware that it is so much more than that and that its impact extends far beyond Siberia. There can be no other railway that has had such a profound influence on the history of not only the nation in which it was built, but that of the world. The Trans-Siberian is well known as the longest railway in the world. It is less well understood that it was the railway line that did most to create today's geopolitical system. It is a heavy burden for a humble iron road.

# BIBLIOGRAPHY

This list is just a short taster to further reading, focussing mostly on my sources for this book. There are, in fact, few books in English on the Trans-Siberian, and no modern history, apart from short accounts in the various guides. The main general account is almost fifty years old: *To the Great Ocean* by Harmon Tupper (Secker and Warburg, 1965), a lovely, eccentric mix of history and anecdote.

Many of the books on the Trans-Siberian describe the author's journey, and there is a concentration on early accounts soon after construction, when travel on the line was quite an adventure. Among the good ones are Annette M. B. Meakin's *A Ribbon of Iron* (BiblioLife, 2009), Arnot Reid's *From Peking to Petersburg* (BiblioLife, 2009), and Robert L. Jefferson's *Roughing it in Siberia* (Sampson Low, Marston & Company, 1987), all of which are available from various sources as modern reprints. From that early period, too, there is the official *Guide to the Great Siberian Railway 1900* (edited by A. I. Dmitriev-Mamanov and A. F. Zdziarski), which was reprinted by David & Charles in 1971. Peter Fleming wrote up his diary of a trip in 1934 some years later as *To Peking: A Forgotten Journey from Moscow to Manchuria* (1952, reprinted by Tauris Parke Paperbacks, 2009). Most recently there is Eric Newby's *The Big Red Train Ride* (Weidenfeld & Nicolson, 1978), a hilarious account of a bleak journey at the height of communism, dodging the minders and being treated to huge banquets.

The best account of the politics leading up to the decision to build the line and the role of the various players is *Road to Power: The Trans-Siberian Railroad and the Colonization of Asian Russia, 1850–1917* (Cornell University Press, 1991) by Steven G. Marks, a truly ground-breaking work. The principal advocate of the line, Sergei Witte, wrote some revealing *Memoirs of Count Witte* (available as a modern reprint), while Theodore H. Von Laue's *Sergei Witte and the Industrialization of Russia* (Columbia University Press, 1963) explains his wider policies, which were an enormous influence on the final years of the tsarist regime.

The Russo-Japanese War is covered well by *Railways and the Russo-Japanese War* (Routledge, 2007) by Felix Patrikeeff and Harold Shukman, and there is a useful little handbook on the war, *The Russo-Japanese War 1904–5* (Osprey, 2002) by Geoffrey Jukes.

There is a reasonably copious literature on the story of the Trans-Siberian during the Russian Civil War that followed the First World War. Peter Fleming's *The Fate of Admiral Kolchak* (1963, reprinted by Birlinn 2001) shows that had he turned his talents to fiction, Fleming would have been the equal of his brother Ian. The American point of view is given in *When the United States Invaded Russia* (Rowman & Littlefield, 2013), and a thorough account of the Japanese role and the politics behind it is given in the academic but excellent *Japan's Siberian Intervention, 1918–1922* (Lexington, 2011) by Paul E. Dunscomb.

On the *Baikal Amur Magistral* or BAM, the feisty septuagenarian Dervla Murphy's account of her journey with a bicycle along the line in *Through Siberia by Accident* (John Murray, 2005) interweaves history with her tribulations on the trip. There is a detailed account of the role of the Young Communists in the building of the line in *Brezhnev's Folly: The Building of the BAM and Late Soviet Socialism* by Christopher J. Ward (University of

Pittsburgh Press, 2009). The thorough account of the history of the line and the wider environment in the *Siberian BAM guide* (Trailblazer, second edition 2001) by Athol Yates and Nicholas Zvegintzov is particularly enlightening.

The literature in English on Russian railways is not copious, either, and is generally aimed at the trainspotter end of the spectrum. There are two books by J. N. Westwood, *A History of Russian Railways* (George Allen & Unwin, 1964) and *Soviet Railways Today* (Ian Allan, 1963), both of which have useful background. For early Russian railway history there is *Russia Enters the Railway Age, 1845–1855*, while *Russian Steam Locomotives* (1960, reprinted by David & Charles, 1968) by H. M. Fleming and J. H. Price needs no explanation.

For a general account of the history of Russia at the time of the construction of the line and its early history up to 1924, Orlando Figes's *A People's Tragedy: The Russian Revolution 1891–1924* (Penguin Books, 1998) is peerless. There is also a compelling description of Siberia before the Trans-Siberian and the story of the Decembrists in Christine Sutherland's *The Princess of Siberia* (1984, reprinted by Quartet 2001).

There are numerous fabulous gobbets of information in *The Trans-Siberian Railway: A Traveller's Anthology* (Century Hutchinson, 1988), edited by Deborah Manley, a book well worth taking on the journey. And for those who do go, the best guide to the Trans-Siberian is undoubtedly Bryn Thomas's *The Trans-Siberian Handbook* (Trailblazer, eighth edition, 2012), which has the most detailed route outline and a good history. The Lonely Planet guide, *The Trans-Siberian Railway* (Lonely Planet Publications, fourth edition, 2012), is very thorough, too.

# NOTES

## ONE: A Slow Embrace

1 There are different estimates depending on whether the distance is being measured as the crow flies, or on the original railway line, or on the present line after various curves had been cut out.

2 J. N. Westwood, *A History of Russian Railways* (George Unwin & Allen, 1964), p. 19.

3 Harmon Tupper, *To the Great Ocean: Siberia and the Trans-Siberian Railway* (Secker & Warburg, 1965), p. 14.

4 Ibid., p. 15.

5 Harry de Windt, *From Pekin to Calais by Land* (1899; available free online).

6 Steven G. Marks, *Road to Power: The Trans-Siberian Railroad and the Colonization of Asian Russia, 1850–1917* (Cornell University Press, 1991), p. 24.

7 Tupper, *To the Great Ocean*, p. 8.

8 Ibid., p. 9.

9 One of these involves a change of two hours.

10 Tupper, *To the Great Ocean.*, p. 7.

11 Ibid., p. 138.

12 Quoted in ibid., p. 159.

13 Westwood, *A History of Russian Railways*, p. 21.

14 Ibid.

15 Ibid., p. 26.

16 Richard Mowbray Haywood, *Russia Enters the Railway Age, 1842–1855* (Columbia University Press, 1998), p. 1.

17 Referred to in chapter 1 of my previous book *Fire & Steam: How the Railways Transformed Britain* (Atlantic Books, 2007).

18 Quoted in Westwood, *A History of Russian Railways*, p. 28.

19 Ibid., p. 33.

20 See my previous book, *Engines of War: How Wars were Won and Lost on the Railways* (Atlantic Books, 2010).

21 Westwood, *A History of Russian Railways*, p. 32.

22 Haywood, *Russia Enters the Railway Age*, p. 451.

23  *The Times*, 10 October 1865.
24  Highlighted in my previous book *The Great Railway Revolution* (Atlantic Books, 2012).
25  Haywood, *Russia Enters the Railway Age*, p. 475.
26  Ibid., p. 5.
27  Ibid., p. 6.
28  See my previous book, *Engines of War*, for an account of the role of this railway.
29  Westwood, *A History of Russian Railways*, p. 41.
30  Ibid., p. 64.
31  Quoted in ibid., p. 65.

## TWO: Holding on to Siberia

1  Eric Newby, *The Big Red Train Ride* (Penguin Books, 1980), p. 62.
2  Quoted in Tupper, *To the Great Ocean*, p. 39.
3  Ibid., p. 40.
4  Ibid., p. 43.
5  Perry McDonough Collins, *Siberian Journey: Down the Amur to the Pacific, 1856–1857* (University of Wisconsin Press, 1962), p. 84.
6  The first was one John Ledyard in the eighteenth century.
7  Marks, *Road to Power*, p. 46.
8  Ibid, p 49.
9  Ibid., p. 50.
10  Ibid., pp. 52–3.
11  Ibid., p. 33.
12  See my previous book, *Engines of War*.
13  Marks, *Road to Power*, p. 39.
14  Quoted in Tupper, *To the Great Ocean*, p. 69.
15  Marks, *Road to Power*, p. 68.
16  Ibid., p. 94.
17  Theodore H. Von Laue, *Sergei Witte and the Industrialization of Russia* (Columbia University Press, 1963), p. 14.
18  Ibid., p. 81.
19  While the total length is 5,750, most of the section west of the Urals had already been built.
20  Quoted in Tupper, *To the Great Ocean*, p. 71.

## THREE: Witte's Breakthrough

1  Then called Tiflis.
2  Sergei Witte (ed. Avram Yarmolinsky), *The Memoirs of Count Witte* (Garden City, 1921), p. 16 (available as a reprint).
3  Ibid., p. 17.
4  Ibid., p. 32.
5  Although technically Witte already had a title.
6  Witte, *The Memoirs of Count Witte*, p. 35.
7  Ibid., p. 52.
8  Von Laue, *Sergei Witte*, p. 77.
9  Ibid., p. 78.
10 Marks, *Road to Power*, p. 125.
11 Ibid.
12 Ibid., p. 126.
13 Witte, *The Memoirs of Count Witte*, p. 52.
14 Marks, *Road to Power*, p. 128.
15 Newby, *The Big Red Train Ride*, p. 68.
16 Tupper, *To the Great Ocean*, p. 83.
17 Marks, *Road to Power*, p. 133.
18 Quoted in A. I. Dmitriev-Mamonov and A. F. Zdziarski (eds), *Guide to the Great Siberian Railway* (1900; David and Charles, 1971), p. 66.
19 Marks, *Road to Power*, p. 139.

## FOUR: Into the Steppe

1  Marks, *Road to Power*, p. 176.
2  Ibid.
3  See my previous book, *The Great Railway Revolution*.
4  Witte, *The Memoirs of Count Witte*, p. 86.
5  Ibid., p. 89.
6  Ibid., p. 94.
7  Ibid., p. 87.
8  Tupper, *To the Great Ocean*, p. 101.
9  Ibid.
10 Marks, *Road to Power*, p. 184.
11 Quoted in Tupper, *To the Great Ocean*, p. 115.
12 *Cassier's Magazine, an Engineering Monthly*, Volume XVIII (May 1900), p. 33.
13 Tupper, *To the Great Ocean*, p. 175.
14 Ibid., p. 106.

15  Ibid.
16  Ibid., p. 112.
17  Ibid.
18  Ibid., p. 113.
19  Cited in my earlier books *Fire & Steam* and *The Great Railway Revolution*.
20  It is, though, barely a 15-minute walk across the river from the station, as I discovered on my trip on the Trans-Siberian in November 2012.
21  Tupper, *To the Great Ocean*, p. 183.
22  Soon after renamed Sir William Armstrong, Whitworth & Co., which eventually became part of Vickers Armstrong.
23  Tupper, *To the Great Ocean*, p. 228.
24  Ivan V. Nevzgodine, 'The Impact of the TS Railway on the Architecture and Urban Planning of Siberian Cities', in Ralf Roth and Marie Noelle Polino (eds), *The City and the Railway in Europe* (Ashgarth, 2003), p. 85.
25  Ibid., p. 87.
26  Martin Page, *The Lost Pleasures of the Great Trains* (Weidenfeld & Nicolson, 1975), p. 169.
27  Felix Patrikeef and Harold Shukman, *Railways and the Russo-Japanese War* (Routledge, 2007), p. 3.
28  Quoted in Nevzgodine, 'The Impact of the TS Railway', p. 86.
29  Patrikeef and Shukman, *Railways and the Russo-Japanese War*, p. 45.
30  Ibid.
31  Marks, *Road to Power*, p. 189.
32  Ibid.
33  From Pushechnikov's account of his work on the line, quoted in Marks, *Road to Power*, p. 190.
34  Ibid., p. 189.
35  Ibid., p. 130.

FIVE: **Travels and Travails**

1  Tupper, *To the Great Ocean*, p. 245.
2  William Oliver Greener in Deborah Manley (ed.), *The Trans-Siberian Railway: A Traveller's Anthology* (Century, 1988), p. 60.
3  Ibid., p. 63.
4  Dmitriev-Mamonov and Zdziarski, *Guide to the Great Siberian Railway*, p. 76.
5  Arnot Reid, *From Peking to Petersburg* (Edward Arnold, 1899;

BiblioLife, 2009), p. 184.

6   Ibid., p. 194. Indeed, I found similar stalls at some stations when I travelled on the line in 2012.

7   This and following references: Robert L. Jefferson, *Roughing it in Siberia* (Sampson Low, Marston & Company, 1897; available in reprint), pp. 104–9.

8   This and subsequent quotes, from Tupper, *To the Great Ocean*, pp. 253ff.

9   The scrolls have been recently restored for display by the Hermitage Museum in St Petersburg.

10  Page, *The Lost Pleasures of the Great Trains*, p. 164.

11  Dmitriev-Mamonov and Zdziarski, *Guide to the Great Siberian Railway*, p. 164.

12  All these are quoted in Page, *The Lost Pleasures of the Great Trains*, p. 183.

13  This was not unique. The American magnate Jay Gould also used to take a cow with him on his own train – see my previous book *The Great Railway Revolution*, p. 188.

14  Oliver G. Ready, *Through Siberia and Manchuria by Rail* (1904; available online at Project Gutenberg), p. 3.

15  Ibid., p. 5.

16  Harry de Windt, 'A Cure for Insomniacs', quoted in Manley (ed.), *The Trans-Siberian Railway*, p. 42.

17  Ibid., p. 42.

18  This and subsequent quotes from Francis E. Clark in Manley (ed.), *The Trans-Siberian Railway*, p. 82.

19  Annette M. B. Meakin, *A Ribbon of Iron* (Archibald Constable & Co., 1901; BiblioLife, 2009), p. 21.

20  Ibid.

21  Marks, *Road to Power*, p. 186.

22  Quoted in Tupper, *To the Great Ocean*, p. 252.

23  Marks, *Road to Power*, p. 187.

24  Ibid., p. 191.

25  Chin-Chun Wang, 'The Chinese Eastern Railway', *Annals of the American Academy of Political and Social Science*, Vol. 122, *The Far East*, (November 1925), pp. 57–69.

## SIX: **Casus Belli**

1 Witte, *The Memoirs of Count Witte*, p. 102.
2 Wang, 'The Chinese Eastern Railway'.
3 Witte, *The Memoirs of Count Witte*, p. 110.
4 Accounts vary between 3,000 and 5,000.
5 Quoted in Tupper, *To the Great Ocean*, p. 330.
6 Witte, *The Memoirs of Count Witte*, p. 124.
7 Tupper, *To the Great Ocean*, p. 341.
8 *Cassell's History of the Russo-Japanese War*, Vol. 1 (Cassell, 1905), p. 67.
9 Quoted in Patrikeef and Shukman, *Railways and the Russo-Japanese War*, p. 51.
10 In contrast, the Japanese organized huge feeding stations for their troops on trains heading for the war.
11 Quoted in Patrikeef and Shukman, *Railways and the Russo-Japanese War*, p. 70.
12 Tupper, *To the Great Ocean*, p. 338.
13 Ibid., p. 337.
14 See my previous book, *Engines of War*, for a longer development of this theory.
15 Patrikeef and Shukman, *Railways and the Russo-Japanese War*, p. 93.
16 Maurice Baring, *With the Russians in Manchuria* (Methuen, 1906), p. 184.
17 Patrikeef and Shukman, *Railways and the Russo-Japanese War*, p. 84.
18 Ibid., p. 16.
19 Ibid., p. 117.

## SEVEN: **The New Siberia**

1 Tupper, *To the Great Ocean*, p. 356.
2 Marks, *Road to Power*, p. 154.
3 Steven Marks, 'Conquering the Great East: Kulomzin, Peasant Resettlement and the Creation of Modern Siberia', in *Rediscovering Russia in Asia, Siberia and the Far East* (M. E. Sharp, Inc., 1995), p. 28.
4 Donald W. Treadgold, *The Great Siberian Migration: Government and Peasant Resettlement from Emancipation to the First World War* (Princeton University Press, 1957), p. 239.
5 Both quotes from James Simpson, cited in Tupper, *To the Great Ocean*, p. 264.

6   Jules Legras, *En Sibérie* (Armand Colin, 1899, but available online), p. 89 (my translation).
7   Treadgold, *The Great Siberian Migration*, p. 145.
8   R. A. F. Penrose, Jr, *The Last Stand of the Old Siberia* (William F. Fell, Co., 1922), p. 106 (available free online).
9   Ibid., p. 110.
10  Marks, 'Conquering the Great East', p. 30.
11  Treadgold, *The Great Siberian Migration*, p. 95.
12  Ibid., p. 7.
13  Ibid.
14  Since fewer arrived in winter, there were periods when the weekly flow reached 25,000.
15  Legras, *En Sibérie*, p. 89 (my translation).
16  Greener in Manley (ed.), *The Trans-Siberian Railway*, p. 63.
17  Westwood, *A History of Russian Railways*, p. 123.
18  It worked by notionally breaking the journey into two, so that the cheaper tariff for produce carried long distances did not kick in.
19  Dmitriev-Mamonov and Zdziarski, *Guide to the Great Siberian Railway*, p. 79.

## EIGHT: Russia all the Way

1   Borghese is quoted in Newby, *The Big Red Train Ride*, p. 190.
2   Tupper, *To the Great Ocean*, p. 347.
3   Mrs John Clarence Lee, *Across Siberia Alone* (John Lane Company, The Bodley Head, 1914), p. 42 (available free online).
4   Ibid., p. 54.
5   From R. L. Wright and Bassett Digby, *Through Siberia: An Empire in the Making* (Hurst & Blackett, 1913), cited in Tupper, *To the Great Ocean*, p. 348.
6   Quoted in Tupper, *To the Great Ocean*, p. 349.
7   Quoted by Steven Marks in 'The Burden of the Far East: The Amur Railroad Question in Russia, 1906–1916', in *Sibirica: The Journal of Siberian Studies*, Volume 1, Number 1 (1993/4), p. 11.
8   Tupper, *To the Great Ocean*, p. 370.
9   Westwood, *A History of Russian Railways*, p. 115.
10  Quoted in Tupper, *To the Great Ocean*, p. 371.
11  Marks, 'The Burden of the Far East', p. 18.
12  Tupper, *To the Great Ocean*, p. 372.

## NINE: The Battle for the Trans-Siberian

1   Carl J. Richard, *When the United States Invaded Russia: Woodrow Wilson's Siberian Disaster* (Rowman and Littlefield Publishers Inc., 2013), p. 18.
2   Now Brest, Belarus. There were in fact two treaties of the same name, the other one involving Ukraine and the Central Powers.
3   R. H. Bruce Lockhart, *Memoirs of a British Agent* (1934; Pan Books, 2002), p. 252.
4   Richard, *When the United States Invaded Russia*, p. 31.
5   Orlando Figes, *A People's Tragedy: The Russian Revolution 1891–1924* (1996; Penguin Books, 1998), p. 577.
6   Accounts differ as to whether he was fatally injured or not; as they do, too, over whether the Hungarian assailant was lynched or simply beaten to death.
7   Paul E. Dunscomb, *Japan's Siberian Intervention* (Lexington Books, 2011), p. 50.
8   Richard, *When the United States Invaded Russia*, p. 46.
9   Peter Fleming, *The Fate of Admiral Kolchak* (1963; Birlinn 2001), p. 31.
10  Richard, *When the United States Invaded Russia*, p. 55.
11  Ibid., p. 88.
12  Figes, *A People's Tragedy*, p. 651.
13  William S. Graves, *America's Siberian Adventure* (1931; Peter Smith Publishers, 1941, and available online), p. 90.
14  Dunscomb, *Japan's Siberian Intervention*, p. 93.
15  Cited by Richard, *When the United States Invaded Russia*, p. 151.
16  Ibid, p. 151.
17  Ibid., p. 153.
18  Fleming, *The Fate of Admiral Kolchak*, p. 146.
19  Graves, *America's Siberian Adventure*, p. 341.
20  Five of whom are buried in Vladivostok.
21  Fleming, *The Fate of Admiral Kolchak*, p. 92.
22  Four of whom are buried in Vladivostok.
23  General Budberg, quoted in Figes, *A People's Tragedy*, p. 586.
24  Ibid., p. 652.
25  Fleming, *The Fate of Admiral Kolchak*, p. 120.
26  Graves, *America's Siberian Adventure*, p. 321.
27  Figes, *A People's Tragedy*, p. 658.
28  Graves, *America's Siberian Adventure*, p. 301.

29  Leon Trotsky, *My Life* (Charles Scribner's Sons, 1930), p. 326; and available online at http://www.marxists.org/archive/trotsky/1930/mylife/1930-lif.pdf.

30  Ibid., p. 325.

31  Ibid., p. 326.

32  Ibid.

33  Ibid.

34  Fleming, *The Fate of Admiral Kolchak*, p. 156.

35  There were platinum and silver, too.

36  Fleming, *The Fate of Admiral Kolchak*, p. 166.

37  Ibid., p. 169.

38  Ibid., p. 170.

TEN: **The Big Red Railway**

1  Richard Taylor, *The Politics of the Soviet Cinema 1917–1929* (Cambridge University Press, 1979), p. 52.

2  Ibid., p. 54.

3  Ibid.

4  Arthur Ransome, *The Crisis in Russia* (1921; available free online via Authorama).

5  Taylor, *The Politics of the Soviet Cinema*, p. 63.

6  Ransome, *The Crisis in Russia*.

7  From Helen Wilson and Elsie Mitchell, *Vagabonding at Fifty* (Coward-McCann, 1930), quoted in Manley (ed.), *The Trans-Siberian Railway*, p. 123.

8  From Junius B. Wood, *Incredible Siberia* (Dial Press, 1928), quoted in Tupper, *To the Great Ocean*, p. 408.

9  All these quotes from Malcolm Burr's 'No Dining Car' (1930), in Manley (ed.), *The Trans-Siberian Railway*, pp. 183–4.

10  From Wood, *Incredible Siberia*, p. 407.

11  From Wilson and Mitchell, *Vagabonding at Fifty*, p. 123.

12  Tupper, *To the Great Ocean*, p. 409.

13  Wang, 'The Chinese Eastern Railway'.

14  Tupper, *To the Great Ocean*, p 426.

15  Robert N. North, *Transport in Western Siberia: Tsarist and Soviet Development* (University of British Columbia Press, 1979), p. 116.

16  David J. Dallin and Boris I. Nicolaevsky, *Forced Labour in the Soviet Union* (Hollis and Carter, 1947), p. 239.

17  Ibid., p. 238.

18  J. N. Westwood, *A History of Russian Railways* (George Allen & Unwin, 1964), p. 235.
19  Tupper, *To the Great Ocean*, p. 407.
20  Westwood, *A History of Russian Railways*, p. 236.
21  Simon Sebag Montefiore, *Stalin: The Court of the Red Tsar* (Phoenix, 2007), p. 356.
22  Thomas Morgan on Suite101.com website.
23  Tupper, *To the Great Ocean*, p. 411.

## ELEVEN: The Other Trans-Siberian

1   Similar ideas for a railway north of the existing alignment had long been mooted, with the first proposal having being made in tsarist times.
2   It has subsequently been shortened as a result of tunnels and cut-offs.
3   Athol Yates and Nicholas Zvegintzov, *Siberian BAM Guide* (Trailblazer, 2001), p. 308.
4   Ibid., p. 297.
5   Christopher J. Ward, *Brezhnev's Folly* (University of Pittsburgh Press, 2009), p. 9.
6   Quoted in Yates and Zvegintzov, *Siberian BAM Guide*, p. 306.
7   Ward, *Brezhnev's Folly*, p. 9.
8   Ibid., p. 7.
9   Quoted in Yates and Zvegintzov, *Siberian BAM Guide*, p. 310.
10  Ibid., p. 313.
11  Ibid.
12  Quoted in Yates and Zvegintzov, *Siberian BAM Guide*, p. 314.
13  Ibid., p. 106.
14  Ibid.
15  Dervla Murphy, *Through Siberia by Accident* (John Murray, 2005), p. 72.
16  Ward, *Brezhnev's Folly*, p. 13.
17  Murphy, *Through Siberia by Accident*, p. 64.
18  Ward, *Brezhnev's Folly*, p. 19.
19  A tradition carried on with many other major rail projects.
20  Murphy, *Through Siberia by Accident*, p. 25.
21  Russian Railways website http://eng.rzd.ru
22  Yates and Zvegintzov, *Siberian BAM Guide*, p. 308.
23  Ward, *Brezhnev's Folly*, p. 152.

24 Quoted in Ward, *Brezhnev's Folly*, p. 152.
25 Ward, *Brezhnev's Folly*, p. 153.

## TWELVE: The Greatest Railway

1 Tupper, *To the Great Ocean*, p. 456.
2 Ibid., p. 459.
3 Newby, *The Big Red Train Ride*, p. 114.
4 Manley (ed.), *The Trans-Siberian Railway*, p. 200.
5 See my previous book, *Engines of War*, p. 274.
6 Tupper, *To the Great Ocean*, p. 468.
7 Michael Binyon, 'Keeping the dream on track', *The World Today* (February and March 2013), p. 11.

# INDEX

Ukraine, 24, 27, 176, 195, 217, 225, 255
  famine, 205, 210, 222
Ulan-Ude, 216, 219, 256
  *see also* Verkhneudinsk
united railway tariff, 26
United States of America
  expansionist policies, 123
  migration, 143–4, 147, 149, 151, 153–4
  railway construction costs, 88
  railway network, 41
  and Russian civil war, 173–4, 180–4,
    187, 190–2, 199
  Southern states, 34–5
  supplies bridges, 77
Ural Mining Railway, 42
Ussuri, river, 87
Ussuri Cossacks, 183
Ussuri Railway, 60, 66–7, 75, 79–80,
  86–8, 96, 101
  and civil war, 180, 187
  costs, 88
  and expansion into China, 122, 125
Ussurisk, 122
Ust-Kut, 234

Vancouver, 64
Verebinsky bypass, 18
Verkhneudinsk, 88, 200
  *see also* Ulan-Ude
Virgin Lands Campaign, 230
Vladivostok
  approach to, 68–9, 71
  and civil war, 172–3, 175, 177–8, 180–
    1, 183, 186–9, 192, 195, 198–201
  and construction of Amur Railway, 165
  and construction of BAM, 230–1
  and containerization, 255–6
  and convicts, 79–80
  and early railway schemes, 38
  descriptions of, 60, 87
  and improved timetables, 163, 223, 251
  inauguration of railway, 59–60
  latitude, 8
  and luxury train services, 108–9, 117
  road connections, 98, 101
  and Second World War, 226
  station, xviii, 60
vodka, *see* alcohol
Volga, river, 39, 42, 73, 203
Volga region famine, 54–5, 210
Volkonsky, Prince Sergei, 2–3
Volkonsky, Princess Maria, 2
Voloshinov, Nikolai, 220
Vyazemsky, Orest, 80, 86–7
Vyshenegradsky, Ivan Alekseevich, 40,
  43–7, 53–5, 58, 97

wagonways, 11
Wang, Chin-Chun, 126–7, 213
Ward, Colonel John, 186
Warsaw Pact nations, 238

Warsaw–Vienna railway, 15–16
waterways, 13, 45, 61, 83
Western Siberian Railway, 65–6, 69, 96,
  102, 105, 150
  construction, 73–4, 81–3
  costs, 86, 88
  propaganda trains, 205
Western Union, 33
Westinghouse, 95
Westwood, J. N., 170, 222–3
Whistler, George, 19
Wilson, Helen, 208, 211
Wilson, Woodrow, 176, 179–81, 187
Witte, Julius, 48
Witte, Sergei, xvii, 2, 47–63
  and Amur Railway, 166–7
  appointed minister of finance, 54–5
  early career, 48–54
  and expansion into China, 69–72, 123–
    5, 127–8, 130–1, 167
  extremist politics, 51
  and freight tariffs, 52
  initiation of railway, 55–63
  and October Manifesto, 139–40
  and railway construction, 83–4, 89, 95,
    97–8, 110
  and Russo-Japanese War, 139, 141, 166
  ruthlessness, 52–3
  second marriage, 50–1
  sense of humour, 52
  train crash and imprisonment, 49–50
Wood, Junius B., 209–10
workforce, 73–6, 78–81, 86–7
  on Amur Railway, 169–70
  on BAM, 232, 234, 246
  casualties, 75–6
  Chinese labourers, 79–81, 125–6, 129,
    137
  conditions, 74–6
  food and diet, 75, 232
  in Manchuria, 125–6, 129, 137
  prisoners and exiles, 78–81
  soldiers' work to rule, 80
  wages, 75, 79, 86
  working hours, 74–5

Yakutsk, 249
*yamschchiki*, 4
Yekaterinburg, 39, 41–2, 72, 185, 195
  execution of royal family, 180, 195
  *see also* Sverdlovsk
Yekaterinburg–Chelyabinsk line, 43, 61
Yenisei, river, 65, 84, 101–2, 106
Yingkou, 126
Yugovich, Alexander, 124–5, 129

Zborov, 176
Zhang Xueliang, 215
Zhang Zuolin, 215
Zhukov, Marshal Georgy, 224
Zmeingorsk works, 11